Pulled Over

The Chicago Series in Law and Society

Edited by John M. Conley and Lynn Mather

Pulled Over

*How Police Stops Define Race
and Citizenship*

CHARLES R. EPP,
STEVEN MAYNARD-MOODY
& DONALD HAIDER-MARKEL

THE UNIVERSITY OF CHICAGO PRESS   CHICAGO AND LONDON

CHARLES R. EPP is professor in the School of Public Affairs and Administration at the University of Kansas and the author of *Making Rights Real*, also published by the University of Chicago Press. STEPHEN MAYNARD-MOODY is professor in the School of Public Affairs and Administration and director of the Institute for Policy and Social Research, both at the University of Kansas. DONALD P. HAIDER-MARKEL is professor in the Department of Political Science at the University of Kansas.

The University of Chicago Press, Chicago 60637
The University of Chicago Press, Ltd., London
© 2014 by The University of Chicago
All rights reserved. Published 2014.
Printed in the United States of America
23 22 21 20 19 18 17 16 15   2 3 4 5

ISBN-13: 978-0-226-11385-2 (cloth)
ISBN-13: 978-0-226-11399-9 (paper)
ISBN-13: 978-0-226-11404-0 (e-book)
DOI: 10.7208/chicago/9780226114040.001.0001

Library of Congress Cataloging-in-Publication Data

Epp, Charles R., author.
    Pulled over : how police stops define race and citizenship / Charles R. Epp, Steven Maynard-Moody, and Donald Haider-Markel.
    pages cm—(The Chicago series in law and society)
    ISBN 978-0-226-11385-2 (cloth : alk. paper)—ISBN 978-0-226-11399-9 (pbk. : alk. paper)—ISBN 978-0-226-11404-0 (e-book)   1. Racial profiling in law enforcement—United States.   2. Traffic violations—United States.   3. Police—Complaints against—United States.   I. Maynard-Moody, Steven, author.   II. Haider-Markel, Donald P., author.   III. Title.   IV. Series: Chicago series in law and society.
    HV7936.R3E77 2014
    363.2'32—dc23

                                                2013022799

♾ This paper meets the requirements of ANSI/NISO Z39.48-1992 (Permanence of Paper).

FOR LORA AND NICHOLAI
— C.R.E.

FOR THOSE WHO ANSWERED OUR QUESTIONS AND TOLD THEIR
STORIES, OUR TEACHERS
— S.M.-M.

FOR MICHELE AND JESIAH
— D.H.-M.

Contents

Tables

Figures

Narratives

Preface and Acknowledgments

"**O**h, your book is about racial profiling." We commonly confront this response when asked to describe our research. "Well, sort of, but not really," we respond. The term "racial profiling" has come to imply that African Americans and Latinos are stopped at higher rates because police officers deliberately *choose* to stop more of them. This is a widely held assumption. As this book was going to press, federal judge Shira Scheindlin ruled that New York City's practice of widespread stop-and-frisks is unconstitutional. New York mayor Michael Bloomberg attacked the decision, declaring that it unfairly treats the New York police as if they were racist holdovers from America's benighted past. "Stop-and-frisk is not racial profiling," the mayor declared. "I signed a law banning racial profiling," he added, and the police commissioner has "zero tolerance" for it.

We hope that this book will show what is wrong with this and similar defenses of what we will call *investigatory stops*, of which the stop-and-frisk is one example. The mayor's claims artfully dodge the real issues, implying that to criticize racial disparities in stops is to attack the motives of individual officers. If it is acknowledged that individual officers are not deliberately racist, according to this view, then there is no problem. But there is a problem, and the common focus on officers' motives misunderstands its source. That source is the police practice of investigatory stops and how this officially guided practice prompts officers to act on implicit stereotypes of who looks suspicious. Investigatory stops are aimed not at enforcing a law but checking whether a person is up to no good. When police departments encourage their officers to make investigatory stops, this necessarily translates into an expectation to make stops on the basis of inchoate suspicions. What happens then, as every law enforcement specialist knows, is precisely what the New York statistics reveal: the vast majority of those stopped are innocent, and racial minorities are disproportionately represented among these innocent victims of intrusive stops. As an officer long ago observed to journalist Gary Webb, "You've got to kiss a lot of frogs before you find that one prince."

And so this book is about much more than racial profiling. As we examined our survey data, listened to police officers and drivers, and read more deeply, we discovered that race shapes and is shaped by police stops in often hidden and subtle but profound and foundational ways. We show how race is embedded in police practice and criminal justice policy even when police departments have taken deliberate steps to prohibit "racial profiling"; how official police practices and training encourage officers to make large numbers of stops merely to check people out; how these practices implicitly incorporate negative stereotypes of African American and Latino criminality; and how these practices, in the context of negative racial stereotypes, lead officers when carrying out criminal surveillance to stop African Americans and Latinos at much higher rates than whites. The people who are subjected to these investigatory stops regard them as deeply unfair and an affront to their equal rights. Ultimately, police stops pursuant to these official practices construct and reconstruct the meaning of rights, citizenship, and race. *Pulled Over* is our effort to describe and understand the racial framing of police stops, especially investigatory stops, a police practice that is the deeper source of racial disparities and is more entrenched and troubling than racial profiling.

Along the way we have had much help. Two extraordinary graduate students, Laura Lucas and Shannon Portillo (now Professor Portillo), assisted and often guided us. Advice from Matthew Zingraff and Chris Crandall helped us to improve our survey design. Glenn Adams, Monica Biernat, and Chris Crandall deepened our understanding of stereotyping. Whenever we were uncertain of data analysis steps, Jacob Fowles and especially Bert Kritzer provided insight and practical advice. This book is much improved by the deep and thoughtful critiques of the University of Chicago Press series editors, John M. Conley and Lynn Mather, and the anonymous reviewers. Marie Provine offered continued insight and advice as we worked through revisions. Our editor, John Tryneski, provided encouragement when we needed encouraging and insight when we needed guidance. At the Institute for Policy & Social Research, Laura Stull refined our figures and Whitney Onasch copyedited our manuscript before we sent it out for review.

We took more years than we care to admit to try to understand our findings. Colleagues too numerous to mention challenged our observations and insights and were generous with suggestions. We are grateful for comments and suggestions from Bentley Allen, Mario Barnes, Dick Brisbin, Paul Chevigny, Lauren Foley, John Gilliom, Joel Grossman, Donald Green, Bernard Harcourt, Margaret Keck, Michael Musheno, Mitch Pickerill, Adam Scheingate, Jerome Skolnick, Lester Spence, and Steve Teles. (And Chuck is grateful for ongoing conversations with Lora Jost over many years.) Portions of this work have been presented at seminars at the following universities: California at Berkeley, Yale, Johns Hopkins, Ohio, West Virginia, Kansas, Lviv (Ukraine), and Aarhus (Denmark). Questions and comments from discussants, panel members, and audiences at the annual meetings of the Law and Society Association, State Policy and Politics Section of the American Political Science Association, and Midwest Political Science Association continually challenged our emerging understanding of the findings.

This material is based on work supported by the National Science Foundation under Grant No. SES-0214199. Any opinions, findings, and conclusions or recommendations expressed in this material are those of the authors and do not necessarily reflect the views of the National Science Foundation.

Thank you all.

CHAPTER ONE

"I Felt Violated"

NARRATIVE 1.1.
Joe, African American male: "I Felt Violated"

One time that I particularly remember, I was just, I don't know how to explain it—I felt violated.

I was doing the speed limit, I got pulled over and was asked for my driver's license and registration. I went and asked why I was being pulled over. He just pretty much stated that there was a warrant check. And pretty much ran my license and asked if I had any warrants for my arrest and I told him, "No." And he ran my plate and driver's license and asked if that was my current address and all that good stuff and then released me.[1]

The stop Joe describes in his brief narrative might appear, at first glance, to be inconsequential. Some might say it was merely a minor inconvenience in the police war on crime. The officer was professionally courteous and, in the end, issued no citation. It was all over in a few minutes. Research tells us stopped drivers are most concerned about police rudeness and sanctions, and on these dimensions, Joe could hardly have fared better. Yet Joe's emotional response was palpable and raw. This African American man was not merely annoyed or angry. He felt violated.

Joe's experience and indignation are common among African American drivers. In this book we will share similar stories from many African American drivers and will verify that their experiences fit widespread patterns revealed in a survey of 2,329 drivers. For example, Deana, an African American woman, was stopped twice within five minutes one night by different officers who only asked where she was going.[2] Lisa was followed home from work at 10:30 every night for two weeks—every night—by police officers who looked closely at her and asked whether she owned the Corvette she was driving. Billy was stopped and questioned and his car was searched on two different occasions.[3] Kenneth was stopped, held in a police car and questioned, and then released.[4] In some cases the stop was more intrusive. Joe, the driver in our opening narrative, told us of a previous stop in which an officer pulled him over, approached him with his hand on his gun, handcuffed him, and ran a warrant check. Darrell was stopped along with several high school buddies while driving through a white neighborhood, held in handcuffs on the sidewalk for an hour, and then released.[5] In most of these stops, the African American driver described the officer as "polite" or even "nice." In none was the driver given a ticket. And yet in each case, the driver described to us fear and resentment of the experience. White drivers rarely share these experiences, making police stops a defining aspect of the racial divide in America.

Police stops matter. No form of direct government control comes close to these stops in sheer numbers, frequency, proportion of the population affected, and, in many instances, the degree of coercive intrusion. The police make some eighteen million traffic stops per year in the United States.[6] Nationally, 12 percent of drivers are stopped per year by the police.[7] Among racial minorities the rate is considerably higher: 24 percent or more by some estimates.[8] In a police stop the driver (or pedestrian) is arrested for the duration of the stop, is not free to leave, and is sometimes subjected to the most searching of inquiries, ranging from intrusive questions (What are you doing in this area?) to a physical pat-down, a search of the vehicle, or handcuffing. Being stopped is a potent experience. Drivers vividly remember the details and share stories of police stops with family and friends. While driving, they note who is stopped by the police and what is transpiring in the stop: a single officer writing a ticket or several officers conducting a vehicle search while the driver stands alone at the front of his vehicle.

Police stops convey powerful messages about citizenship and equality. Across millions of stops, these experiences are translated into common stories about who is an equal member of a rule-governed society and who is subjected to arbitrary surveillance and inquiry. With the growing push to use local police in immigration enforcement, Latinos are increasingly likely to share African Americans' long experience of inquisitorial stops. "Show me your papers" will become a common command to people who look stereotypically Latino. When people like Joe, Deana, Lisa,

Billy, Kenneth, Darrell, and others we will introduce in this book are subjected to intrusive, arbitrary inquiries when stopped, and other people—white people—are largely free of these inquiries, police stops actively re-create and enforce the country's racial divide. Stops contribute to what Michael Dawson has called African Americans' "linked fate," or the sense, based directly on experience, that racial discrimination is still a defining feature of American life.[9]

In a country that celebrates democracy and racial equality, this police-defined racial divide is a deep and festering wound. In an era of police reforms, among them community policing and the growing diversity of the ranks of officers, it represents an institutional failure. From the controversies over highway drug interdiction in Maryland and New Jersey in the 1990s to the recent debates over racial profiling of Latinos in Arizona and racially discriminatory stopping and frisking of pedestrians in New York City, it is well established that racial minorities are more likely than whites to be stopped by the police.[10] But disparities in who is stopped are only the most obvious indicator of how police stops both reflect and define racial division in the United States. In stops, racial minorities are questioned, handcuffed, and searched at dramatically higher rates than whites are; they are much more likely than whites to perceive the stop as unfair; and they distrust the police in general at much higher rates than whites do. On each of these dimensions the racial gap is wide. These patterns appear in the frisking of pedestrians by big-city police, stops and searches of vehicles on interstate highways by state patrols, and, our focus, stops of drivers on city and suburban streets by local police. Although these types of stops differ in some ways,[11] they are united by their essential racial characteristics: in each, police officers disproportionately stop racial minorities and act more intrusively toward them during the stop.

Why do racial disparities in police stops persist despite a widespread legal and moral commitment to *non*discrimination? This question is the subject of considerable research and controversy, much of it conducted via increasingly sophisticated statistical studies. The standard answers fall roughly into two competing camps. One is that racial disparities reflect racism (whether deliberate or implicit) on the part of individual officers, the other that officers are rationally justified in stopping black people at higher rates than whites because they commit crimes at higher rates.[12]

Missing from much of this commentary is attention to how police

stops are organized and conducted, and how the people who are subjected to these stops think about them. This study returns the focus to
these basic issues. Here, the focus is on the lived *practice* and the lived
experience of police stops.

This shift in focus has led us to believe that current debates over "racial profiling," as it is commonly called, rest on two basic assumptions
that are, at best, incomplete. By enlarging the discussion, we hope to increase understanding and open new possibilities for reform. The first
assumption is that what African Americans find offensive—and what
ultimately distinguishes a racially problematic stop from a racially legitimate stop—is primarily officer rudeness and disrespect, not other elements of the stop itself. This assumption reflects the widespread belief
that racism is mainly a personal animus and is expressed in interpersonal rudeness. It is further based on the psychological theory of procedural justice, which teaches that people evaluate the legitimacy of official decisions on the basis of whether the process seems fair, not whether
they got a favorable outcome.[13] For example, a driver is likely to accept
the legitimacy of a traffic ticket if he or she feels the officer acted fairly.

Drivers do value fair treatment and feel demeaned when treated
unfairly, and this fact supports a legal theory that runs parallel to the
psychological one: fair procedures are valuable not only because they
minimize mistakes but also they affirm the inherent dignity of the individual.[14] According to this legal theory, an essential purpose of fair procedure is to treat the people subjected to official procedures as *"people,"*
not *"things."*[15] In the narrative above, Joe's sense of violation reflected
his sense that he was not accorded this dignity.

But we emphatically depart from how the psychological version of
this theory has been interpreted in the context of police stops. In that
context, it has been claimed that since people have difficulty knowing
whether a stop is truly fair, they make an inference based on whether
the officer seemed respectful. As Tom Tyler, the leading scholar of procedural justice, has put it, while officers should *be* fair as well as politely
respectful, *appearing* to be respectful "is especially advantageous in reducing public dissatisfaction about [racial] profiling."[16]

This claim that people will view police stops as legitimate if the officers are polite and respectful has allowed the widespread stopping of racial minorities to fester. William Stuntz, the noted Harvard criminal law
professor, said as much: "If Tyler's claims are even partly true, the police could simultaneously increase the number of *Terry* stops [stop-and-

frisks], decrease the injury those stops cause, and substantially reduce complaints of police discrimination—all without changing the way they select search targets. . . . Worrying about how street stops happen makes more sense than worrying about how many of them happen."[17] By saying officers could gain acceptance of investigatory stops "without changing the way they select search targets," Stuntz suggests that officers could continue to target large numbers of racial minorities for these stops—so long as investigatory stops are "carried out more politely" and suspects are "treated with more dignity."[18] As we will show in chapter 2, the leaders of professional policing responded to the racial profiling controversy by urging departments to train their officers to be unfailingly respectful when stopping people—as if this would address the problem.

Joe, Deana, Lisa, Kenneth, Billy, and many other African Americans who we will introduce in this book certainly prefer to be treated politely in police stops. But in their experience, official politeness could not convert an otherwise offensive police stop into a fair and legitimate one. Some police stops are recognized to be fundamentally unjust no matter how "polite" or "nice" the officer. The deeper problem in these polite but unjust stops is that they are part of a broad, continuing pattern in which racial minorities are disproportionately subjected to suspicious inquiries without any particular basis or justification. Pervasive, ongoing suspicious inquiry sends the unmistakable message that the targets of this inquiry look like criminals: they are second-class citizens. Law professor Sherry Colb called this "targeting harm": the person targeted by such a stop "is left wondering, 'Why me? Why have the police singled me out when they lacked an evidentiary basis? Why didn't they search someone else instead or as well? What gave them the gut feeling that I am a criminal?'"[19] These harms are compounded when the person targeted believes, on the basis of widely known patterns, that he or she has been selected because of race. Targeting in this way generates especially pernicious social costs, as Bernard Harcourt observes, by turning increasing numbers of the targeted groups into convicted criminals or innocent but distrustful subjects of surveillance who feel treated like criminals—and by giving others the comparative freedom from such control.[20] Accompanying these harms is the invasion of privacy imposed by the officer's questions and searches. To the question "Why are you in this neighborhood?" most people will think with considerable justification, "Why is that any business of yours?" But when the questioner is a police officer, they will offer an answer while feeling their privacy invaded and their dignity eroded. Patting down a person's body in search of a weapon or a bag of drugs or rifling through the contents of a vehicle only on the basis of the hope that by chance some such searches will turn up contraband are even deeper intrusions of privacy and assaults on dignity.

The earliest psychological research on procedural justice acknowledged that politeness may not be enough. If people who are subjected to an ongoing, discriminatory pattern learn to recognize it as such, they will come to conclude that the process is deeply unfair *even if the officials carrying it out are unfailingly respectful and polite.* As Tyler put it in an early, prescient caveat to the psychological theory of procedural justice, even if officials appear to be respectful "a procedure that consistently produces unfair outcomes will eventually be viewed as unfair itself."[21]

This deeper truth has been forgotten in the effort to legitimate inquisitive police stops by making the officers more polite. What makes inquisitive police stops so offensive to so many African Americans and Latinos is not that the officers carrying them out are impolite or even frankly bigoted, but that these stops are common, repeated, routine, and even scripted. This scripted practice treats its targets not as individuals worthy of dignity but as numbers to be processed in search of the small percentage who are carrying contraband or have an outstanding warrant.

This leads to the second faulty assumption in current debates over "racial profiling": it is the belief that racial disparities in police stops are the product of discriminatory *police officers* rather than an *institutionalized practice* that is inherently unfair and discriminatory. The focus has been on identifying and reducing "intentional" discrimination. Was the officer who stopped Joe frankly racist but careful to hide it? If not deliberately bigoted, was he acting on the basis of implicit negative stereotypes of black people, stereotypes that he may not have been aware that he held? Or was he acting rationally, on the assumption that his warrant checks would be more efficient if focused on black men? These are the positions in a growing debate over the source of racial disparities in police stops and, more broadly, on the status of racism in American society.[22]

The Supreme Court, too, assumes that discriminatory intent, rather than discriminatory practice, is the problem.[23] Under the constitutional law governing fair procedure in police stops, if an officer deliberately stops a person only because that person is black, then the officer is acting with discriminatory intent and the stop is illegitimate. But this is only a theoretical possibility, because the court requires direct evidence that a stop is intentionally biased. If the officer has some legal justification for the stop, however trivial—for example, the driver's car has a burned-out license-plate light—and does not frankly admit to targeting minorities, then the stop is constitutionally acceptable, according to current standards.

The search for discriminatory intent is a distraction. Few people, and virtually none in positions of authority, frankly acknowledge racist intent. Occasionally people make a verbal slip, and then their opponents and the media cry "gotcha!" But these gotcha moments do not speak to the real issues at stake. For Joe and other minorities, it matters little if we somehow know whether the officer merely recognized that Joe was black or *actually* thought, "I'm going to check out that black guy *because* he's black." The distinction is exceedingly fine and virtually unknowable, yet constitutional law gives any police stop a free pass unless it can be shown that the officer *did* think such a thing.

This book rests on the different assumption that every member of our society, police officers included, recognizes the social fact of race and widespread stereotypes of blacks and whites.[24] Who doesn't know the prejudicial stereotype that blacks are lazy, prefer to live on welfare, are prone to complaining, and are aggressive or violent? Awareness of these stereotypes is enough to make acting on the stereotypes a *possibility*. Fifty-eight percent of whites in a recent survey even acknowledged agreeing with at least one of these common negative stereotypes of black people.[25] But even if people do not agree with these stereotypes, the existence and persistence of these stereotypes is enough to make acting on their basis a possibility.

Instead, attention should focus on institutionalized practice: how the structure of incentives, training, and policy in contemporary policing makes it more likely that officers will act on the basis of bigotry or implicit stereotypes, leading to racial disparities in outcomes. It is our thesis that a specific, well-entrenched, institutionalized practice of the *investigatory stop* is the main source of racial disparities in police stops and why the racial minorities subjected to these stops view them as deeply unfair even if carried out by a politely respectful officer. The investigatory stop is the deliberate creation of police leaders, led by police professional associations, policing researchers, and police chiefs. It is implemented through professional training and the fostering of shared professional norms and culture. Following directives and guidance, officers on the street widely use investigatory stops to check out people who look suspicious. The investigatory stop is made not to enforce traffic laws or vehicle codes but to investigate the driver. Is this driver carrying a gun or illegal drugs? What is he up to? Why is he in this neighborhood? Is there a warrant for his arrest? Because officers are not supposed to stop a driver without a legal justification, most investigatory stops are nominally justified by minor violations: a burned-out license-plate light, failing to signal a lane change, driving 2 miles per hour over the speed limit, and the like. (In the case of Joe's stop, the officer was uncommonly frank and offered no pretextual justification.) But the purpose of these stops is to criminally investigate the driver in the hope of making an arrest.

The investigatory stop is why blacks are stopped at much higher rates than whites and why police pursue intrusive lines of questioning and searches more commonly in stops of blacks than of whites. While whites mainly experience conventional traffic-safety stops, racial minorities—blacks especially—commonly experience investigatory stops. As a result of this and shared stories of police stops, African Americans and Latinos have developed a shared knowledge of the investigatory stop: how to know when one has been stopped in such a way, how to endure the experience, and how to go on with life. This racial difference in police practices and people's lived experience and shared knowledge of these practices is why black people commonly rate stops that they have experienced as unfair, while whites are generally more sanguine about the stops that *they* have experienced. It is a key reason why, compared to whites, African Americans so distrust the police.

Although police officers have carried out investigatory stops for decades, police leaders introduced a new twist in the 1980s that considerably heightened the level of racial discrimination in these stops, and then made this reinvented investigatory practice a core tactic in the wars on drugs and crime. This innovation was to encourage the typical street-level officer to engage in proactive stopping of many drivers (and pedestrians) so as to carry out as many intrusive investigations of people as possible. "Proactive" is the key word. It means that officers are to stop drivers and pedestrians not only, or even primarily, when they do something wrong; officers are to stop as many people as possible so as to be able to investigate them more closely. As one of the early supporters of this tactic advised, officers are to "maximize the number of citizen contacts" in the hope that some yield fruit.[26] But because officers cannot possibly stop *all* drivers or pedestrians and scrutinize *all* communities, they must focus on some, and, in the context of enduring racial stereotypes of black criminality and violence, they tend to target racial minorities and their neighborhoods. The vast majority of these stops and searches yield no contraband or illegal guns, and, as Jon Gould and Stephen Mastrofski found in an observational study of street searches, a high proportion are clearly unconstitutional.[27] The officer who stopped Joe had little justification for the stop but hoped to be able to arrest him, and Joe had experienced precisely this pattern before. These facts underlie Joe's feeling of violation.

Simply put, what has emerged in the past two decades is an institutionalized practice rather than the haphazard activity of individual officers. As police professional associations and leaders in the past twenty years deepened their commitment to investigatory stops, the practice has become more widespread, frequent, and racially discriminatory. This deepening of the pattern reflects the growth of research, court decisions, and especially professional training and guidance that all support the practice of racially biased investigatory stops. We trace the origins of this practice to the period of deep institutional reforms in policing and crime-control policy in the late 1970s and 1980s. In that period, the police faced widespread critiques that they were too insular and unresponsive to local communities, that their officers were exclusively white and male even when policing minority communities, and that officers engaged in brutality and spoke insultingly to people they had stopped. Under intense pressure from these critiques, police departments widely adopted a number of reforms. They adopted "community policing" initiatives that emphasized listening and responding to the concerns of ordinary people and neighborhoods. They hired racial minorities and women. They developed extensive rules, training, and oversight to control excessive use of force.

At the same time, however, police departments began more harshly enforcing laws against ordinary street disorder and drugs, and these initiatives relied on police stops as their key enforcement tool. The "broken windows" initiative encouraged police to crack down on loitering, public drinking, and graffitiing, viewing these things as precursors to serious crime. The Reagan and first Bush administrations launched a war on drugs that fostered large numbers of arrests of ordinary drug users and low-level dealers. This war was built from the start, as Doris Marie Provine argues eloquently, on the empirically false imagery of black people as the main users and sellers of dangerous drugs.[28]

Contemporary police departments are far less frankly racist, less blatantly abusive, and less insulated from the communities they serve than even a generation ago. They are also more intent on proactive control of the population and discovery of drugs held by the ordinary citizens on the street and their enforcement has focused disproportionately on young black men. The result has been a massive growth in investigatory stops, arrests, and imprisonment of racial minorities. "Stoked by fear and political opportunism, but also the need to address a very real social problem," Glenn Loury writes, "we threw lots of people in jail, and when the old prisons were filled we built new ones."[29] The increase and pervasiveness of various forms of criminal supervision, from heightened surveillance to prison and probation, have led scholars to refer to the current institutionalized criminal justice policy regime as the "carceral state."[30] The carceral state both reflects our history and culture of racial subjugation and helps define the contemporary meaning of race.

While the investigatory stop was a key part of this broader context, it was neither a natural nor inevitable consequence of these other initiatives: it was a deliberate, specific invention that directly contributed to the explosion in arrests and imprisonment of racial minorities. The inventors of this practice honed techniques for targeting some types of drivers for stops, for questioning the driver and passengers, for inquisitorial observation of the visible contents of the vehicle, and for getting the driver to "consent" to a search of the vehicle. While some officers had done some of these things in the past, the inventors of the investigatory stop turned these actions into a systematic, formalized practice, pioneered formal training in how to do it, and spread this knowledge widely among police departments through a committed campaign of proselytization. The inventors of this practice knew it would disproportionately target racial minorities for reasons that we will summarize below and spell out in more detail in the second chapter. Nonetheless, they honed the practice and encouraged its widespread adoption.

Although police departments differ in many ways—big cities versus small towns, urban departments versus state highway patrol agencies, traditional versus progressive agencies—the investigatory stop has spread widely among these agencies. This type of stop is increasingly and widely deployed in other countries in much the same way it is used in the United States: to target racial minorities for intrusive, inquisitorial stops. Thus, the widespread use of investigatory stops of pedestrians in Britain fueled deep resentments among urban minority youth and sparked the huge riots that engulfed that country's major cities in 2010.[31]

In focusing attention on the specific invention of the investigatory stop, this study joins a growing body of scholarship on how institutions contribute to racial (and other) disparities. An old body of writing attributes racial disparities to "institutional" or "institutionalized" racism.[32] These theories rightly recognize that individuals' beliefs are part of broader patterns, but they are justifiably criticized for failing to identify how these broad patterns produce specific disparate outcomes, especially when, as in the present case, few individual police officers acknowledge being deliberately racist (and few probably *are* deliberately racist).[33] The alternative has been to focus on either the voiced beliefs of individuals or the articulated policies of particular organizations. But too often this fails to recognize that patterns of *practice* may be widespread (even if not formally expressed), may have distinct racial implications (even if containing no frank racial expression), and may contribute to racially disparate outcomes (even if few individuals carrying out these practices specifically intend to produce these outcomes).

Important recent studies bridge this gap by showing how some racial disparities result from official policies that, in turn, reflect and reproduce racial stereotypes. The policies that are the focus of these studies are more specific than the abstract and inchoate "institutional" racism of the older writings. Thus, Doris Marie Provine showed how the federal government's war on drugs, and specifically the extraordinarily heavy penalty for possession of crack cocaine, reflected racial stereotypes and directly produced horrific racial disparities in criminal sentencing and imprisonment.[34] Likewise, Joe Soss, Richard Fording, and Sanford Schram have shown how specific state welfare policies reflect racial stereotypes and in turn directly produce troubling racial disparities in welfare benefits and the punitive control of its beneficiaries.[35]

Like these studies of policies, ours strives to identify the specific sources of racial disparity; but unlike them, we identify these sources in official practices that are not directed by specific official policy but which nonetheless are institutionally supported and endorsed. Borrowing from sociological studies, we call these less-formal sources of disparity *institutionalized practices*. Institutionalized practices are common ways of doing things that, while not required by any specific official policy, are supported and legitimated by rules, training, and law, and that spread widely to become a commonly accepted activity.[36] As practices gain increasing support via rules and law, they assume "value beyond the technical requirements of the task at hand,"[37] in the words of

Philip Selznick, which is to say that they come to be viewed not only as effective, but as *professionally right and proper.* These practices enjoy the endorsement of key formal institutions: in the present case, of professional associations and the courts. Through the mechanisms of shared professional recommendations and formal training, these norms, rules, and procedures are translated into individuals' actions. Individuals' perceptions and activities turn these rules and norms into practice on the street. Institutionalized practices are thus a form of what some have called "inhabited institutions," which is to say, institutional norms, rules, and procedures expressed in the shared practices of individual officials and employees.[38]

Institutionalized practices are racially framed when they grow from and reproduce negative racial stereotypes. These stereotypes influence peoples' perceptions, but in often-hidden ways. Even people who are opposed to racism often implicitly perceive others in racially stereotypical ways. We will have more to say about these psychological processes in chapter 2, but for now the important point is that implicit negative racial stereotypes help to support punitive practices like the investigatory stop. In turn, these practices contribute to racial disparities in who is stopped by encouraging officials to act on implicit stereotypes when deciding whom to stop.

The investigatory stop is such a racially framed, institutionally supported practice. It is supported by scholarly research, numerous individual departmental policies, state-level training regimens, professional association resolutions, federal agency support, and judicial approval all the way up to the Supreme Court, and it is widely viewed in policing as a quintessentially professional practice. While it generates racial disparities in who is stopped, these disparities are seen (by many) as acceptable because the practice is professionally and judicially endorsed, is claimed to be necessary to fight crime, and is thought to be controlled by professional training aimed at eliminating intentional racism. Police officers particularly believe that investigatory stops are among their most effective tools for finding and arresting criminals and preventing crimes. In many departments, very large proportions of all arrests are made in "routine" investigatory traffic stops.[39]

The "show me your papers" provision of Arizona law S.B. 1070 extends the racial framing of investigatory stops into the area of immigration-law enforcement.[40] Like investigatory stops generally, this Arizona law and others like it are likely to encourage officers to target people for immigration inquiries on the basis of ethnic stereotypes. Here, too, the issue is not whether an individual officer has intentionally selected a person for inquiry on the basis of the person's race or ethnicity. States like Arizona will claim that they carefully train officers to be "unbiased." But in the context of culturally defined ethnic stereotypes, the vast majority of officers are likely to conflate illegal immigrant status and looking "Hispanic." A policy that directs officers to ask for documentation when they are suspicious of a person's immigration status will inevitably lead officers to focus on Latinos and Hispanics for investigatory stops. A recent survey revealed that 79 percent of registered Hispanic voters—*American citizens all*—believe that Arizona-style laws will increase the likelihood that the police will target legally present Hispanics for inquiries.[41]

This is not a hypothetical fear. Marco Sanchez, a psychologist who is a U.S. citizen, reported the following experience that parallels many of our observations in this book:

> I didn't know the reasons why this police officer stopped me. Of course, I was very surprised, anxious, tried to understand what I did wrong. And the first the police officer asked me was, "Do you have legal documents?" Sure, I'll give you my driver's license, my registration and my insurance. And he asked me, again, did you have legal documents? I thought that he meant my insurance documents were expired. We received these insurance documents periodically, and I'm not always on top of the newest one in the wallet compartment. So, I'm, again, looking for those documents. He asked me directly, are you legally in the country? That got me by surprise and I started asking him why did you stop me? . . . He didn't say anything. Walked back to the patrol car with my driver's license.[42]

Others report similar experiences.[43] While our data do not address the emerging issue of ethnic disparities in police enforcement of immigration law, our focus on investigatory stops helps to explain these disparities and how experiencing these "show me your papers" stops shapes people's sense of their place in American society.

Our unique dataset, described at the end of this chapter, makes it possible to empirically distinguish investigatory police stops from their conventional counterpart, traffic-safety stops, and doing so brings into clear focus a number of things that have only been hinted at in previous studies. One is that racial disparities in police enforcement are singularly concentrated in investigatory stops. When the police are enforcing

traffic-safety laws, they are *not* more likely to stop black drivers. Whatever are the psychological and cultural sources of racial disparities in police stops, these forces do not appear in traffic-safety enforcement, the
most common street-level activity of police officers. But when the police
are carrying out investigatory stops, they are dramatically more likely to
stop black and other minority drivers. In speeding stops, the most important influence on who is stopped is how fast you drive. In investigatory stops, the most important influence on who is stopped is not what
you do but who you are: young black men are by far the most likely to be
stopped. This inquisitorial focus on young black men is a classic instance
of what scholars call "intersectionality," or how disadvantages associated with race, gender, and youth are compounded when combined.[44]
Our data reveal such intersectional compounding throughout the several
stages of the investigatory stop.

Likewise, inquisitive intrusions, like probing questioning and searches,
are not scattered across all types of stops. They are concentrated in investigatory stops, and officers are much more likely to pursue these intrusions of African Americans than whites. Among drivers stopped for
excessive speeding, black people are *not* significantly more likely to be
questioned or searched. Intrusive questions and searches are concentrated in investigatory stops, and in these stops African Americans are
significantly—dramatically—more likely to questioned and searched.
And, again, young black men are the most subject to these heightened
investigatory intrusions.

Another issue clarified by this key distinction between types of stops
is whether people are more accepting of police stops if the officer is professionally courteous and respectful. As we will discuss more fully in
chapter 2, this claim has helped to legitimate investigatory stops in the
eyes of the police and policy makers. Stopped drivers do prefer polite
to rude officers, but our findings reveal a more fundamental source of a
driver's evaluation of a stop's legitimacy. From the perspective of people
who are stopped, black and white, traffic-safety stops are a proper use of
state power. In contrast, investigatory stops are at best dubious and often
seen by those who are stopped as violations of rights and dignity. Black
drivers reported to us that they recognized the patterned character of investigatory stops and feared and resented these stops even when the officer remained professionally courteous and respectful.

Distinguishing investigatory from traffic-safety stops also brings
into clearer focus why African Americans are considerably less trust-

ing than whites of the police overall. Our evidence suggests that the different types of police stops experienced by whites and African Americans contribute to this trust gap. Whites almost exclusively experience traffic-safety stops and generally judge these stops to be basically fair. In addition to routine traffic-safety stops, African Americans also experience investigatory stops and generally judge *these* stops to be fundamentally *unfair*. These differences in underlying experiences and judgments of fairness have broader implications. Psychological research shows that people care about procedural fairness because *they view whether they are treated fairly as a measure of their standing in the community*.[45] Fair treatment implies that a person is viewed as a full and equal member of the community who is deserving of respect. Unfair treatment implies lower status, that you do not belong or deserve respect. Some psychological research suggests that people who are members of traditionally stigmatized groups, like racial minorities, are especially attentive to whether they are treated fairly.[46] Knowing that they and their group have long been viewed as second-class citizens (or worse), members of traditionally stigmatized groups are attentive to whether *this* official in *this* instance is treating them with the respect due a full and equal member of the community. It should come as no surprise that a police stop based on a pretext to criminally investigate the driver causes the person so targeted—Joe, for example—to feel violated. His rights and dignity *were* violated; he was treated as a thing, not a person.[47]

The broadest implication of distinguishing traffic-safety from investigatory stops is our observation that these two types of stops have profound consequences for people's sense of their place and status in American society. A pioneering study by Joe Soss found that when people's experience of government is limited to programs with arcane rules and arbitrary decision making, they come to believe that government in general is arbitrary and unfair and that they have little efficacy in shaping their own fate in its hands; but when people experience programs with predictable rules and reasonable decision making, they come to believe in their personal efficacy and equal status in a fair democratic system.[48] Other studies, on such diverse topics as the post–World War II GI Bill and Social Security, similarly have found that these egalitarian policies contributed to their beneficiaries' sense of efficacy and political engagement.[49] It is increasingly clear that policies shape politics and even the basic conditions of democracy.

But as Joe Soss, Jacob Hacker, and Suzanne Mettler show, a growing number of public policies *undermine* democratic equality and erode people's sense of political efficacy.[50] The investigatory stop is a key one of these *inequality*-inducing policies. Vesla Weaver and Amy Lerman have found that experiencing a police stop reduces one's likelihood of voting.[51] But this may go too far: the problem is not police stops in general but investigatory stops in particular. Our data show that while white drivers' experience of predictable, reasonable traffic-safety stops contributes to their perception of their equal status in a rule-governed democracy, African Americans' common experience of investigatory stops contributes to their perception that they are not regarded as full and equal members of society. Investigatory stops, we find, are significantly more likely to foster the perception that the police are "out to get people like me," and they render people significantly more likely to change the clothes they wear and avoid driving in some areas of the city for fear of how the police might treat them and to feel less comfortable calling the police for help. The notorious pass laws in South Africa under apartheid, which allowed black people into white areas only if carrying a pass authorizing entry, worked a similar evil, and no amount of professional courtesy and respectfulness can hide the deep violation at the core of this practice.

Leaders of professional policing occasionally have acknowledged these deeper truths, as we will explore in more detail in chapter 2. In a conference among police chiefs in 1999, just as racial disparities in police stops first reached national attention, two police leaders observed:

> Despite the constitutionality of the practice [of investigatory stops], motorists understand that they are being stopped for a different reason than the one provided and are angered by the inference needed to make the stop. The resulting anger could escalate hostility and risk greater physical danger for both the officer and motorist. The anger continues after the stop and is shared within the motorist's peer group. As more anecdotal stories circulate about such stops, the long-term effect on race relations must be balanced against the short-term effect on drug enforcement. Police managers may legitimately weigh race relations as more important than the potential arrest of a drug user or street level dealer.[52]

These comments acknowledge our central thesis: investigatory stops are an institutionally supported practice under the control of police leaders, not the isolated acts of individual police officers. This practice *by de-*

sign sacrifices the liberty and dignity of large numbers of innocent people, who are disproportionately racial minorities, in pursuit of a small number who are dangerous or carrying contraband. The innocent victims of this practice rightly feel that their status as free and equal members of society has been diminished, and they resent this implication and the police for enforcing this message.

Driving as a Condition of Democratic Citizenship and Equality

Racially defined investigatory stops, even if little more than a brief question or records check, are thus far more than a minor inconvenience. They strike at the heart of democratic citizenship and racial equality.

Outside our most densely populated urban cores, Americans drive to work, to see family and friends, to shop, and to visit places for recreation, worship, and political involvement.[53] We drive to parks where we can walk or bike safely distant from cars and their noise, pollution, and the road-scarred landscape. We drive to commit crime, and we may even drive to protest the building of a new highway. In the United States and increasingly around the globe, the mobility provided by cars has become essential for participation in economic and civic life. As John Urry writes, the car "is a sign of adulthood, a marker of citizenship and the basis of sociability and networking."[54] Our car-based social system is so pervasive, Urry continues, that we should reconceptualize the social landscapes "as a civil society of 'car-drivers' and 'car-passengers.'"[55]

In comparison to the essential democratic rights to speak, vote, and run for office, the freedom to drive may seem less important. Most traditional views of urban public spaces, such as Hannah Arendt's polis or Jurgen Habermas's coffee house, emphasize the democratic *discourse* in these settings.[56] From this deliberation-based perspective, driving—which is about getting places, not about shared deliberation—may seem less essentially democratic. Individual drivers, in their steel mobile living rooms insulated from others are, in many ways, the antithesis of engaged, deliberative citizens. Cars and roads thus can be viewed as "non-places of super modernity," to borrow Mimi Sheller and John Urry's phrase.[57]

Still, to many Americans, the freedom to drive is just as basic as the freedom to speak, and we should take seriously this popular assumption. "It's not just your car—it's your freedom!" Thus proclaimed an advertising campaign for a major auto manufacturer. It powerfully conveyed

Americans' dependence on, and celebration of, driving. While American law treats driving as a privilege, not a right, and personal vehicles as meriting less privacy from police intrusion than the constitutionally sacrosanct home, the American economy and culture treat driving and the car as something more. Given American society's limited public transportation systems, driving and the car are at once *economic necessities* and *prerequisites for personal freedom*. The economic necessity of driving is obvious. Eighty-six percent of working Americans drive to work; only 5 percent use public transportation.[58] Driving is not merely a choice; it is a requirement imposed on most Americans by the structure of our metropolitan areas and economy.

But driving is more than an economic necessity. It is for many in our car-centered society a prerequisite of freedom and full citizenship. For most Americans, coming of age is marked not by the right to vote or drink or the obligation to register with the selective service system. Earning a driver's license proclaims the step into adulthood with its opportunities for freedom and self-determination and its obligations of responsible behavior. In the 1950s, early advocates of drivers' education focused not just on safety and etiquette but also on how good driving is an expression of good citizenship. In teaching to stop and yield, to obey traffic laws, and to respect others on the road, drivers' education aimed to create the good citizen necessary to our mobile society. Safe drivers are safe citizens, these writers claimed, while inattentive or reckless drivers are dangerous citizens.[59]

As economic success became increasingly dependent on mobility, automobility became associated with upward social mobility. Cars, and now vans, trucks, and SUVs, have come to signify economic standing, lifestyle choices, and even political beliefs. Even choosing not to drive is a social or political statement as much as a practical choice. For most Americans the personal auto is a measure of status, and it has been so for decades.

The freedom to drive is especially important for African Americans and other racial minorities. "From its earliest days, the automobile symbolized mobility and freedom for blacks," Thomas Sugrue has observed.[60] "Cars became a powerful symbol of 'making it,'" and, by driving, African Americans could escape the rampant segregation of public buses, subways, and trains.[61] In September 1949, *Ebony*, the magazine of African American upward mobility, published an essay, "Why the Negro Drives a Cadillac." At a time when no ads for Cadillac appeared in

Ebony and Cadillac hired only white salesmen, the big expensive car was the symbol of economic success.[62] Jeremy Packer comments, "The automobile is the quintessential sign of American success, and for African Americans this was especially the case, as it also signified freedom from the restriction on mobility blacks had suffered since their arrival in the Americas centuries before."[63] Long into the post–civil rights era Cadillacs and other classic American luxury cars, along with the freedom to drive, have symbolized freedom and equality for many African Americans.[64] Likewise, in Latino communities, as Ben Chappell has shown, the carefully crafted lowrider is both an expression of personal artistry and a proud symbol of "making it."[65] In the lowrider, as in the lovingly restored classic Cadillac in African American neighborhoods, mobility, equality, and expression come together.

Perhaps the strongest evidence of the link between mobility and citizenship is found in the enduring effort of societies to manage the mobility of groups deemed unworthy of full citizenship. Long before U. S. governments issued driver's licenses, passports, or visas and decades before emancipation, African Americans, both slave and free, were issued traveling papers to document who was free to travel to what locations. As Packer notes, "This documentation was a form of both verification and surveillance."[66] Even as driving gave newfound freedom to African Americans, Sugrue observes, it exposed them to a new form of discrimination: intrusive police stops of vehicles.[67] During the long years of apartheid, South African pass laws mapped where blacks were allowed to live and travel. "Effectively, to be African and not employed in such areas [near or in white population centers] became a crime against which police forces could be used," writes Julia Wells. "Passless Africans faced fines, imprisonment, forced labour or expulsion from the area until they contracted employment."[68] In the United States, controversy recently followed the decision by some states to allow undocumented immigrants to have driver's licenses, as if having a driver's license was tantamount to becoming a citizen. For example, Utah created special "driving privilege cards" that declared in bold red ink, "'cannot be used as a legal identification' to allow the undocumented necessary mobility while restricting their citizenship."[69] Moreover, denying a driver's license created one more layer of illegality to the status of undocumented immigrants: driving to work, church, or the grocery store were no longer routine aspects of living, but breaking the law.[70]

Study Design and Methods

This book is based on an extensive survey of drivers and dozens of traffic stop narratives told by drivers and police officers. We surveyed by phone a stratified random sample of the driving population in the Kansas City metropolitan area in 2003 and 2004; 2,329 drivers completed the survey. Approximately 12 percent of drivers are stopped over the course of a year, and to achieve an adequate sample of stopped drivers, we oversampled those who reported being stopped in the past year. Among drivers, we contrast the police-stop experiences of white and African American drivers. To adequately sample African American drivers, we oversampled these drivers as well. We received responses from 708 drivers who reported being stopped in the year prior to answering the survey. Among these stopped drivers, 497 (70 percent) were white and 211 (30 percent) were black.

Using a driver survey allows us to address several problems vexing much past research on racial profiling.[71] The first is whether the deep racial disparities observed in pedestrian stop-and-frisks, as has occurred in New York City, are typical of police activities *generally*. Unfortunately, the studies of stop-and-frisks, although methodologically state-of-the-art, are not able to address this fundamental question, because their data are limited that one particular activity; they have no data on racial disparities in other police activities. Our survey of drivers allows us to compare patterns in investigatory stops and more-conventional traffic-safety stops. A second problem vexing past research is the difficulty of measuring a population baseline for comparing the stop rates of whites and African Americans. Many studies rely on the racial composition of the local population in general, but it is widely recognized that the driving population may be quite different from the residential population. Our survey allows careful measurement of the baseline. The third problem is the lack of information in past studies on drivers who are *not* stopped: do they drive better than those who are stopped, or are they free of stops for some other reason, like being white? Our survey allows us to address these questions. Fourth, many studies lack adequate data on many key aspects of the stop experience. Past studies have relied on official traffic-stop data, but these do not include information on driving behavior, value and condition of their vehicle, how the driver and officer acted during the stop, and drivers' perceptions and evaluations of the stop. Again, our survey offers data on these key matters. In developing our survey, we drew on a handful of earlier survey-based studies,[72] but ours goes beyond these by eliciting from drivers a broader range of information about their own personal characteristics, the nature of the stop experience, their evaluations of it, and their level of trust in the police and their perceptions of their own place in society.

Survey questions are necessarily limited, however, and we dig deeper into drivers' perceptions and the dynamic character of police stops by drawing on drivers' narratives of stops. After completing the survey, we conducted in-depth follow-up interviews with a systematic, unbiased subsample of drivers who had been stopped in the past year. The narrative opening this chapter is one such story. For these follow-up interviews we sampled both whites and African Americans, young and old, and responsible and risky drivers. We specifically did not select these respondents based on their survey responses regarding their experiences in police stops. These interviews yielded narratives of stop experiences in the drivers' own words. As Richard Delgado and Mario Barnes have argued, narratives often offer a more complete view of peoples' experiences and perceptions of discrimination than can be gained by analyzing statistical patterns alone.[73] Drivers' narratives also help us to avoid placing our own interpretations on peoples' perceptions and experiences. While journalistic accounts of racial profiling often rely on drivers' narratives,[74] skeptics may fairly ask whether the narratives chosen for presentation are extreme and unusual: how often—really—do officers stop drivers for tiny violations and then immediately search the vehicle? Our survey-based sampling for drivers' narratives helps to ensure that the narratives we present in this book represent typical patterns rather than extreme examples. In sum, unlike other studies that report patterns in traffic tickets (but thereby ignore all of the stops that result in no ticket) or report a handful of anecdotes of horrific or simply offensive pretextual stops, our random survey and systematic sampling strategy for the follow-up interviews ensures that our conclusions are drawn from a broad cross-section of the population.

Two other methodological issues deserve brief discussion. One is why we focus on black/white differences. Other ethnic and racial differences are essential research topics but are beyond the scope of this book. Punitive anti-immigration policies and police surveillance increasingly target Latinos, and the prison population of Latinos is growing rapidly. But investigatory stops have targeted primarily African Americans, and several studies of patterns in police stops observe that the black/white disparities are the heart of the problem; Latino/white disparities are somewhat less severe.[75] Likewise, as observed by noted books on racial disparities in the criminal justice system, among them Michelle Alexander's *The New Jim Crow*, Michael Tonry's *Punishing Race*, and Jerome Miller's *Search and Destroy*, the heart of the problem is the disparity between whites and African Americans.[76] Further, while the Latino population in the Kansas City metro area is growing, it remains proportionally small and difficult to feasibly study via a survey focusing on drivers. By concentrating on differences between white and black drivers, we focus on the area of deepest racial disparity.

The other issue is whether our research site, the Kansas City metropolitan area, is somehow unique and thus may skew our findings. We think it is not unique. With some two million residents in a multicounty area, it is like many throughout the country, and there is every reason to believe that our findings apply elsewhere as well. The Kansas City area is typical of urban-suburban sprawl cities that cover many jurisdictions and vary dramatically in racial composition and wealth. The contiguous city boundaries of the Kansas City metro area span two states, Missouri and Kansas, six counties, and forty-four cities. Median household income just prior to the survey varied by city from a low of $33,011 in Kansas City, Kansas, to a high of $188,821 in Mission Hills, Kansas.[77] African Americans represent a low of zero percent of the population in several small, extremely wealthy suburban city jurisdictions and a high of 31 percent in Kansas City, Missouri.

Nor are the sharp racial disparities that we find in Kansas City-area police stops unique. Numerous studies have found racial disparities in police stops throughout the country: in the dense, multiracial and multiethnic coastal cities of Los Angeles and New York City, but also the large Midwestern sprawls of Wichita, Kansas, and St. Louis, Missouri; in progressive, reform-oriented police departments like those in some of the Kansas City jurisdictions, but also traditional "political" departments like that of Boston; on major interstate highways in Maryland and New Jersey but also rural highways in Louisiana.[78] We argue that the institutional rules undergirding investigatory stops and the practice of these stops are not unique to Kansas City but instead are national phenomena, and in chapter 2 we will examine the development of these institutional rules. Here, one point from that discussion is relevant: investigatory stops have been widely implemented throughout the country,

and the Kansas City metro area is in this respect no different. One way
to illustrate this is to highlight the expert sources used by police consultant Charles Remsberg in developing his widely followed training manual *Tactics for Criminal Patrol*, a recipe book for how to make investigatory stops. Remsberg drew on the contributions of police trainers and
patrol officers in dozens of police agencies around the country, among
them the state police in the West (California and Oregon), Midwest (Illinois and Ohio), Northeast (New Jersey and New York), the Great Plains
(Kansas), Southwest (Arizona), and the South (Louisiana, Arkansas,
and Alabama).[79] Among city police departments and local sheriff's departments, his sources are again drawn from every region of the country
and every size of city: Tupelo, Mississippi; Chicago, Illinois; Washington DC; Anaheim, Los Angeles, and San Diego, California; Jacksonville
and Ft. Lauderdale, Florida; Little Rock and West Memphis, Arkansas;
Phoenix, Arizona; Milwaukee, Wisconsin; Tillamook County, Oregon;
and Albany, New York, among many others.[80] Police departments in all
of these areas were the source of professional knowledge about how to
carry out investigatory stops. The Kansas City metropolitan area is no
different from communities across the nation with regard to investigatory stops.

When we report that the vast majority of African American drivers
have experienced at least one highly intrusive police stop, and when we
offer illustrative examples of these stops in the drivers' own words, we
can be reasonably sure that these are representative patterns. We discuss
our research design and methods in more detail in the appendix.

Meaning of "Race"

The United States is historically divided by race, but who is "black" and
who is "white" and who belongs to other racially defined groups has no
fixed meaning. Shared understandings of these categories are shaped by
culture, politics, and policy. For this reason scholars increasingly question the common practice of defining "race" in binary terms (black/
white), treating these terms as if they had an obvious meaning, and assuming that race is a cause—of different rates of high school graduation,
for example—rather than an effect—of school policies, for example.[81]

We have incorporated some of these lessons in this study. We asked
our survey respondents to self-identify their race, and we allowed them

to identify whatever category or categories of race or ethnicity they wished.[82] But we also recognized that a person's race, in the current ordinary language meaning of that term and in the specific context of a police stop by an officer who does not know the driver, may be as much a matter of how the person looks, or, to put it slightly differently, may be a matter of the person's street presentation. This may include not only skin pigmentation, hair type, and so forth, but also style of dress, linguistic accent, and perhaps even type of vehicle. Therefore, we also asked our survey respondents to tell us what race they would appear to be in the view of somebody who had just met them on the street and did not know them.

We also asked respondents to tell us how much they look like a number of different types of people: construction worker, lawyer or doctor, hip-hop artist, factory worker, retiree, professional athlete, businessperson, twenty-something college student, working person trying to make ends meet, and so forth. These are not racial categories, per se, but that is in part the point. In the eyes of a police officer, what it means for a driver to be "black" might be shaped by how much the person looks like a lawyer or a hip-hop artist.

But a basic point of the recent research on the meaning of race is that the racial divide in American society is not simply a carryover from the past, but is also a product of *current practices and policies.*[83] We share this view. When the police stop an African American man, require him to stand at the front of his car, perhaps in handcuffs, while the officer searches the car and other drivers stare as they whiz by in comparative freedom, the drivers' race may have been a key part of what sparked the decision to make the stop. But it is also likely that this widespread practice shapes perceptions of stopped driver and passers-by alike of who is black and the meaning of race. Blacks and other minorities are ones who are held by the side of the road while police officers rummage through their cars. In this way police stops shape the meaning of race in an ongoing way.

The Plan of the Book

Police stops flow in several stages, and we have devoted a chapter to each of these stages. Chapter 2 examines the planning and development of the investigatory police stop, placing it in the context of police reform in the wake of the civil rights movement and the urban riots of the 1960s and in the context of what is known about the psychology of implicit racial stereotypes. Chapter 3 examines the decision to stop a driver and how investigatory stops and traffic-safety stops yield different patterns in who is stopped; while the key explanation of who is stopped in traffic-safety stops is how you drive, the key explanation of who is stopped in investigatory stops is who you are. Chapters 4 and 5 examine what transpires during the stop. It is an interactive process shaped by the actions of both driver and officer. Chapter 4 shows that the type of stop determines the script governing this interaction; both officers and drivers follow different scripts in investigatory stops versus traffic-safety stops. Chapter 5 goes on to show that officers' investigatory inquiries are largely targeted at African Americans and that these inquiries unfold in a rationally managed pattern, under the control of officers, rather than emerging in response to provocations by drivers. Chapter 6 examines how drivers evaluate the legitimacy of police stops. It shows that white and black drivers view stops through different evaluative frames that reflect their very different patterns of experiences in these stops. Black drivers, having a familiarity with intrusive investigatory stops, recognize when they are being subjected to such a stop and evaluate it negatively no matter how polite or respectful the officer. Chapter 7 expands the view to show that the experience of investigatory stops erodes drivers' overall trust in the police, willingness to call the police for help, sense of their own freedom to drive, and sense of their place in society. Chapter 8 offers a concluding analysis and suggestions for reform.

In the debate over whether (or how many) individual police officers are racists, whether stopping black people at higher rates is helpful in fighting crime, and how stop-and-searches can be made less offensive by training officers to be polite and respectful, two basic points have been missed. Racial disparities in who is stopped and searched are the product not simply of myriad individual officers' decisions but of coordinated guidance from above. The investigatory stop is an *institutionalized* practice. And investigatory stops cause harm—real, palpable harm to real people, most of whom are innocent.

Looking Beyond the License Plate

Police stop and search racial minorities at disproportionately high rates, and these disparities have grown wider in recent years; these well-established observations are not only troubling but puzzling. With the civil rights era the United States embarked on a historic effort to eradicate racial discrimination and fulfill its promise of equal protection of law. The vast majority of Americans have come to view overt racial bias as immoral, and virtually all major institutions have sought to end past policies and practices of racial discrimination. Racial discrimination has been reduced to an obvious wrongness that would have seemed impossible fifty years ago. The police, too, engaged in searching reform to eradicate overt racial discrimination among their ranks and become more responsive to local communities, white and black alike.

Why racial disparities in police stops remain so wide is the subject of this chapter. The answer, we believe, is not the reemergence (or continuation) of frank racism within the ranks of the police. Instead, the source of these disparities is a police practice, the investigatory stop, that is regarded by many police leaders and frontline officers as quintessentially "professional," but in its implementation targets African Americans and Latinos. It does so because implicit racial stereotypes of black and Latino criminality were built into the practice's design from the start, and these implicit stereotypes continue to shape how officers act while employing the practice. While overt racism did not *produce* this poisonous interaction between professional practice and implicit racial stereotypes, the failure of professional policing to address the racial disparities generated by it is less easy to absolve. We proceed by examining first the creation of the investigatory stop, and second, how implicit racial biases are expressed in it.

Inventing the Investigatory Stop

To understand how professional policing has come to celebrate the investigatory stop in spite of its racial consequences, it is useful to put the development of this policing technique in the context of the institutional structure of policing and of the police reforms of the past generation. After summarizing this context, our focus turns to the police rules, norms, and beliefs that support the practice of investigatory stop.

We focus particularly on how the idea and practice of investigatory stops developed and gained professional legitimacy. We understand legitimacy, in the words of Mark Suchman, as "a generalized perception or assumption that the actions of an entity are desirable, proper, or appropriate" in reference to a larger system of beliefs or ideas.[1] Since the civil rights era the key standards for legitimacy in policing have been responsiveness to the community (thus, "community policing") and fidelity to the nondiscrimination imperative. As these twin standards gained ascendance, and after the Kerner Commission identified the practice as racially discriminatory and a key trigger of the urban riots of the 1960s, the practice of investigatory stops, which was widespread in the 1960s, suffered a loss of legitimacy.[2] In the 1980s and 1990s police leaders worked to revive and relegitimate the practice of investigatory stops, with the consequence that this practice has come to enjoy more widespread use and support than ever before.

Three developments contributed to the revival and relegitimation of the investigatory stop, and we will examine each in turn. The first was the wave of institutional reforms of policing in the wake of the civil rights era. The second was research by policing scholars claiming that investigatory stops were among professional policing's most effective crime-fighting tools. Accompanying this research was the development of remarkably detailed knowledge about how, *tactically*, to effectively carry out these stops. This body of knowledge grew out of the federal government's war on drugs and the police training provided as part of that initiative, which spread ideas about how to carry out investigatory stops so as to discover contraband in vehicles. This research and the accompanying improvements in stop tactics and training convinced police leaders that investigatory stops were an effective strategy. Proving their effectiveness, at least in the eyes of police professionals, contributed to what Suchman has called "instrumental" legitimacy, a preliminary stage in a process of legitimation.[3] Still, some effective practices are prohibited and morally scorned, and so more was needed than a belief in the practice's effectiveness. The third development consisted of higher-order efforts to legitimate investigatory stops as right and proper in relation to the nondiscrimination imperative. This final stage was supplied by key judicial decisions and, ironically, by the police profession's response to the racial profiling controversy of the late 1990s. In that response, police leaders argued that racial disparities in police stops are the product of deliberate discrimination by (relatively few) individual officers—not broader institutionalized practices—and they pledged to stamp out this sort of individual racism with professional training and oversight. At the same time they defended investigatory stops as essentially professional and faithful to the principle of nondiscrimination when controlled by professional training and oversight. This final development thus took the form of what Suchman has called "normative" legitimation, or supporting a practice by tying it to higher-order (here, legal) norms.[4]

The upshot was that investigatory stops, a practice widely maligned in the late 1960s as discriminatory and counterproductive, enjoyed increasing support within policing in the 1980s and 1990s as a quintessentially professional innovation.

The Institutional Context: Localized Policing Shaped by Waves of Reform

Policing in the United States is extraordinarily decentralized among tens of thousands of local police departments and dozens of state police agencies. This hyper-local structure has long frustrated the efforts of police reformers. Still, successive waves of reform have swept through police departments, bringing a common form and common policies. The leading reforms of the mid-twentieth century worked to insulate departments from direct political control, professionalize the selection and training of officers, and bring officers under the control of the department's central command.[5] Policing retains much of the legacy of this paramilitary, hierarchical, bureaucratic structure. By the mid-1960s, policing seemed increasingly insulated, unresponsive, and racially biased.[6] For example, leading big-city departments deployed teams of mainly white officers to carry out aggressive patrols and large numbers of police stops in poor, minority neighborhoods. The practice caused intense resentment and, as we will describe in more detail shortly, triggered the urban riots of that decade.

Unknown to many Americans, in the succeeding decades professional police departments worked to eradicate racial discrimination by officers and become more open to community concerns. Where fifty years ago the ranks of police officers in most departments were entirely white and male, many departments are now remarkably diverse, made up of men and women, African Americans, Latinos, Asian Americans, and gays as well as straights.[7] This diversification was once a key flashpoint of controversy, but it is now an accomplished social fact. Decades ago, police departments were regarded as bureaucratically insular and resistant to community concerns, but most departments now celebrate community policing, a cluster of reforms aimed at making police policies and practices more responsive to public concerns through decentralization, community engagement, and a focus on addressing neighborhood problems.[8]

In the mid-twentieth century, police departments allowed their officers to use force as they felt appropriate, and, as a result, many young black men were shot or beaten by the police; now virtually all departments try to control their officers' uses of force with detailed rules, training, and internal oversight.[9] As a direct result the number of shootings and beatings has declined. More generally, police departments now condemn any open expression of racism by officers or any decision to stop a driver solely on the basis of the driver's race.

On each of these dimensions—diversity, community responsiveness, regulation of the use of force, and eradication of racist views among officers—some departments are rightly criticized. But many, vastly more than would have been considered possible in the 1960s, earn well-deserved praise.[10]

Still, some aspects of policing are more entrenched and enduring, and they provide the conditions for what we are about to describe. The most basic of these enduring features is that the mission of the police is to fight crime, and, following this, that individual officers are celebrated and rewarded for making arrests. Policing's crime-fighting mission developed as a core feature of professional reform in the twentieth century; it was the key replacement to the older police mission of service to the urban political machines.[11] This mission remains alive and well in the twenty-first century, even as police departments evolved to be more responsive to their communities and more oriented toward addressing underlying problems that give rise to crime. A key consequence of this mission is to reward officers for making arrests; making a "big bust" will inevitably remain among officers' most desired goals.

Second, as Jerome Skolnick and Michael Tonry have emphasized, making arrests and big busts will always be easier in the disorderly context of poor urban neighborhoods than in wealthier urban and suburban neighborhoods.[12] Official efforts at crime control, therefore, will inevitably focus on poorer neighborhoods. For one thing, residents of poor urban neighborhoods spend more of their time and conduct more of their transactions—illegal as well as legal—out of doors where they are more vulnerable to surveillance and arrest. Drug sales are as frequent in wealthier neighborhoods, but they occur indoors. If arrest is the goal, and it is, then this goal is far more easily met on the street in poor urban neighborhoods than inside suburban homes.

Third, perhaps the most basic enduring feature of street-level police work is what Skolnick described as the combination of authority and danger.[13] Officers exercise and seek to impose the authority of the state in situations that are often uncertain and sometimes dangerous. They learn to be suspicious of members of the public and are prepared to use force, including deadly force, to maintain control of a situation and protect their own life and that of others. Underneath contemporary police reforms and the latest criminal justice innovations are the enduring features of police work: a strong commitment to the mission of fighting crime, a focus of this mission on poor and disorderly neighborhoods, and the visceral, personal, and collective belief that authority must be exercised firmly in order to head off threats of violence.

Riots and Reinvention

Among the most important of the recent innovations is the investigatory stop: a police stop where the intent is not to sanction a driving violation but to look for evidence of more serious criminal wrongdoing. In a general sense the police have carried out investigatory stops for decades. Officers have long stopped suspicious-looking characters and asked what they are up to, and since the development of car patrols in the 1930s and 1940s, they have sometimes stopped suspicious-looking drivers to do the same. In the 1960s, some big-city departments took these efforts to extremes and encouraged their officers to stop large numbers of people in minority ghettoes.[14] These heavy-handed stops created intense resentment in minority neighborhoods. The presidential Kerner Commission famously identified police stops and searches as the trigger for many of the devastating urban riots of the 1960s.[15] Surveys of the riot-torn cities showed that large numbers of African Americans and Latinos reported being stopped, searched, and even hit by the police.[16]

In the wake of the riots professional policing reinvented the investigatory stop in a more systematic, seemingly legitimate form. A first step was to back off the widespread use of these stops. By the 1970s, studies commonly reported police indifference rather than aggressive stops in the nation's inner cities.[17]

At the same time, police leaders and scholars began to rethink how to do police stops. The key early study was the Kansas City Preventive Patrol Experiment of 1973, which removed police patrols from some neighborhoods while leaving them in place in others.[18] The study's surprising conclusion was that suspending preventive patrols affected neither the crime rate nor residents' perceptions of police protection. While no department stopped using preventive patrol, the experiment provoked many police leaders to begin asking whether the police should take a different approach to fighting crime.

By the late 1970s the germ of a different, more "proactive" approach to making police stops emerged. James Q. Wilson and Barbara Boland in 1978 called on police to shift from random patrol to what they called — still using the old term — "aggressive patrol." Aggressive patrol consisted of "maximiz[ing] the number of interventions in and observations of the community," or, in other words, of surveilling, stopping, and searching as many drivers as possible, "especially suspicious ones."[19] Such aggressive stops, Wilson and Boland argued, would reduce crime by increasing the likelihood that the police would "find fugitives, detect contraband . . . and apprehend persons fleeing from the scene of a crime."[20] Several subsequent studies reported empirical support for the idea that aggressive stops might reduce the crime rate.[21]

By the early 1980s, Wilson and another colleague, George Kelling, pushed the aggressive patrol proposal further, calling on departments to make arrests in troubled neighborhoods for such minor violations as public drinking, graffitiing, and loitering.[22] They based this proposal on what they called the "Broken Windows" theory, which posited that low-level disorder like loitering contributes to a shared perception in a neighborhood that order in general has broken down. This perception, they

argued, encourages offenders to take the risk of committing more serious offenses. To forestall this dynamic, Wilson and Kelling argued that
police should arrest people for contributing to public disorder: for public drunkenness, loitering, and the like. In 1994, Wilson went further and
called on the police to use widespread stops and searches as a means to
seize guns so as to reduce the murder rate.[23]

Within a year, a research team led by Lawrence Sherman, one of the
country's leading policing scholars, confirmed that traffic stops aimed at
seizing guns could reduce the crime rate. The study, called the Kansas
City Gun Experiment, found that police stops for the purpose of searching vehicles for guns in high-crime neighborhoods directly contributed
to reductions in gun-related crime in those neighborhoods.[24] Officers
participating in the study were instructed to use any legal pretext to stop
suspicious vehicles and then use any legal reason to carry out vehicle
and person searches and seize guns. These vehicle stop-and-searches
yielded a significantly higher number of seized guns than in comparison
neighborhoods, and gun-related crimes declined significantly in comparison to these other neighborhoods. It is hard to overstate the influence of the Kansas City Gun Experiment. For the first time in the wake
of the Kansas City Preventive Patrol Experiment, a carefully designed
study had demonstrated that not all police patrol activities were a waste
of time and resources: patrol aimed at stopping and searching vehicles
"worked." An Indianapolis study soon claimed to confirm the Kansas
City study,[25] and then other studies showed that proactive stops in crime
hot spots could reduce the rate of crime in targeted areas.[26]

The evidence favoring investigatory stops' effectiveness in general,
though, was mixed. The Indianapolis replication of the Kansas City Gun
Experiment in part failed, a point we return to in this book's conclusion.[27] A second replication in Pittsburgh was initially thought to confirm some (albeit modest) crime-reduction effects of investigatory stops,
but a recent scientific review concluded that these effects were probably
exaggerated by limitations in the study's methods, and police stops in
fact may have led to no significant decline in crime.[28]

Still, scholars and police leaders widely viewed this line of research,
stretching from Wilson and Boland's 1978 paper through the Indianapolis replication of the gun experiment and targeted hot spots policing,
as demonstrating the utility of aggressive stop-and-searches, especially
in high-crime areas. Thus, in a widely cited policy analysis submitted
to Congress of what works in police crime-prevention, Sherman and his

colleagues reported that directed patrol and proactive arrests, including arrests for low-level violations by young men, showed promise in reducing crime.[29] Regarding proactive arrests in traffic stops and foot-patrol stops, these scholars reported that "there appear to be substantial results from focusing scarce arrest resources on high risk people, places, offenses, and times."[30] This conclusion came with a prescient caveat: the long-term social costs of proactive police stops and arrests may overwhelm their short-term crime-fighting benefits. Those stopped and arrested for minor offenses may have more trouble getting a job, may learn to distrust the police, and may become more "defiant."[31] But this early doubt was not widely noted.

Stops Enlisted in the War on Drugs

The research just summarized coincided with a massive federal war on drugs. This "war" targeted low-level drug dealers and users, but in practice this was deeply biased. As Doris Marie Provine has shown, while drug-use surveys consistently find that whites, blacks, and Latinos use illegal drugs at similar rates, the war on drugs rested on the assumption that racial minorities are the primary users and traffickers of illegal drugs.[32] Virtually all of the imagery used to support this policy identified African Americans and Latinos as the source of the problem and its principal victims.[33]

A key innovation in this war was to turn the ordinary police and highway patrol officer into drug law enforcers. Previously this role had been played by specialist squads of drug or vice detectives. Departing from that practice, the federal Drug Enforcement Agency developed a specialized knowledge on how ordinary front-line officers could be taught to carry out investigatory stops and make drug arrests. With "Operation Pipeline," the DEA trained ordinary state and local officers to use drug-courier profiles to select drivers for investigatory traffic stops.[34] While the elements of this profile included a number of behavioral characteristics, they also included ethnicity and race: trainers and training films identified Hispanics and African Americans as more likely to be carrying drugs.[35] By the late 1990s the DEA had trained some twenty-seven thousand state and local police officers in the practice of investigatory stops, and many of these officers went on to train others in their local departments.[36] In recent years the use of investigatory stops has spread to immigration-law enforcement, as local police and sheriff's departments in some areas have encouraged their officers to stop people suspected of lacking immigration papers.[37]

While investigatory stops are not new, the practice gained renewed acceptance and widespread adoption after the mid-1980s. Although the DEA had used profiles to select airline passengers for drug searches as early as 1976, both David Harris and Gary Webb concluded that the informal experiments by a Florida Highway Patrol officer in 1984 encouraged the general the use of these stops by regular police officers in the war on drugs.[38] The emergence in the late 1980s and early 1990s of legal controversy over these stops also suggests the spread of the practice. In 1987, New Jersey public defenders began receiving large numbers of drug cases arising out of traffic stops on the New Jersey turnpike and civil liberties groups collected over two hundred complaints from drivers who had been stopped and searched with no justification.[39] In 1990, a New Jersey public defender office opened the first formal investigation into the pattern.[40] Several studies of police practices reported growing use of investigatory stops by urban police departments in the early 1990s.[41] Our own interviews with officers indicate a shift over this period from limited to more widespread use of investigatory stops. For example, a senior command-level officer told us, "sure, years ago [the early 1980s], if we were investigating a particular dirt-bag, we would sometimes use a traffic stop to get him, but now, in particular areas of town, which we select based on crime statistics, *we stop everything that moves.*"[42]

The Courts Weigh In

Investigatory stops raise questions of illegal searches and seizures, but by the mid-1990s, the federal courts ruled that investigatory stops did not violate Fourth Amendment and other protections of individual rights. The key Supreme Court decision was *Whren v. United States* (1996).[43] In that case police officers were trolling for illegal drug sales in a poor African American neighborhood in Washington DC and saw the occupants of a small pickup truck apparently looking down at something on the pickup's seat as they lingered at a stop sign. When approached by the officers, Michael Whren, the driver, quickly made a turn without signaling and drove away. The officers pulled him over for failing to signal a turn and searched the pickup, found illegal drugs, and arrested him and his passenger, James Brown, both black men, for drug possession. Both were convicted.

A unanimous Supreme Court ruled that stops are legitimate if based on *any* objective violation of the law, no matter how minor, and officers may use minor violations as pretexts to seek evidence of more serious criminal wrongdoing. Although the court acknowledged the significance of Whren's allegation of racial bias, the justices suggested that a traffic stop would be unconstitutionally discriminatory only if the defendant could show that officers had intentionally used race as the primary reason for selecting him for a stop.[44] Proving intentional discrimination requires in practice that officers admit in court what is unspeakable and what no socially attuned officer will ever say: that their primary reason for stopping a car was the race of the driver. *Police Chief* magazine immediately reported that *Whren* "preserve[s] officers' ability to use traffic stops to uncover other criminal activities."[45] Enrollments in Operation Pipeline grew rapidly,[46] and a California Highway Patrol training officer crowed, "After *Whren* the game was over. We won."[47]

In key follow-up cases, the Supreme Court expanded police powers to use traffic stops for investigations. *Knowles v. Iowa* (1998) authorized officers to conduct pat-down searches of the occupants of a vehicle and the areas within their reach so long as the officer justifies these searches as necessary to guard against a perceived risk of attack.[48] *United States v. Arvizu* (2002) authorized officers to stop and search a vehicle if the "totality of the circumstances" supported reasonable suspicion of criminal activity, even if no single element of those circumstances rose to the level of probable cause to justify the stop.[49] After this string of decisions it is difficult to identify what sorts of police stop-and-searches are not constitutionally legitimate. The line between illegal and legal is reduced to little more than whether or not the officer "articulates" a set of plausibly suspicious driver behaviors as the justification for a stop and search. *Police Chief's* report to its readers of the *Arvizu* decision said as much: "Our [police chiefs'] responsibility is to assure that officers include all of the relevant observations in their reports and testimony in court," which is to say, train your officers to give legal justifications for their decisions.[50] Likewise, *Police Chief* reported that *Knowles* means that to justify a vehicle search: "Police chiefs and administrators should always have their officers articulate the dangers they are facing and how those dangers affect their decisions. Often, that will be the difference between winning and losing a case."[51] In other words, the difference between a legal and illegal stop is not *what the officer saw and did* but *how he or she describes it.*

Institutionalized Police Practice

By the 1990s the investigatory stop had become scripted, predictable, and deeply institutionalized. By this we mean that investigatory stops are not the creation of individual officers' discretionary decisions but of organized training, professional norms, and shared expectations. *Police Chief* magazine, the official voice of the International Association of Chiefs of Police (IACP), repeatedly and enthusiastically encouraged police departments to adopt this practice. As the director of the IACP's traffic-enforcement program put it in 1996:

> Savvy police administrators have rediscovered the value of traffic enforcement. They see it not as simply an end in itself, but also as a valuable tool—as a means to an end and an integral part of both criminal interdiction and community policing. An alert police officer who 'looks beyond the traffic ticket' and uses the motor vehicle stop to 'sniff out' possible criminal behavior may be our most effective tool for interdicting criminals.[52]

This is but one of many ringing endorsements of the investigatory stop to appear in IACP publications.[53] In 2000, the association created the Looking Beyond the License Plate award, given annually to officers who made major criminal arrests in traffic stops.[54]

Training in how to make investigatory stops was equally systematic, enthusiastic, and detailed. To illustrate, we draw on a book-length police training text, *Tactics for Criminal Patrol* by Charles Remsberg, which has been described by a leading police consultant and former Los Angeles deputy police chief as "authoritative" and "used by police agencies throughout the nation."[55] The investigatory stop, Remsberg teaches, is a type of police traffic stop that "seeks to maximize the number of citizen contacts in vehicle stops during each shift and, through specific investigative techniques, to explore the full arrest potential of each."[56] In carrying out investigatory stops, officers proceed through the following sequential steps that form what Remsberg called the "Criminal Patrol Pyramid":[57]

1) Develop suspicion (or, typically, merely curiosity) about a driver.
2) Discover a legal justification to stop the driver (typically this justification is some minor violation of the traffic laws or vehicle code), and make the stop.
3) Decide, after making the stop, whether to seek to search the vehicle based on

the close observation of the vehicle and its visible contents and dialogue with the driver (and passengers). Officers use this dialogue to assess the truthfulness of the driver.

4) Search the vehicle ("usually by consent").
5) Discover contraband or weapons.
6) Make an arrest.
7) Seek "bonus benefits" (forfeiture of vehicle, cash, etc.; information about additional criminal offenses).

Police training materials offer detailed guidance for each of these steps. These boil down to Remsberg's basic recommendation to "train yourself to regard out-of-the-ordinary as potentially criminal."[58] In this training, reasonable suspicion of criminal activity, in a legal sense, is not the basis for an investigatory stop. Officers are to pursue stops and searches on the basis of little more than unsatisfied curiosity. As a federal judge observed in *Ligon v. City of New York*, the New York police department's training in how to conduct stop-and-frisks "has taught officers the following lesson: Stop and question first, develop reasonable suspicion later."[59]

Regarding which drivers to pull over, Remsberg identifies a number of things that should arouse an officer's curiosity: vehicle modifications, unusually dirty vehicles, unusual driving behaviors, and drivers or vehicles that appear to be out of place.[60] The race of the driver is implicitly—and sometimes explicitly—a factor.

The training manual describes in detail the subsequent stages of the investigatory stop. After the stop is made, the key decision facing the officer is how far to push the investigation, and it is to be made by observing the vehicle and its contents and by asking questions of the driver. When the officer's initial suspicion or curiosity is resolved through these inquiries, the driver is quickly let go. But when the officer's initial curiosity grows during the course of the inquiries, he or she is to push the investigation through to a search of the vehicle. Thus, upon approaching the vehicle, the officer should conduct a "sensory pat down" of the vehicle and driver. "This is the pivotal period when you must quickly decide whether the subject you've just stopped is 'just' a traffic violator who should be warned or ticketed and sent on his way—or a felony suspect who warrants the full Criminal Patrol treatment."[61] The officer should visually inspect the vehicle's interior and then engage the driver in casual conversation—Remsberg calls it a "concealed interrogation"—for the purpose of sniffing out evidence of deception.[62] Another guide encourages the officer to "ask non-threatening questions, such as 'Where are you going? What is the purpose of your trip? Are you on vacation or is this a business trip?'"[63] Then, "as you are talking to the motorist . . . look around the vehicle for items supporting the person's story."[64]

The ultimate stage of the investigation is a search of the vehicle. Remsberg's discussion assumes that in most stops the officer will fail to establish probable cause for a search and so must gain the driver's "consent" to conduct a search. Remsberg offers multiple tactics to obtain consent. He describes how to ensure that the driver consents to a general search of the entire vehicle and its contents, explains how to document that the consent was given and that it was "voluntary," and provides extensive guidance on how to pressure the driver into consenting if he or she initially declines.[65] *Tactics of Criminal Patrol* trains officers on how to "position" the driver "emotionally to grant you his permission." Officers cannot legally ask drivers for consent to search while they are detained, but Remsberg suggests that officers keep up a casual conversation while handing back the driver's documents, the point at which the driver is free to go. "With a 'seamless' transition" at this critical point "the suspect is less likely to register the fact that his status has officially changed" to being free to leave. "Psychologically, though, the chances are overwhelming that the average person won't leave at that 'break' point. . . . After all, you're the police and you're still talking to him. As a practical matter, his freedom to disregard your questions and split simply doesn't occur to him."[66]

Then casually set the driver up for consent to search. "One option is to pretend that the idea of searching has occurred to you as an afterthought. . . . Turn, as if you're going to walk away after you've returned his papers, then, still acting the good ol' boy, turn back and broach the subject cordially, lightly, almost as a joke: 'Say, can I ask you a question?' Wait for him to agree, then: 'You know, I sure run into a lot of strange things out here. You don't have any bazookas or drugs or atomic bombs in the car, do you?. . . . When the driver says 'No,' then casually but quickly pop the $64,000 question: 'Well, you wouldn't mind if I took a look, would you?'" "This phrasing, too, employs psychology in your favor. The implication is that the subject will look guilty if he *does* mind. . . . It's psychologically harder to decline."[67]

Four key elements of this carefully prescribed model of the investigatory stop will figure prominently in our analysis. First, investigatory stops are an *institutionalized practice*: while undoubtedly some individual officers may learn the technique on their own, it is taught and propagated by formal police training and shared educational materials. Official police policies and the shared norms of professional policing encourage and support this practice. Thus, Remsberg observed that success "is not a matter of luck or accident or some birth gift of unerring instinct. It's a matter of *training* and *motivation*." While training is necessary, it is not difficult to apply: "The principles are simple enough, when known, that just a week after a rookie was instructed in Criminal Patrol tactics at a Kansas academy, he busted 300 pounds of marijuana on one of his first traffic stops."[68]

Second, successful use of the tactic requires stopping lots of vehicles. "Criminal patrol in large part is a numbers game; you have to stop a lot of vehicles to get the law of averages working in your favor."[69] "Vehicle stops are golden opportunities for unique field investigations which, with the right volume of contacts, the right knowledge and creativity, and the right approach, can lead to major felony arrests."[70] "Remember, you need a *lot* of contacts to find the relatively few felony offenders you're most interested in. To get the volume you want, you're going to have to intensively enforce the traffic laws. You may need to call upon more *trivial* violations or public safety considerations, like having a taillight out or a cracked windshield, changing lanes without signaling, impeding traffic, following too closely, failing to dim lights, speeding 3 to 5 mph over the limit . . . and so on."[71] Or, as an officer observed, in trying to find contraband by stopping and searching vehicles "you've got to kiss a lot of frogs before you find that one prince."[72] As we will observe throughout this book, the recommendation to stop lots of drivers simply in order to carry out intrusive investigations is a recipe for giving deep offense to many people.

Third, officers cannot possibly stop all drivers, and they cannot possibly search every vehicle that they stop: officers must focus on some, and the race of the driver figures prominently in many discussions of where to focus. Thus, in a fascinating section of *Tactics for Criminal Patrol* titled "Looking for Mr. Wrong," Remsberg walks a fine line between explicitly recommending that officers should *not* focus on minority drivers and offering detailed discussions of how and why focusing on minority drivers is widely done and makes sense. He opens the guidance by suggesting that "the profile as a reliable absolute has been discredited."[73] One reason is that nearly any type of person may be carrying drugs, and another is the political controversy over racial profiling. "Today, officers rarely utter the 'P word' [profiling] except among themselves. For good reason, profiling has sparked controversy, lawsuits and condemnation and is now officially prohibited by most agencies." He then quickly pivots to a deeper practical truth: "Yet in practice the old 'traditional profile pattern' continues frequently to be used. There's no doubt that targeting vehicles and occupants who match the profile has yielded countless caches of hidden drugs and cash and has resulted in numerous spectacular arrests. Traditional profile characteristics still *do* correlate closely with a sizable portion of drug couriers." Michael F. Brown's training guidebook offers a similar analysis: while "the practice of detaining people based on characteristics" (for example, "a male with particular racial characteristics in a Florida rental car, northbound on a major interstate highway") is controversial, "it seems safe to say that stops can be based on information including profiles, which when viewed from the totality of circumstances perspective, will be considered valid."[74]

And finally, a key to successful use of the investigatory stop according to Remsberg is establishing a friendly rapport with the driver. The officer should be unfailingly courteous and polite. Too often officers try to be "coolly professional." Instead, "people loosen up and talk most easily to those they consider friendly, understanding, trustworthy, helpful, and nonthreatening."[75] Likewise, an early guide to the practice advised officers to "slow down your approach, attempt to put the motorist at ease. Be polite and courteous. It is extremely important to develop rapport with the person."[76]

By the 1990s police researchers and leaders were hailing the investigatory stop as among professional policing's most effective "crime-fighting tools."[77] But how that tool is employed in practice depends on the choices made by tens of thousands of individual police officers. Whether their choices are biased by race depends on how they see the social world: who is seen as "suspicious," "out of place," or simply "unusual" determines who is stopped, questioned, and pressed for consent to be searched. Unfortunately, a large body of research demonstrates that most people in the contemporary United States, police officers included, cannot help but assume that racial minorities are more likely to be dangerous or engaged in criminality. An institutionalized practice that directs front-line officers to stop those who look suspicious will inevitably trigger these assumptions, called "implicit social cognitions," into action.

The "Cognitive Monster"

Police stops begin with a glance. Something—often something fleeting and inchoate—catches a police officer's attention, which then leads to either a decision to look elsewhere or to a cascade of events and interactions that become the stop. The concept of framing and research on implicit bias helps us understand what catches an officer's attention and how this shapes the experience and outcomes of police stops. Framing occurs when stereotypes or schemas define, or place in context, events and encounters. Frames structure how we anticipate and interpret interactions. They grow out of a larger social and historical context; they are the cognitive and cultural baggage we bring to each new experience. They do not determine actions and experiences, nor are they impervious to change, but they have a powerful hold on our judgments and interpretations. Frames are especially powerful and persistent when they arise out of, and in turn shape, institutions and institutionalized practices. They are not just relics of our social past, but are continually recreated. Indeed, everyday actions, like police stops, reinforce institutionalized frames and define—or "socially construct"—the meaning of "race."[78] As Erving Goffman long ago observed, frames "are not merely a matter of mind" but are shaped by, and shape, "the way in which . . . an activity is organized."[79]

Attitudes and perceptions about race incorporate deeply embedded cultural stereotypes. Indeed, the concept of "race" more meaningfully reflects cultural and cognitive frames than any objective differences between people.[80] The modern civil rights era brought many legal and social changes to American society, but did not erase generations of prejudice.[81] Donald Kinder and Lynn Sanders observe that the "public form and private meaning of prejudice" has undergone important transformations since the mid 1950s. They write that "animosity towards blacks is expressed today less in the language of inherent, permanent, biological differences, and more in the language of American individualism, which depicts blacks as unwilling to try and too willing to take what they have not earned."[82] Contemporary racial attitudes, termed "color blind racism" by Eduardo Bonilla-Silva, are based less on classical biological racism and more on the language of social pathology.[83]

In the post–civil rights era, whites express strong support for formal

racial equality.[84] Similarly, Americans of all races report that they believe racial profiling by police is wrong. If the modern civil rights era
marked the decline in the legitimacy of biological racism, the social turmoil of the 1960s and 1970s and the resentments of the 1980s and 1990s
gave greater voice to the belief that blacks are trapped by social pathologies which, in the view of many whites, are largely of their own making.

Of the various social pathologies attributed to blacks, one directly im-
plicates the police: the enduring stereotype that blacks are more likely to
be violent, aggressive, and engage in crime.[85] As Elijah Anderson writes,
the image of blacks, especially black men, as "predator" has become a
"vivid shape" in the public mind.[86] These stereotypes are the basis of racial framing.

David Hamilton and Tina Trolier define "stereotype" as a "cognitive
structure that contains the perceiver's knowledge, beliefs, and expectations about human groups."[87] Stereotypes are generic descriptions that
we use to comprehend and categorize people and groups. They form and
accumulate from various sources, including our broader social and cultural context as expressed through media and other institutions, such
as families, friends, and communities. Some cognitive stereotypes are
based on personal experience, but most are imprinted second- and third-
hand. For better or worse, they are part of our cultural and cognitive
inheritance. Focusing specifically on racial stereotypes, Patricia Devine
observes, "ethnic attitudes and stereotypes are part of the social heri-
tage of a society and no one can escape learning the prevailing attitudes
and stereotypes assigned to major ethnic groups."[88]

From the beginning of the scientific study of stereotypes, these men-
tal images have been seen as a normal and essential aspect of thinking.[89]
Stereotypes minimize the difficult cognitive task of responding to every new and unique individual.[90] But to the extent that stereotypes of a
group meaningfully diverge from the reality of its individual members,
social judgments become biased. Thus, the necessary and natural process of relying on cognitive frames to comprehend experience leads in-
exorably to prejudice.[91] As Michael Billig bluntly summarized, "people
will be prejudiced so long as they continue to think."[92] In essence, the
nature of how we perceive and think about the world requires us to look
at people and experiences through the often distorted lens of cognitive
stereotypes. Normal thinking is the basis for some of human kind's most
destructive and pernicious traits, termed by John Bargh an uncontrolla-
ble "cognitive monster."[93]

Implicit intergroup bias—this cognitive monster—powerfully alters socially meaningful interactions and has enduring material consequences for individuals and groups.[94] In a now classic study, Birt Duncan showed a video of a minor interpersonal conflict, a slight and ambiguous shove. Whites considered this shove more aggressive and violent when performed by a black actor than when the identical shove was performed by a white actor. He concluded that the negative stereotype that classifies blacks as more violent "primed" this biased social judgment.[95] White observers literally saw more aggression and violence in the same act when it was performed by a black person. Andrew Sagar and Janet Schofield replicated Duncan's research with sixth graders. Like adults, these preadolescents rated the same ambiguously aggressive behavior—in this case, an accidental bump in a school hallway—as more mean and threatening when the hallway bump was with a black boy rather than a white boy. Sagar and Schofield's research also added another piece to the stereotyping puzzle: in addition to confirming Duncan's work, they found that "black students reflected the same anti-black bias as those by white students."[96] This suggests that implicit and widely available cultural stereotypes can alter the social judgment of all members of a community, even those negatively affected by the stereotypes: tragically, black children can express anti-black bias common in our culture.

Psychologists distinguish automatic and controlled cognitive processes. Although this distinction is somewhat arbitrary, controlled processes are intentional and require active attention: they are most evident in problem solving, decision making, and in learning new behaviors.[97] To the extent that intergroup bias and prejudice are controlled, they can be more easily altered or suppressed. By contrast, automatic processes are spontaneous and unintentional; they do not require conscious effort and are activated by environmental cues.[98] Although not entirely outside conscious control, racial stereotypes and intergroup bias are activated automatically. After carefully reviewing several decades of cognitive and social psychology research, Irene Blair concluded, "We have come to understand that intergroup bias may operate more quickly and efficiently than previously thought, and it can influence without our awareness or intention. . . . Rooted in a lifetime of socialization and maintained through efficient and silent cognitive processes, intergroup biases are well entrenched."[99]

The nonconscious and automatic nature of intergroup bias has important implications for the understanding of prejudice: individuals who express little overt prejudice—and indeed may consider racial prejudice morally wrong—may still respond on a gut level to racially biased stereotypes. Devine showed that there were no differences in stereotypical responses from low- and high-prejudiced individuals when black stereotypes were subliminally primed, "suggesting that once activated, the application of a stereotype to others may be unavoidable."[100]

The automatic activation of implicit negative stereotypes—especially those conjuring images of black criminality and violence—may have profound and enduring effects on social judgment and people's lives. Stereotypes can have literally life-or-death consequences. Joshua Correll and colleagues used a video game to simulate the snap judgment to shoot or not shoot an ambiguously dangerous target. Reporting on four different experiments, they documented racially biased shooting. When the only difference between the video presentation of a potentially armed subject was the shading of the skin, "Participants fired at an armed target more quickly if he were African American than if he was White . . . , and they decided not to shoot an unarmed White more quickly than an unarmed African American target."[101] They attributed this "shooter bias" to the widely shared cultural stereotype that blacks are more dangerous and threatening than whites. Providing additional evidence that everyone in a particular society—whether prejudiced or not, whether black or white—learns these culturally defined stereotypes, the authors found no meaningful difference between black and white shooters. It is important to note that these troubling findings did not use trained police officers as subjects. As the authors acknowledge in a later article, police training does mitigate shooter bias, yet overall the findings underscore the dangers of implicit negative racial stereotypes on policing.[102]

These findings about prejudice and implicit intergroup bias come from the controlled setting of the psychology lab. Outside the lab, Dean Dabney and colleagues inadvertently discovered the power of implicit racial stereotypes in their study of shoplifting.[103] Their study aimed at identifying the behaviors of shoplifters so as to better predict which people in a store are planning to steal something. Ten trained white and nonwhite observers observed 1,555 shoppers on a closed-circuit TV as they walked through a large suburban drug store that was open 24 hours a day, 7 days a week. During the first 6 months of the study, observers picked shoppers at random, carefully recording their behavior and noting their physical characteristics. Halfway through the data gathering, the researchers realized that pure random selection did not identify enough shoplifters

for meaningful research. They revised the protocol to allow trained observers to focus on shoppers who acted suspiciously, defined as dressing
in a way that could conceal stolen merchandise and doing at least one of
the following things: looking for such store countermeasures as security
cameras, "scanning" or "scoping" for onlookers, or playing with product
packaging. These are similar to the cues that experienced police officers
use when trying to identify suspicious citizens. Directing the trained observers to select suspicious-looking shoppers produced an unanticipated
result: the observers began selecting a significantly larger proportion of
young black men. This occurred even though the selection protocol contained no overt racial elements, and none of the observers felt that their
judgments were racially biased. Despite intensive training and specific
instructions to ignore shopper race, age, and appearance, observers were
unable to resist the pull of the stereotype of black criminality in shaping
their selection of potential or probable offenders.[104]

Research on stereotyping and implicit bias has important implications for understanding race relations and, in particular, the enduring
problems of racialized policing.[105] Through a mix of training and what
they absorb from other cops and experiences on the street, police officers learn to identify clusters of traits and behaviors they believe are
associated with increased risk of committing crimes or posing a danger to others.[106] In *Justice Without Trial*, Jerome Skolnick referred to individuals so targeted as "symbolic assailants."[107] Although he laments
the outcome, Skolnick admits that in the real world of social and racial stratification and the cognitive association of race and crime "it is
inevitable that police will continue to use race as an indicator [of crimi-
nality] . . . [and] if courts say that police cannot use race as an indicator,
they won't report that they did, and will testify that what they saw was
solely odd behavior."[108] In a carefully controlled experiment, C. L. Ruby
and John C. Brigham found that police officers were significantly more
likely than lay-persons to perceive evidence of guilt and deceptiveness in
the ambiguous actions of African Americans, compared to similar actions of whites.[109]

Most Americans—and especially white Americans—believe that
crime has a black face. Justin Levinson and Robert Smith marshal wide-
ranging evidence to show that implicit bias helps explain the troubling
evidence that African Americans are overrepresented in all aspects of
our criminal justice system, from decisions to prosecute to incarceration.[110] Jennifer Eberhardt and her colleagues report that evidence of

implicit bias that African Americans are violent and criminal is consistent and robust over a wide range of studies spanning many years of research.[111] In one study they showed police officers pictures of faces and asked, "Who looks criminal?" These police officers identified more black than white faces as "criminal," and the more "stereotypically" black (based on skin color and facial features), the more likely they were labeled "criminal."[112] Tom Tyler and Cheryl Wakslak surveyed residents of Oakland, Los Angeles, and New York City regarding citizen attitudes towards the police. In general, whites and blacks agreed that racial profiling is wrong. Nonetheless, when asked to explain why cops are more likely to stop and detain blacks, whites were more likely than minorities to justify the actions as legitimate policing based on the increased likelihood of black criminality. Few whites suggested that racialized policing is an explanation.[113]

The stereotype of black criminality has a powerful hold on police and public perceptions of minorities.[114] When survey respondents were asked by researchers to imagine a typical user of illegal drugs, over 95 percent pictured an African American.[115] Among television viewers shown a news story about crime that contained no image of a criminal suspect, 60 percent of these viewers erroneously remembered seeing an image and 70 percent of these viewers reported that the suspect was black.[116] High unemployment and the related family disruptions are associated with higher crime rates in both African American and white neighborhoods, and yet Americans do not commonly associate poor white populations with crime.[117] When controlling for actual crime rate, survey respondents in several major cities expressed exaggerated fear of crime in proportion to the presences of racial minorities.[118] The overrepresentation of blacks as suspects and offenders in media and police crime alerts reinforces the enduring stereotype of black criminality.[119]

Implicit bias can shape perceptions of places as well as people, and the modern urban ghetto is widely seen as a setting of social disorder requiring greater policing.[120] Poor black neighborhoods do have higher crime rates than other neighborhoods,[121] and African Americans are disproportionately represented in all aspects of the criminal justice system.[122] Careful survey-based studies of victims of crimes and of peoples' self-reports of whether they have committed crimes confirm that African Americans, on average, are somewhat more likely than whites to commit some types of crimes.[123] But police focus aggressive stops on African Americans and Latinos considerably more than can be justified by neighborhood crime statistics alone, as careful research in New York City by Andrew Gelman, Jeffrey Fagan, and Alex Kiss has shown.[124] Widespread assumptions about black criminality undoubtedly contribute to who is arrested and for what crimes.[125] Contrary to common belief, African Americans do not use illegal drugs at higher rates than whites, and yet the war on drugs has disproportionately targeted African Americans.[126] The greater the proportion of African Americans in a city's population, the higher are expenditures on policing and the higher are arrest rates, even after taking into account official crime rates.[127] David Eitle, Steward D'Alessio, and Lisa Stolzenberg found that felony arrests rise in association with black-on-white violence but not black-on-black violence, even though the percentages of cases with black perpetrators and white victims is relatively low, on average less than 10 percent.[128]

African American drivers, just like the officers who pull them over, perceive and interpret the encounter through a racial frame. Black driver views are based in part on what scholars have termed "metastereotypes," or black views of white views of blacks.[129] Blacks, especially black men, older blacks, and lower-income blacks, believe that whites hold negative racial attitudes about them. This general assumption is heightened during police stops based on the widely held belief among blacks of police racism and racialized policing.[130] Most have experienced investigatory stops or have heard friends or family members describe their experiences in these stops. Based on personal and shared experiences, blacks believe that the police are constantly watching them and treat them as if they don't belong; blacks fear that every small offense will result in a stop and that every encounter with the police can escalate and turn ugly.[131] They fear that they are seen as criminal. Katheryn Russell-Brown reminds us that "stories of [African American] encounters with 'the law' in which a relative was left bruised, battered, or buried, have been passed down through generations like heirlooms."[132] Thus, just as cops anticipate the possibility of violence, however remote, during a police stop, black drivers fear that any encounter with the police can, based an inadvertent action or remark or misunderstanding, escalate into a humiliating and threatening experience.

White drivers also bring cognitive frames to their encounters with police. Their frames, like black driver frames, reflect their history and, regardless of social and economic status, are based on white privilege.[133] Whites begin their encounters with police assuming that they have full citizen rights and leave these experiences with their status undiminished. They anticipate many of the negative consequences of a stop: the embarrassment and annoyance of being pulled over and the possibility of an expensive ticket or, in rare occasions, greater sanctions, especially if intoxicated. But for white drivers stops have no further significance for their standing in society. As we will show in the chapters that follow, for whites a stop is just a stop.

What the Police Response to the Racial Profiling Controversy Revealed

In the context of implicit racial stereotypes, the growing police commitment to investigatory stops predictably led to an explosion of racial disparities in police stops—and controversy. By 1999 "racial profiling" had become a national issue. Profiling controversies boiled in dozens of localities; the New Jersey attorney general issued a report condemning racial profiling in that state's highway patrol; the U.S. Department of Justice opened investigations into racially discriminatory police stops in three states and began overseeing stops by the New Jersey state police; the ACLU filed a class-action lawsuit against the Maryland state police based on statistical evidence of deep racial bias in vehicle stops.[134] On June 9, 1999, President Clinton issued an executive order condemning racial profiling, and many states and local governments followed with similar denunciations.[135]

Professional policing faced a crisis. How its leaders responded to this crisis contributed to investigatory stops' legitimacy within professional policing. This response is telling in another way: it lends additional support to our contention that racial disparities in police stops reflected official practice, not the isolated actions of errant officers. In July, 1999, the IACP, in its first official response to the breaking crisis, acknowledged that the controversy reflected "the increasing prevalence of proactive enforcement."[136] Rather than abandoning the practice as inherently problematic, the leaders of professional policing defended it. "There can be no question as to the benefits of proactive traffic enforcement," Bobby Moody, IACP president, declared. "So the question confronting law enforcement executives is this: How does law enforcement enact a proactive program of traffic enforcement without antagonizing segments of the community and exposing our agencies to claims of bias?"[137]

These leaders offered several answers. They tried to shift the responsibility to a few intentionally biased officers.[138] Following Tom Tyler's procedural justice thesis, they called on departments to get their officers to act more politely in investigatory stops.[139] Thus, Moody declared, "If handled poorly, this already tense situation can turn into the basis for charges of bias and result in costly litigation for the police department."[140] Another writer in the *Police Chief* suggested that if a department trains its officers to be exceedingly polite during proactive stops, communities may accept a program of intensive investigatory stops.[141] The IACP's model policy on racial profiling recommended both a firm departmental commitment to proactive stops and "a requirement that all persons be treated with the utmost courtesy in traffic stops."[142] Police leaders also sought to show that those living in the neighborhoods targeted for investigatory stops accepted, even welcomed, them as a means to reduce violence and crime.[143]

But what is most telling is that every official condemnation of racial profiling by the leaders of professional policing was accompanied *in its official text* by a full-throated defense of investigatory stops. In its first forum on racial profiling the IACP declared, "Proactive traffic enforcement is an effective strategy to protect the public from the devastation caused by drug abuse, street and highway traffic-related death and injury, illegal trafficking in and possession of weapons, and the continued freedom of fugitives, as well as to otherwise promote and maintain an orderly and law-abiding society."[144] Likewise, the IACP membership's first official resolution on the issue, adopted in 2000 and titled "Condemning Racial and Ethnic Profiling in Traffic Stops," devoted the first half of the text not to such a condemnation but to a full-bore defense of proactive stops. It begins:

> "WHEREAS, intensive traffic enforcement efforts
> have been proven to reduce traffic crashes and increase
> the apprehension of the criminal offender; and
> WHEREAS, law enforcement agencies have seized more
> illegal drugs resulting from traffic enforcement than they
> have from undercover enforcement strategies; and
> WHEREAS, traffic stops utilizing plain view and consent
> searches annually lead to the interdiction of millions
> of dollars in illegal substances and stolen property."[145]

A second resolution, on "Professional Police Contacts," declared:

"WHEREAS, traffic stops have been proven to reduce street and
violent crimes, increase the apprehension of criminal offenders,
combat illegal drug activities, illegal guns and other crimes."[146]

The IACP Highway Safety Committee's recommended model policy
on racial profiling in the same breath condemns individual officer bias
and celebrates the investigatory stop as a core practice: "It is the policy
of this department to patrol in a proactive manner, to aggressively investigate suspicious persons and circumstances, and to actively enforce the
motor vehicle laws."[147]

Summary: Institutionalized Racial Framing

Some institutional structures of law and official policy ameliorate or op-
pose negative racial stereotypes, as is the case with civil rights law. Other
institutional structures build on and accentuate these negative stereotypes, as we will show is the case with investigatory police stops. Policies
favoring proactive investigatory stops, by directing officers to look not
for violations of the law but suspicious individuals, activate departments'
and officers' implicit stereotypes of which neighborhoods and which individuals are suspicious.

Law and police policies not only reflect cultural meaning, but also
create and change how we see and act upon racial stereotypes. Thus, in
complex ways, police policies racially frame who is stopped by the police, the nature and interpretation of the stop encounter, and the outcome of the stop. We will explore each element of racial framing in the
pages that follow, but it is useful to summarize our core thesis.

Institutionalized racial framing is the process by which widely implemented official practices activate culturally embedded racial stereotypes
which then shape police perceptions of people's criminality and threat,
and, in turn, people's perceptions of their place in society. The "aggressive policing" policy favoring investigatory stops encourages officers to
disproportionately select African Americans for investigatory stops and
the intrusive questions, searches, and physical restraints often imposed
during these stops. Disproportionate levels of investigatory stops of African Americans, in turn, encourage these drivers to bring to their encounters with police expectations of unequal and intrusive treatment,
and to leave these stops deeply distrusting the fairness of the police and

doubting their own equal status and liberty in society. The comparative freedom of whites from these stops encourages them to view police stops as a legitimate form of traffic enforcement. The interaction—confrontation—of these culturally embedded assumptions about the other during the police stop reconstructs the meaning of law, equal citizenship, and racial identity.

The Decision to Stop a Driver

DEANA: OK. I have been, like, driving home from work at night and get stopped by the police for no reason, just stopped me to see where I was going. . . . I was getting off work at like 11:30, 12:00.

INTERVIEWER: So you were driving home, and do you remember how you were driving?

DEANA: Um, I wasn't driving fast; they didn't give me a ticket or anything. They just wanted know where I was going. What I had been doing and where I was going.

INTERVIEWER: Do you remember about where this was?

DEANA: Yes, I29 and 635. Actually, one night I got stopped twice, the same night, by two different police. . . .

INTERVIEWER: Do you remember what they said or how they acted?

DEANA: Well, they just wanted to know where I was going. And the second time they stopped me, I was pretty upset, you know. The same night, just about five minutes apart. And they wanted to know why I was upset.

I said, I'm like, "You just stopped me up the street." And you know I was scared, I knew they had just stopped me, and it was a different police. . . . They just wanted to know where I was going and where I had been.

INTERVIEWER: Do you remember how they acted? Were they . . .?

DEANA: They were nice, they were nice.[1]

Why did the police stop this driver, but not that one? Why me, but not you? What was the officer thinking? Did I look suspicious or like I didn't belong here? Did he stop me because I'm black? Why *me*?

Many studies find that the police stop African Americans at higher rates than whites.[2] In our sample, 12.2 percent of white drivers reported being stopped in the past year, while 24.5 percent of African American drivers were pulled over, almost exactly double the rate for whites. These crude racial disparities, however, tell us little about the racial framing of police stops; most studies do not help explain *why* this is so, and why matters.

This chapter examines who is stopped by the police and why, and it is the first step in showing that investigatory stops are the source of racial disparities in police stops. Police officers cannot possibly stop everybody violating traffic and other laws; they pick and choose.[3] But in carrying out traffic-safety and investigatory stops they pick and choose *differently*. In traffic-safety stops, officers target especially egregious violators, leaving the rest of us to mosey on at merely 3 or 4 miles per hour over the speed limit. In investigatory stops, officers target people who look suspicious.

What counts as looking suspicious—and thus who is stopped in investigatory stops—is the heart of our analysis in this chapter. The decision to stop you but not me is a pure test of whether and how the visible indicators of racial and social status affect police suspicion. This is because the decision about who to stop is based entirely on what the officer has seen, often at some distance, before the officer and driver have exchanged any words. Whether the driver is polite or a jerk, apologetic or indignant, cultured or profane, and whether the driver and officer eventually have a nice chat or get into a nasty tit-for-tat may influence the officer's decision to issue a ticket, but it has no possible influence on the decision to make the stop.

Our core thesis is that officers' racial biases, which are shared in common with the rest of the population, are not *generally* influential but instead are activated by and in the practice of making investigatory stops. In these stops officers target what we described in chapter 2 as the stereotypical "criminal": African Americans and, especially, young African American men.

In traffic-safety stops, by contrast, officers' discretionary choices are focused on traffic-law violations. In these stops officers target significant traffic-safety violators. It is the contrast between these two sets of factors—the factors that predispose a driver to a traffic-safety stop versus those that predispose a driver to an investigatory stop—that shows especially clearly how the investigatory stop activates and gives expression to racial stereotypes.

Our analysis of who is targeted builds on research by Robin Shepard Engel and Jennifer Calnon, who found that racial disparities in po-

lice stops are greater in stops made for low-level violations, like failure
to signal a turn, than in stops for speeding violations.[4] Likewise, Albert
Meehan and Michal Ponder found that officers in a large West Coast city
were significantly more likely to run computerized license-plate checks
and make stops of African American drivers in "white" neighborhoods
than anywhere else, and especially more likely to run these checks and
make stops of "out of place" black drivers than "out of place" white drivers.[5] This is a classic investigatory-stop pattern. Still, neither of these two
otherwise excellent studies could take into account key competing explanations, and it is necessary to do so if we are to be sure that investigatory stops are the source of the racial-disparity problem.

We consider several competing explanations for who is stopped.
Some writers claim that African Americans are stopped at higher rates
because they are worse violators of traffic laws. If so, we should find that
African Americans speed and run through red lights (and so forth) more
than whites; that African Americans are stopped at higher rates than
whites not only in investigatory stops but also in traffic-safety stops; and
that the apparent racial difference in who is stopped should disappear
when controlling for speeding, running through red lights, and so forth.

Alternatively, it is possible that African Americans are stopped at
higher rates because of class, not race. While scholars in the United
States justifiably focus on racial biases, the claim that the police are biased by class is common in other countries and may be true in the United
States, as well.[6] African Americans are on average poorer than whites,
and being poorer may translate into a higher rate of stops either because
the vehicles of the poor have more problems (like burned-out headlights) or because the police are simply more suspicious of poor people
in general. If poverty or class—not race—is the underlying explanation,
then we should expect to find that any apparent racial disparities in who
is stopped will disappear when taking into account the visible indicators
of class: the nature and character of drivers' vehicles. If there is a class
bias in who is stopped, then this is a problem but it is a different problem
than racial bias.

A third possibility is that police racial biases are *generally* influential
rather than activated by, and in, the investigatory stop. Certainly a large
body of research on implicit racial stereotypes seems to suggest that
these biases are everywhere and commonly influential. For example, recall the study noted in chapter 2 that found that people perceive a child's
bump of another child as more deliberate and mean-spirited (as opposed

to accidental and benign) if done by a black child than a white child. A bump by a child is a low-level kind of violation, if it is even a violation at all. If racial stereotypes similarly frame *all* police enforcement activities rather than being isolated in the investigatory stop, then police are likely to view *any* traffic-law violation as more serious or dangerous if done by a black driver than a white driver. Such a generally influential bias could be expected to prime officers to view a moderate violation of the speed limit, or a failure to signal a turn, as more dangerous and worthy of sanction if done by a black driver than a white driver. If so, we might expect racial disparities to be present in all kinds of stops even after taking into account how much drivers violate the traffic laws. If the bias is generally influential rather than activated in the investigatory stop, we should expect racial disparities *not* to be concentrated in investigatory stops.

To begin, consider how discretionary choices permeate even traffic-safety enforcement, as described by an officer who was "working speed."

NARRATIVE 3.2.
Traffic officer, white male: "It Happened to Be an African American Female"

I observed a silver Volvo with one headlight not working properly. That's actually a violation here, for not having both headlights working; it's an equipment violation. But I was working speed, so I hit it with the laser; honestly, it was a while ago, so I don't know exactly how fast she was going.

I pulled her over and walked up to the vehicle, and it happened to be an African American female. And when I told her I stopped her for speeding, she assumed that I stopped her because of her race.

And she goes, "Why didn't you get the vehicle next to me?"

And I said, "Well, you drew attention to yourself because you only have one working headlight."

She didn't believe me. I said, "Well, if you don't believe me turn on your headlights." And I walked to the car and I pointed to it and said, "That one right there is not working. If you don't believe me, you can get out and look at it."

And so, I went back and she saw it, and it was like, "Whoops," you know.

And I walked back to my car, wrote her a ticket for the speeding and said, "Sign here by the 'X,' the city will send you the fine, blah, blah, blah."

And that was it. She pulled off.[7]

By this officer's description, even a typical speeding stop is subject to discretionary choice: a burned-out headlight drew his attention to *this* speeding driver rather than another. If the car's burned-out headlight attracted suspicion, is it possible that the driver's black face did too? The point is that officers *could* disproportionately stop African Americans in all kinds of stops, for speeding as well as for criminal investigation. They could—but as will be revealed, they don't. African Americans do not speed more than whites, and officers do not stop them at higher rates than whites in any stop except investigatory stops.

Do African Americans Violate Traffic Laws More Often than Whites?

"Black drivers on the New Jersey Turnpike are twice as likely to speed as white drivers, and are even more dominant among drivers breaking 90 miles per hour," according to the Manhattan Institute's Heather Mac-Donald. "This finding demolishes the myth of racial profiling."[8] *Do* African Americans violate traffic laws more than whites? Surprisingly little research has addressed this question. The earliest study found that whites and blacks did not differ in their tendency to speed. This study defined "speeding" as any violation of the posted speed limit and is unreasonably broad, because officers are more likely to stop excessive speeders than those who drive 1 or 2 miles per hour over the limit.[9] Another study (the basis for MacDonald's claim) tried to address this limitation by defining speeding as driving 15 miles or more per hour over the 65 miles-per-hour limit on the New Jersey Turnpike; by this definition, black drivers were more likely than whites to speed.[10] But the New Jersey study went on to observe that few drivers of either race drive this fast and this difference cannot explain the wide racial disparity in who was stopped on the New Jersey Turnpike. An intriguing study of North Carolina drivers that relied on the self reports of drivers who had been stopped for speeding found that African Americans were not more likely than whites to speed.[11] A recent observational study of Cincinnati drivers found that African Americans were marginally more likely to speed than whites, but the differences were not large (although blacks were somewhat more likely than whites to speed at higher rates of speed).[12] In all, these studies suggest that if black drivers violate traffic laws more than whites—and this is by no means certain—the difference is not great. Nor have studies tested for whether this difference explains why African Americans are stopped at higher rates (if in fact there is a racial difference in traffic-law violation). It is possible, for example, that how much you speed has little to do with whether you are stopped; many drivers exceed the speed limit for months, even years, without being stopped.

We designed our survey to address these issues. The survey responses reveal that African Americans do not typically violate traffic laws more than whites. While the majority of both whites and blacks acknowledge speeding, whites report somewhat greater violations than blacks: whites report driving 5 percent above the speed limit and blacks report on average driving at a rate 3 percent above the limit. In a 65-mile-per-hour zone, this translates, on average, into driving about 68 miles per hour for whites and 67 for blacks. And while 72 percent of whites report routinely and knowingly violating the speed limit, only 57 percent of blacks do so. On average, *black drivers speed less than whites.* What about truly excessive speeding? Almost precisely the same proportion of black and white drivers—about 6 percent of each group—report driving more than 15 percent above the speed limit.

What about other traffic rules, like coming to a complete stop at a stop sign, not speeding up to get through yellow lights before they turn red, signaling lane changes and turns, and so forth? Do African Americans violate these rules of the road more than whites? No. While both black and white drivers acknowledge violating these sorts of rules, the level of acknowledged violation is significantly higher among white drivers than black drivers. While 11 percent of African American drivers acknowledge that they often speed up to get through a yellow traffic light, 17 percent of white drivers acknowledge this, a statistically significant difference ($p < .001$, two-tailed t-test). All of this adds up to the expectation that it is not higher levels of traffic-law violation that explain why African Americans are stopped at higher rates than whites.

What about time spent driving? The more time spent on the road, the more a driver is exposed to the risk of a police stop. Thus, somebody who speeds at 15 miles per hour over the limit but drives only 10 minutes a day to and from a nearby job is less likely to be stopped than somebody who drives this fast but does so through the course of an hour-long commute. According to our survey responses, African Americans on average spend significantly more time driving than whites: almost 2 hours per day for blacks but only 1.5 for whites, a significant difference ($p < .001$, two-tailed t-test). By this measure, African Americans are almost 30 percent more exposed to police stops simply by virtue of spending more time driving. We will take this into account in our discussion below.

Vehicle as Class Indicator

"Why are you stopping me?" Billy asked an officer. "Because I'm a poor man in a ragged car?"[13] Billy's question gets to the heart of the class-based hypothesis: it is not race but class that leads to higher rates of police stops among African Americans. If so, poor whites are as likely to be stopped as poor blacks; wealthy blacks are as likely to be as free of stops as are wealthy whites. African Americans on average have less income than whites, and this is true as well of the drivers who responded to our survey: black respondents reported on average earning between ten and twenty thousand dollars less per year than whites. This is a large difference. Is it visible in the character of peoples' vehicles?

For many, one's car presents a visible symbol of social status, although the status conveyed is equivocal. Among African Americans, this self presentation took a specific form. As historian Thomas Sugrue observed, in the post World War II period, "The Cadillac assumed iconic status among the black elite as a symbol of having made it," and, more recently, luxury cars "continued to have special status in black popular culture."[14] As Sugrue observes, black popular culture has especially celebrated the luxury domestic car: the Cadillac or high-end Oldsmobile. This symbol of having made it, as Sugrue observed, played into a pernicious stereotype of "welfare queens" driving Cadillacs. Not surprisingly, then, while we found no statistically meaningful difference in the percentage of whites and blacks who drive a foreign luxury car, African Americans are almost twice as likely as whites (7.2 percent versus 4.5 percent) to drive a domestic luxury car, a significant difference ($p < .01$, two-tailed t-test).

On further examination, Sugrue points out, since in general African Americans are less wealthy than whites, they have less money to spend on their vehicles—and it shows. According to our survey, African Americans' vehicles are less valuable, more run-down, and more subject to vehicle code violations than are vehicles driven by whites. Whites' vehicles on average are worth \$1,250 more than African Americans' vehicles, a large and statistically meaningful difference ($p < .01$, one-tailed t-test). This basic difference leads to other differences in the vehicles of whites and blacks. Blacks and whites tend to drive vehicles with similar levels of customization and unrepaired accident damage (the slight differences are not statistically significant). But compared to whites, blacks drive vehicles with more code violations, such as a burned-out taillight, which are legal bases for a stop (this difference by race is statistically significant, $p < .05$, two-tailed t-test). In sum, the vehicles driven by blacks and whites differ in some noticeable ways that express, however faintly, economic class.

Distinguishing Traffic-Safety and Investigatory Stops

The distinction between traffic-safety and investigatory stops is the key to sorting out how and when race matters in police stops. We need, therefore, a way to empirically differentiate these two types of stops. Recall, as we described in chapter 2, that these stops are distinguished by their purpose, character, and justification. The *justification* given by officers to drivers is the basis for our working distinction. Officers making investigatory stops commonly have decided to carry out a criminal investigation before they make the stop; they then identify, or create, a pretext to justify the stop. The difference between a pretext and a true justification thus marks the line between an investigatory stop and a traffic-safety stop. When making a traffic-safety stop, officers give a traffic-safety justification; when making an investigatory stop, officers justify the stop with a minor, low-level violation—or they provide no justification at all.

Following this definition, we have classified stops as traffic-safety enforcement if justified by the following: speeding at 7 or more miles per hour over the limit, suspicion of driving under the influence of drugs or alcohol, running a red light, reckless driving, and random roadblock checks for driving under the influence.

We have classified stops as investigatory if they are justified by: the failure to signal a turn or lane change, a malfunctioning light (including license-plate light), driving too slowly, stopping too long, expired license tag, and to check for a valid driver's license or to conduct a warrant check. We have also classified as investigatory any stop in which the officer gave no justification for the stop. For example, in this chapter's opening narrative, the officer gave Deana no reason for the stop and proceeded immediately to an investigatory question.

A variety of miscellaneous justifications fall on either side of this line. For example, we classified checking to see why the driver was parked in the shade—an actual justification reported in our survey—as being an investigatory stop. In cases where an officer gave a driver more than one reason for being stopped, we classified it as a traffic-safety stop if any of the justifications is a traffic-safety reason. Thus, if a driver is stopped for "10 over" and failure to signal a lane change, we classified it as a traffic-safety stop.

The basis for our lists of traffic-safety versus investigatory justifications is our interviews with officers. Traffic-safety justifications were derived from officers' focus group answers to a question we posed: what sorts of infractions are a "must stop?"[15] Must-stop violations are serious risks to safety. Likewise, the list of justifications for investigatory stops is derived from officers' focus group answers to the question, "What justifications do you use when you really want to stop somebody?"[16] These justifications are remarkably *de minimis*, for instance, a burned-out license-plate light. Regarding speeding, we opted for a conservative dividing line: 7 or more miles per hour over the limit is a "true" speeding stop, and at less than that the justification is a pretext. This line is halfway between drivers' self-reports of how fast they typically drive (on average, about 4 miles per hour over the limit) and officers' reports to us of the speed they consider a must-stop (typically about 10 or more miles per hour over the limit).[17]

Figure 3.1 shows how these different justifications as indicators of the type of stop differ by race of the driver. African American drivers are significantly less likely than whites to be given a traffic-safety justification for the stop; while 58 percent of stopped whites are given a justification that is clearly a traffic-safety justification, only 35 percent of blacks are offered similar explanations. This disparity is largely because whites are substantially more likely than African Americans to be stopped for excessive speeding. But other traffic-safety stops are also skewed in this way by the race of the driver. For example, while 3.4 percent of whites are stopped for reckless driving, 1.4 percent of blacks were stopped for this reason. By contrast, the stops of African Americans are substantially more likely to be justified by the low-level violations that are characteristic of investigatory stops. For example, the officer provided no justification to whites in 8 percent of their stops, and gave no reason for the stop to 18 percent of blacks. The justifications for investigatory stops are scattered across a range of low-level violations. While 2.2 percent of whites are stopped for a minor equipment violation like a burned-out taillight, 3.8 percent of blacks are stopped for such a reason. Disproportionate stopping of black drivers for these sorts of

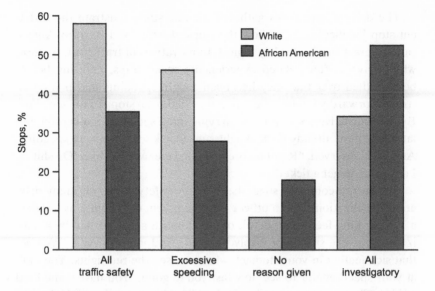

FIGURE 3.1. Justifications for most recent police stop, by race of driver ($N = 709$). All differences are statistically significant ($p < .001$; two-tailed t-test).

miscellaneous low-level violations adds up, however, to a striking overall disparity in such stops: while 34 percent of whites were stopped for a *de minimis* reason; 52 percent of blacks were stopped for similar low-level reasons.

To reduce concerns that these stark differences are shaped by drivers' selective recall, we took pains to ask a grounded, objective questions: "Did the officer give a reason for the stop?" And if so, "What was that reason?" It is hard to interpret these strikingly different reports of the reason given by the officer for the stop as being simply a matter of perception or selective recollection by the driver. No matter how trusting or distrusting of the police, a driver is not likely to convert an officer's declaration that the stop was made for "15 over" into "your license-plate light is out," or vice versa. Additionally, we tested whether drivers' level of distrust in the police (an index that we discuss in detail in chapter 7) helps explain whether they reported that the officer gave no reason for the stop. There is no significant relationship, suggesting that drivers' reports of whether or not the officer gave a reason for the stop are not systematically skewed by drivers' level of trust in the police.[18]

The drivers' narratives gathered for this study illustrate the different stop justifications and how the stops of white and African American drivers differ in this key regard. In narratives of traffic-safety stops, white drivers often related experiencing speed traps, knowing before being pulled over that they had been caught speeding, and being told straightforwardly by the officer that they had been stopped for speeding. By the time drivers see officers carrying out a speed trap, it is often too late: they have already been caught, and they know they were speeding. As Laura observed, "Right before he pulled me over I'm like, 'Oh shit . . . I am going to get a ticket!'"[19]

As Laura's comment suggests, in traffic-safety stops, for many drivers the realization that an officer is pulling them over comes as a shock: a sick, sinking feeling in the pit of the stomach accompanied by a realization that the stop is probably justified. As John observed, "You get that sick feeling in your stomach when you see the red lights. You look at your speedometer to see how fast you're going. You have some kind of idea. Then you just sit and wait. And it's a bit unnerving."[20] Helen observed that the officer seemed very young and "scared to death," perhaps because "I was pissed off . . . I mean . . . I was mad, but, you know, it was my fault."[21] "I was kind of speeding," Donald admitted, "And the lights go on and of course, personally you know, you think they got you and of course you have that sinking feeling."[22]

This sense that "they got you," that "I was mad, but, you know, it was my fault," is entirely foreign to the investigatory stop. In narratives of investigatory stops, African American drivers like Deana in this chapter's opening narrative express puzzlement and fear: knowing that they have done nothing wrong, they realize that the stop is based not on what they did but on the officer's seemingly arbitrary power to pull them over, and they fear what the officer has in mind and what he will do. Investigatory stops are often simply given no justification by the officer. Lisa, an African American woman, provided her story.

NARRATIVE 3.3.
Lisa, African American female: "Followed Me Home for Two Weeks"

I get off [work] at 10:30 at night. They followed me all the way to the house and I spotted them in the mirror and I knew I wasn't speeding. So I just took my time. When I got home, I pulled in front of the house and they stopped right next to me. And so I'm looking at them and tried to decide if I wanted to get out of the car or sit there. So there is no one else around and I don't want to sit in the car. It took me, like, fifteen minutes to get home. So I get out of the car and I just looked at them. And they said, "Is this your car?" And I said, "Yes." And they sat there for a minute. . . . They ran the tags [and] I walked on in the house. . . . But I thought it was odd and they did it for about a couple of weeks.[23]

Billy, an African American man, reported being stopped for driving 2 miles per hour over the speed limit, "67 in a 65," a stop that led to a search of his car.[24] In another stop on the interstate, several officers pulled his cousin over (Billy was a passenger), gave no reason for the stop and immediately proceeded to gain the driver's consent for a search.[25] Kenneth, too, told of a stop in which the officer gave no justification and immediately asked for identification.

NARRATIVE 3.4.
Kenneth, African American male: "Nobody Move"

I was riding down the street and I saw the police going in the other direction. And I pulled over. I stopped to talk to some friends. He [the officer] was going the opposite direction, like, in another street . . . and he came back around a block. He stopped and sat down the street for a few minutes and then he came down the street. And then he was, "Everybody hands up. Give me your ID"—that kind of thing, you know? Now, you know, obviously there was no reason for him to stop because the tags and the registration, it was good on the car, you know.

He asked what was I doing down there with these guys. I mean, these guys are guys I grew up with. You know what I mean? It wasn't a drug area, nothing like that. It was just six black guys standing, you know, in front of a house.[26]

A small number of white drivers provided narratives of investigatory stops, but, with only two exceptions, these stories are best described as cases of mistaken racial identity or something akin to it. Notably, these white drivers suspected that they were stopped because of their street identity—what they "look like" on the street. Donald, a white man, put it this way: "I had a girlfriend of mine and she is an African American . . . and we were driving from downtown out to where I live . . . and they followed us, and I was actually driving her car, and they followed us, I mean for like two to three miles, and they stopped us because they said I made too wide of a turn. . . . I know that they say that there is not such a thing as racial profiling, but I really, speaking as a white man looking on, I would definitely agree that there was."[27] Another white man, James, described an investigatory stop that he attributed to his "scruffy," long-haired appearance. While stopped for speeding (at 7 miles per hour over the limit, which is just on the traffic-safety side of our dividing line), the officers immediately asked to search his car.[28]

Racial Disparities and Investigatory Stops

While we cannot answer definitively whether Deana was stopped because she is black, we can identify how much race, class, age, and law violations shape the likelihood of being stopped. We can further determine the extent racial disparities are concentrated in investigatory stops or scattered across all types of stops. As noted in chapter 1, we surveyed several thousand drivers and asked whether they had been stopped by the police while driving in the past year. We also asked a host of other questions that fill in a complete picture of each driver: race, class, character of vehicle, and how each driver tends to drive. Using these responses we can sort out how much each factor increases or decreases the likelihood of being stopped, and how the different factors taken together shape the likelihood of being stopped. For example, it is helpful to know not only whether and how much African Americans are more likely than whites to be stopped, but how much more likely a 20-year-old African American man is to be stopped than a 20-year-old white woman.

We report our findings in table 3.1. The factors associated with being stopped vary dramatically by type of stop. In traffic-safety stops, the most important influences on who is stopped are *how people drive* and not how they look. The more that people violate the traffic laws the more likely they are to be stopped, regardless of their race, gender, age, or type of vehicle.

In stark contrast, in investigatory stops, the most important influences on who is stopped are not how people drive but *how they look*. African Americans are far more likely to be stopped than whites, men more likely than women, and younger drivers rather than older drivers. Of these broad groups, African Americans face the greatest risk. They are 2.7 times more likely than whites to be stopped in investigatory stops. Women are about half as likely as men to be stopped, and as people age, each additional year decreases their likelihood of being stopped by over 2 percent. For simplicity's sake we do not include a number of miscellaneous factors in the table, but it is worth noting that drivers of domestic luxury cars—cars that are symbolically associated in popular culture

TABLE 3.1. **Likelihood of being stopped for traffic-safety and investigatory reasons.**

Characteristic	Exceeding speed limit by ≥7 mph	Traffic safety stops generally	Investigatory stops
African American	1.308	1.059	2.710****
	(.243)	(.200)	(.460)
Female	0.855	0.944	0.532****
	(.141)	(.152)	(.093)
Age	0.977****	0.979****	0.974****
	(.005)	(.005)	(.006)
Vehicle value (lowest	0.951	1.118	1.710**
quartile)	(.190)	(.223)	(.355)
Domestic luxury car	1.255	1.116	2.223**
	(.530)	(.476)	(.756)
Foreign luxury car	0.717	0.951	0.607
	(.413)	(.487)	(.454)
Time spent driving	1.106**	1.072	1.040
per week	(.048)	(.048)	(.052)
Extent of speeding	1.059****	1.040***	1.006
	(.014)	(.013)	(.013)
Rule-abiding driving	0.662**	0.814	0.586***
	(.121)	(.146)	(.119)
Vehicle damage	1.011	0.958	0.799
	(.165)	(.155)	(.133)
Vehicle customization	0.876	0.852	0.860
	(.099)	(.094)	(.101)
Illegal vehicle conditions	0.791	0.909	1.551***
	(.116)	(.121)	(.210)
Constant	0.0005****	0.004****	0.097
	(.0008)	(.005)	(.146)
Log pseudolikelihood	−356.48	−380.29	−296.84
Wald χ² (13)	107.84****	74.72****	155.47****
p	<.0001	<.0001	<.0001
N	1597	1597	1597

Note: Results were obtained using logit estimation. Reported results are odds ratios, with robust standard errors given in parentheses.
*$p < .10$; **$p < .05$; ***$p < .01$; ****$p < .001$

with African Americans—are 2.2 times more likely than drivers of other vehicles to be stopped in investigatory stops. They are not more likely to be stopped in speeding stops.

The best way to illustrate these large differences in the influence of race, gender, and age by the type of stop is with simple figures. Figure 3.2 illustrates the likelihood of being stopped for speeding at 7 or more miles per hour over the limit, by race, gender, and self-reported tendency to exceed the speed limit, controlling for all other factors. The likelihood of being stopped for speeding increases significantly in direct relation to the driver's tendency to exceed the speed limit, but is not greatly different for African Americans and whites, or for men and women. Over the course of a year, the likelihood of being stopped for speeding is well under 5 percent for drivers who report generally driving below the speed limit, but it rises to more than 18 percent for drivers who report commonly exceeding the speed limit by 16 percent or more (for example, 16 percent above a 70 mile-per-hour limit is just above 81 miles per hour). To be sure, the likelihood of being stopped for speeding is slightly higher for African American drivers than whites, as the figure illustrates, but the difference is neither large nor statistically meaningful and it pales in comparison to the differences by race and gender in discretionary stops.

In investigatory stops, race, gender, and age interact, so that young African American men are by far the most likely to be stopped for investigatory reasons. This pattern is illustrated in figure 3.3. For drivers under age 25, the likelihood of being subjected to an investigatory stop

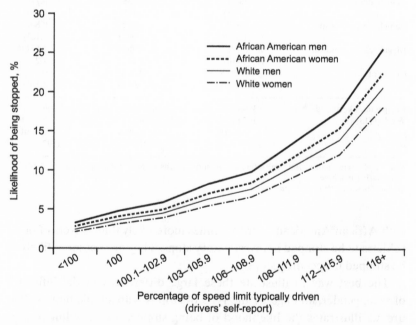

FIGURE 3.2. Likelihood of being stopped for speeding at ≥7 mph over the limit, by race, gender, and self-reported tendency to speed ($N = 1597$). Estimates were generated by postlogit estimation using prvalue (Stata, version 11). The differences by race and gender are not statistically significant, while the variation by tendency to speed is statistically significant ($p < .05$).

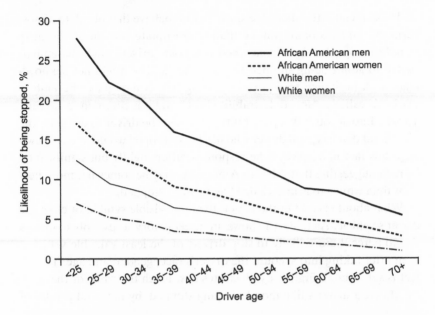

FIGURE 3.3. Likelihood of being stopped for an investigatory reason, by race, gender, and age, controlling for all other factors ($N = 1597$). Estimates were generated by post-logit estimation using prvalue (Stata, version 11). All differences by race are statistically significant ($p < .05$).

over the course of a year varies considerably, from 28 percent for black men to 7 percent for white women. By age 70, the likelihood of such an investigatory stop drops to 6 percent or less for all types of drivers. But the difference by race remains wide even for older drivers: black men must reach age 50 or older to have the same likelihood of being stopped for an investigatory reason as white men under age 25. This finding supports a widely expressed complaint of black men: no matter their age or station in life, police seem to be suspicious of them.

African Americans are also much more likely than whites to be stopped multiple times over the course of a year. Figure 3.4 shows that the likelihood of being stopped more than once over the course of a year varies dramatically by race and gender: over 40 percent for black men under age 25, but only 7.8 percent for white women of the same age (again, controlling for other factors). While the likelihood of experiencing multiple stops declines with age, the racial gap remains wide throughout life. Black men over 50 have the same rate of multiple stops in the past year as white men in their 20s.

These racial differences are stark, but we believe that our data almost certainly *underestimate* rather than overestimate the racial disparity in police stops. We were concerned that some drivers might be embarrassed to admit being stopped by the police and so might not acknowledge it. A hesitancy to report something that is thought to be embarrassing is called a "social desirability bias," and it is common in surveys. To take into account this possibility, we asked the driver to estimate the likelihood that a typical driver who has been stopped would not acknowledge this fact in a survey. The responses differ slightly but significantly by race, suggesting that African Americans may be somewhat more hesitant than whites to acknowledge having been stopped.

What about class? On the street, the most visible symbol of class is a driver's vehicle. As table 3.1 shows, in investigatory stops, police officers are 70 percent more likely to stop drivers of the least valuable vehicles, even after taking into account the driver's race, gender, and age. The effect is substantial. Figure 3.5 illustrates how much the value of the vehicle affects a driver's likelihood of being stopped, by race and gender of

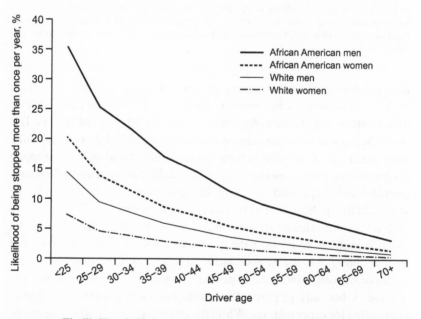

FIGURE 3.4. The likelihood of being stopped more than once in the past year, by race, gender, and age, controlling for all other factors ($N = 1580$). Estimates were generated by post-logit estimation using prvalue (Stata, version 11). Below age 65, all differences by race are statistically significant ($p < .05$).

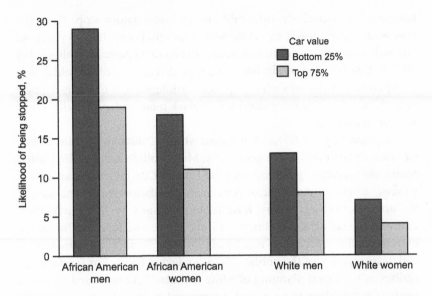

FIGURE 3.5. The effect of vehicle value: the likelihood of an investigatory stop over the course of a year among drivers under age 40, by race, gender, and vehicle value, controlling for all other factors ($N = 1597$). All differences are statistically significant ($p < .05$).

the driver. Over the course of a year, an African American man under age 40 has a 19 percent chance of being stopped in an investigatory stop if his car is not especially low-value; his chance of being stopped jumps to 29 percent if his car is among the bottom quartile in vehicle value. For black women, the likelihood of being stopped jumps from 11 to 18 percent; for white men, from 8 to 13 percent; and for white women, from 4 to 7 percent.

Drivers of such domestic luxury cars as Cadillacs, which, as we have noted, are a cultural marker of minority race, are also more likely to be stopped in investigatory stops. Driving such a car greatly increases one's chances of an investigatory stop, as illustrated in figure 3.6. Over the course of a year, an African American man under age 40 has a 21 percent chance of being stopped in an investigatory stop if his car is some make or model other than a domestic luxury car; his chance of being stopped jumps to 36 percent if he drives a domestic luxury car. For black women, the likelihood of being stopped jumps from 12 to 24 percent; for white men, from 9 to 18 percent; and for white women, from 5 to 10 percent.

A young African American man driving an old, run-down domestic luxury car is especially vulnerable to an investigatory stop. Over the course of a year, an African American man who is less than 40 years old and is driving an older domestic luxury car has a 44 percent likelihood of an investigatory stop. A similar white man driving any other vehicle has an 8 percent chance of such a stop, and a white woman has only a 4 percent chance. Investigatory stops target black men, and, especially, lower income black men.

They also target African Americans who are "out of place" in America's racially bounded urban geography. Metropolitan areas in the United States are racially segregated, and the Kansas City metropolitan area is a classic example: the African American population is concentrated in the urban core (Kansas City, Kansas, and Kansas City, Missouri), while many of the suburbs are almost entirely white. The Kansas City area's extreme racial segregation is a legacy of white flight accompanying racial desegregation of the public schools and what Kevin Fox Gotham describes as the racial planning of white suburbs.[29] As we noted earlier, a study of police stops in a similarly segregated metropolitan area in California found that police officers targeted African American drivers for

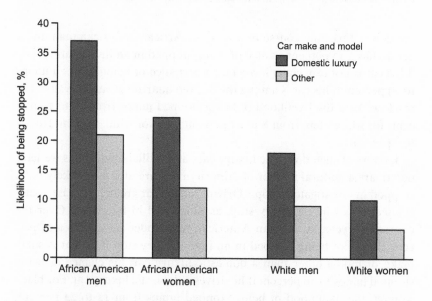

FIGURE 3.6. The likelihood of an investigatory stop while driving a domestic luxury vehicle over the course of a year among drivers under age 40, by race, gender, and vehicle make and model, controlling for all other factors ($N = 1597$). All differences are statistically significant ($p < .05$).

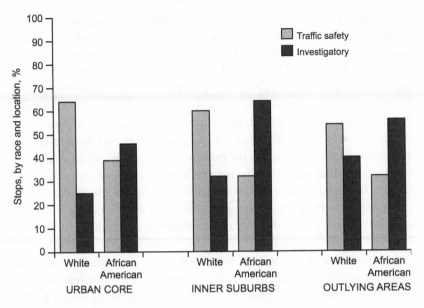

FIGURE 3.7. Stops of African American drivers, by type of stop and location (black drivers, $N = 212$; white drivers, $N = 497$).

investigatory stops when they were in "white" areas of town.[30] In precisely the same way, investigatory stops especially target African Americans in Kansas City's white suburbs. While the proportion of stops of African Americans and whites that are made for speeding does not vary much by location, stops of African Americans are especially skewed toward investigatory stops in the inner suburbs (see figure 3.7).

*   *   *

The traffic stop is a nearly universal experience shared by all drivers. Describing stops, drivers appear to speak a common language. They tell of being yanked from a state of near freedom to one of virtual imprisonment on the side of the road, of sudden shock and indignation at this seemingly arbitrary exercise of state authority. Nearly every driver has experienced being stopped, and most see stops almost on a daily basis, punctuating the wide reach of police patrol.

But this shared experience obscures a deep racial chasm in drivers' experiences of police stops. For most white drivers, the stop is an uncommon experience: only about 12 percent are stopped over the course of a year, and the vast majority of them will experience only one such event that year. For black drivers, the stops are more common: nearly one in four will be stopped over the course of a year, and half of these will experience more than one stop in that year. For black men, stops are especially frequent. Well over a third are stopped every year, roughly triple the rate for white women. Over 40 percent of black men under age 25 experience more than one police stop over the course of a year, approximately six times the rate for white women of the same age.

More fundamentally, while for the vast majority of stopped white drivers the police stop is an understandable response to a clear violation of traffic-safety laws, large proportions of stopped African American drivers are pulled over for more arbitrary, and often unexplained, reasons. Nearly 50 percent of white drivers who are stopped reported that this was for driving 7 or more miles per hour over the limit; roughly half that number of black drivers are stopped for a similar reason. Only about 8 percent of white drivers are given no reason by the officer for the stop; almost 18 percent of black drivers are given no reason. When officers give reasons for making the stop, roughly twice as many African American drivers as white drivers are stopped for a miscellany of highly discretionary reasons, among them driving too slowly, stopping too long, having a burned-out license-plate light, or simply to check whether the driver has an outstanding arrest warrant, which is not a legal basis for a stop.

Beneath these disparities there is one comforting observation. When police are engaged in traffic-safety enforcement, they make stops without regard to the driver's race. In stops for excessive speeding, for instance, the driver's race (and gender) has no relevance to the likelihood of being stopped. It is driving behavior, pure and simple, that determines whether a driver is stopped to enforce the traffic-safety laws.

But this means that virtually all of the wide racial disparity in the likelihood of being stopped is concentrated in one category of stops: discretionary stops for minor violations of the law. Police have told us they use drivers' minor violations of the law to justify stops when they want to investigate the driver on suspicion of criminal activity. The Supreme Court has accepted the legitimacy of pretext stops, but only on the condition that race is not a primary reason for the officer's suspicions. Nonetheless, race is a strong element in discretionary investigatory stops: African American drivers are more than two and a half times more likely than white drivers to be subjected to these stops. Gender compounds this disparity in pretext stops: African American men are almost four times more likely than white women to be subjected to these stops.

We now turn to what happens during traffic stops and show that differences in types of stops lead to racially defined differences in the experience of drivers after the officer approaches the vehicle.

CHAPTER FOUR

Experiences During the Stop

KEITH: Lights came on. Thought I was speeding. Pulled over. You know he whipped a U-ee and came in behind me.

INTERVIEWER: Whipped a U-ee!

KEITH: Well, yeah, he caught me coming at him. He had me dead to rights, there's no running. Didn't have anything to run with. You know, pulled over and as it would happen that particular time I had talked to that officer like an hour earlier. He was on an alarm call at the house next door. And he comes walking up [to the car] and he saw who it was and he started grinning. I was shaking my head. He was like, "I'm going to have to give you a ticket." And I says, "Cool." He got me and it wasn't any great big deal. I didn't get browbeat or rubber-hosed or anything like that. So you know, he did cut me a little slack. Instead of writing it for the full 72 or 3 or whatever it was, he only wrote it for 70. So, $25. Which I'm not going to say it was pleasurable but it didn't suck as bad as it could have. And then he left. I got more ribbing from my daughter and her friend, who was in the car—"Dad got a ticket!" . . . It was all friendly. It was just like, "You know why I stopped you." "Yeah, I was going a little fast." It was just typical. Wasn't anything out of the ordinary.[1]

DARRELL: Probably the time when I was a sophomore in high school, me and a couple of buddies of mine were driving through, like, a predominantly white neighborhood. And we got pulled over because, I guess, somebody's house supposedly got broken into and whatnot a couple of days ago and . . . I guess it was the circumstances. He really had no reason to pull us over, but I guess it's because we were all blacks and whatnot!

INTERVIEWER: Oh my!

DARRELL: Yeah. And they said that we fit the profile for, I guess, for whoever broke into somebody's house that one night. I mean, it's not like he was pulling us over for a traffic violation. He was pulling us over because we were black and, I guess, we met the profile for whatever had happened whenever it had happened. I mean, that was just like an uncomfortable experience for me.

INTERVIEWER: Do you remember what the officer did?

DARRELL: He made us get out of the car and made us wait, I guess, for some people to come, and verify if it was us or not. We never found out if they have to retain us or if he could've let us go. He said that it was negative ID. He let us go. I didn't say anything. I didn't want to make anything worse than what it was.

INTERVIEWER: Do you remember what he said when he came up?

DARRELL: Yeah, he asked us for [our] driver's license and all that stuff. Then he asked if we lived around here because, I guess, my driver's license address wasn't from around where we was. Then he asked us where we lived and why we were over here. And he made us get out of the car and stuff. I mean I just kept cool about it, I guess. I kept my composure. Because I didn't want to make something out of nothing. I mean it was something, now that I look at it. But I didn't wanna, you know, give him a reason to do anything else. So I just play along with it. But after all, I felt really bad. We just had to sit outside on the curb for like an hour.

INTERVIEWER: Oh my goodness.

DARRELL: Yeah, we just sat out there. And they put handcuffs on, too.

INTERVIEWER: They what?

DARRELL: Yeah, they put us in handcuffs. And we sat outside for about an hour, and then they just let us go.

INTERVIEWER: Did the people who were supposed to make the identification ever come? Darrell: They wouldn't tell us. They just said that the ID was negative. So, they just let us go. And I remember one of my friends said, "Did nobody come by?" And he said, "Don't worry about it; you are free to go." All right, whatever.[2]

Why did the police ticket this driver but not that one? Why ticket this driver but search that one? Why engage in friendly jokes with one driver, but threaten the other with arrest, put him in handcuffs, and hold him on a sidewalk for an hour? Why, in short, are some drivers routinely processed while others are subjected to long and intrusive investigations? This and the following chapter examines how and why drivers are treated differently during the stop, and together they take the second step in showing that investigatory stops are the source of racial disparities in police stops.

To show how investigatory stops are the source of these racial disparities, we need to take into account a key alternative explanation: the possibility that they grow instead from unintended tit-for-tat interactions between officers and black drivers. Relations between the police and African Americans have long been conflict-laden, and this may predispose officers and black drivers to respond testily to each other. The arrest in

2009 of the distinguished Harvard University professor Henry Louis Gates Jr., a black man, on the doorstep of his home illustrates this possibility. Returning home from a trip, Professor Gates found his front door stuck and tried to force it open with the help of his driver, who was also black. A passerby, suspecting an attempted break-in, called the police. Sergeant James Crowley, the responding officer, and Professor Gates began to argue; the argument quickly escalated to shouting, and Crowley arrested and handcuffed Gates for disorderly conduct. Professor Gates alleged that Sergeant Crowley treated him disrespectfully; Crowley, in turn, alleged that Gates did not cooperate in his investigation. "The situation deteriorated rapidly," according to a panel of experts on policing and law convened by the city of Cambridge to address what went wrong. The report concluded that "Sergeant Crowley and Professor Gates each missed opportunities to 'ratchet down' the situation and end it peacefully."[3]

Like the Gates incident, stops are inherently *interactive* encounters, in Goffman's use of that term; during the stop, officers and drivers test each other, seeking gains.[4] The officer seeks to stay in control, maintain his or her authority, and impose a sanction; the driver seeks to escape with as little punishment and loss of dignity as possible. How drivers speak and act during the stop affects their own fate, but the driver's words and actions, in turn, are influenced by the officer's. Both officer and driver are especially attentive to signs of respect or disrespect from the other; both want to be respected, both resent signs of disrespect. Sometimes tensions escalate as each party engages in what Stanford Lyman and Marvin Scott have called a "face game."[5] Many studies, and our focus groups with officers, have found that officers act more punitively against the belligerent and disrespectful than the contrite and deferential.[6] In a recent survey in over a hundred police departments, over half of the officers acknowledged that sometimes police officers arrest somebody simply for expressing a "bad attitude" toward an officer.[7]

In these interactive exchanges, African American drivers fare substantially worse than whites. Many studies find that African Americans experience deeper investigatory intrusions, heavier sanctions, and greater impoliteness by the officer, and our study confirms this.[8]

What are the sources of this greater intrusion and punishment of African American drivers? Is it racism by white police officers, pure and simple? Or is it a product of unintended tit-for-tat escalations between officers and black drivers? Or, as we will argue, is it due to how investigatory stops encourage officers to pursue deeper intrusions of black drivers?

Because all police stops are interactive encounters, we take seriously the suggestion that officers treat black drivers more harshly because they are *reacting* to African Americans' disrespectful actions or words, and so this chapter is devoted to considering and eliminating this possibility.[9] It is true that African Americans trust the police much less than do whites. This distrust, it is said, may lead to expressing greater disrespect toward police officers. Here is how it is said to work. To maintain control, officers often speak in a curt and authoritarian manner; while a trusting white driver might view this demeanor as businesslike, a less trusting African American might view it as disrespectful.[10] A resentful driver, perceiving police disrespect, may in turn be more likely than a trusting driver to lash out verbally. And as we have noted, a long line of studies suggest that officers respond more harshly to people who act disrespectfully toward them. From this it is only a small step to the speculation that the source of police harshness toward black drivers is these drivers' disrespectful behavior toward officers.[11] If so, this is a tragic dynamic, since neither the black driver nor the police officer deliberately plans to act in this way. It is an unintentional tit-for-tat escalation.[12]

Some ethnographic studies of the "street code" in impoverished urban areas lend support to this tit-for-tat hypothesis. Elijah Anderson and Philippe Bourgois observe that poor, racial minority youth in high-crime areas believe that signs of disrespect are a great affront and should be met with violence or at least aggressive displays of confidence as a means to regain respect.[13] Deanna Wilkinson and Jeffrey Fagan found that poor youth in high-crime areas commonly follow available scripts that prescribe threats with guns and shootings as the appropriate response to disrespect.[14] These observations may reflect a long-standing norm. In the 1970s, David Luckenbill found that murders commonly are the culminations of escalations in response to signs of disrespect by one of the parties.[15]

Still, as Rod Brunson and Ronald Weitzer have shown, while youth may favor aggressive responses to signs of disrespect by a *peer*, these youth and their parents also recognize that aggressive responses to disrespect by *police officers* is extremely risky and self-defeating.[16] In dealing with police officers, the favored norm is: "(1) show respect toward the officers, (2) comply with police directives, (3) volunteer no information to officers, (4) avoid sudden movements, and (5) keep one's hands in plain sight."[17] Although the tit-for-tat hypothesis is plausible, so is the contrary expectation, that African American drivers *avoid* making challenges to police officers.

Most studies lack any data on officer-driver interactions during the stop, and so the claim that black drivers bring harsh police treatment on themselves is simple speculation. They cannot tell whether searches are done in response to a driver's belligerence or, vice versa, this belligerence is a response to officers' intrusions and impoliteness. Our survey questions and narratives shine a clear light on these interactions.

This chapter and the next show that the dominant factor shaping these interactions is not driver distrust, indignation, or disrespect; it is not the race of the officer. Nor do the seriousness of the offense, the personalities of the officer and driver, whether the driver is a man or woman or young or old, or the driver's type of vehicle meaningfully change the interaction between cop and driver. The dominant influence on these interactions is the type of stop: traffic-safety enforcement or criminal investigation.[18] These other dimensions are relevant, but whether and how the driver's race, gender, and age matter depends on the type of stop. In traffic-safety stops, gender and age matter hardly at all and race has no significant influence. In investigatory stops, the driver's race, gender, and age are the key influences: officers pursue investigatory intrusions far more deeply when the driver is a young black man. And while expressions of disrespect can sour any stop, the type of stop frames this, too: investigatory stops dramatically heighten tensions and disrespect between officer and driver. To be sure, occasionally interactions between officers and black drivers escalate unpredictably, but this is rare because most officers and black drivers try very hard to avoid it.

Illustrating the Basic Patterns

Traffic-safety and investigatory stops follow different scripts. In traffic-safety stops, officers are brief and to the point. They inform the driver why he or she was stopped (or ask whether the driver knows why he was stopped, a question aimed at testing for contrition); ask for the driver's license, insurance papers, and vehicle registration; write a ticket or deliver a warning; and release the driver. In investigatory stops, officers are rarely so to the point: they ask questions, look about the car's interior, prolong the encounter while looking for anomalies and evidence of wrongdoing, and, if suspicious, search the vehicle. Officers proceed coolly and rationally with these investigatory intrusions, rather than being drawn into them as a way to punish disrespectful drivers.

Drivers, too, follow different scripts in these different types of stops. Those stopped for speeding may be contrite and self-effacing, like Keith in narrative 4.1, or indignant, like others we'll introduce below, but in either case their words focus on the alleged violation. While the difference between contrite and indignant in a speeding stop may marginally influence how severe is the sanction, it is unlikely to convert the speeding stop into an investigatory stop. In investigatory stops, the scripts available to drivers are quite different: contrition is rarely the measure against which drivers are judged because the "violation" that justified the stop is typically below the level that requires a show of remorse, and both officers and drivers know this. Nobody seriously expects a driver to feign apology for a burned-out license-plate light or for driving 2 miles per hour over the limit. Instead, drivers' options in investigatory stops are either to accept their role as the subjects of investigation and defer to officers' investigatory intrusions or to challenge the basic fairness of these intrusions.

Other explanations of racial disparities in what happens during the police stop mistake the ephemeral for the deeper structure. Yes, black drivers are more disrespectful toward officers than white drivers, but how disrespectful is the driver is mainly a product of the type of stop: drivers are more disrespectful in investigatory stops, because they resent being stopped on a pretext. Yes, officers sometimes speak in racially bigoted ways, but these expressions are rare and are confined to investigatory stops. Widespread investigatory intrusions of black drivers appear to be less a product of bigotry than of deliberate planning.

Keith and Darrell experienced very different types of stops and, as a consequence, played different roles and followed different scripts. Keith believed he was "caught dead to rights" for speeding and traded jokes with the officer, who almost apologized that he was "going to have to" give Keith a ticket. This suggested that Keith was in the land of objective rules neutrally applied. The officer asked no intrusive questions, carried out no probing examination of the interior of Keith's car, and conducted no search. Keith was frankly contrite and the officer issued a ticket for less than Keith's admitted speed. Keith felt the stop went about as well as might be expected. His experience was consistent with a long-standing observation: police officers are often lenient to traffic-law violators.[19]

Darrell, by contrast, believed accurately that he was stopped not for how he was driving but for being a black teenager in a white neighborhood: the officer explained that he stopped Darrell because he and his friends "fit a profile" for the suspected perpetrators of a recent home burglary. The stop deteriorated from there. Officers asked the young men what they were doing in the neighborhood, held them in handcuffs on the sidewalk for an hour, and then released them with no explanation. The long period of uncertainty and lack of explanation indicates that Darrell was not experiencing objective rules neutrally applied, but arbitrary control. Darrell recognized this: he reported that he did not complain because he wanted to avoid any provocation that might make the situation worse. In doing so, he followed the script of the deferential subject of investigation, a script that we will see repeatedly employed by black drivers. By Darrell's description the officer was not rude, did not use insulting language, and did not say any racial slurs. Still—and not surprisingly—Darrell left the stop feeling "really bad."

How common are these different sorts of experiences? Was Keith's experience common and Darrell's rare? To answer this question we asked our random sample of drivers who reported a stop in the past year what happened during the stop. Most previous survey-based studies have focused on citations, searches, and arrests; some examined whether stopped drivers perceive the officer as acting respectfully or disrespectfully.[20] The narratives of Keith and Darrell, and several excellent ethnographic studies by Rod Brunson, Jacinta Gau, and Jody Miller, illustrate how these limited measures do not fully capture the experience from the driver's perspective.[21] We want to know not only about citations, searches, and arrests but also about handcuffing and intrusive questions ("Why are you in this area?"). And we want to know how the officer spoke and acted. We call these two sorts of things "intrusions and sanctions" and "officer demeanor."

Drivers' answers to these questions are summarized in figures 4.1 through 4.4. The first pair of figures illustrate the incidence of intrusions and sanctions in the two different types of stops, traffic safety and investigatory. The second pair of figures illustrate the officer's demeanor, again divided by these two different types of stops. On all dimensions—intrusions, sanctions, and officer demeanor—the patterns differ considerably between traffic-safety and investigatory stops. Officers almost never pursue intrusive questions and actions in traffic-safety stops, but pursue them regularly in investigatory stops. In traffic-safety stops,

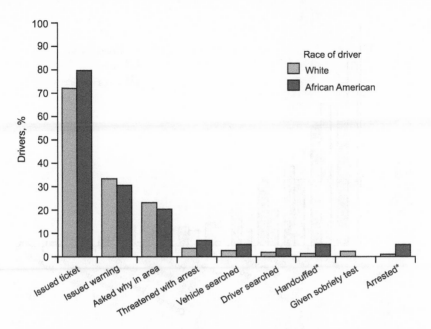

FIGURE 4.1. Intrusions and sanctions by race in speeding stops ($N = 284$–288). *Difference, by race, of driver is statistically significant ($p < .05$; two-tailed t-test).

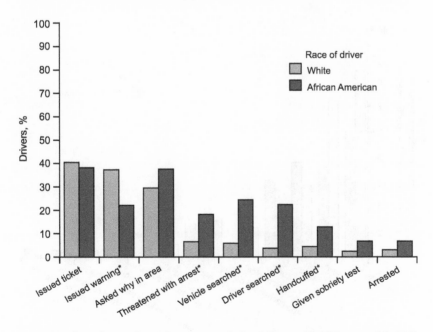

FIGURE 4.2. Intrusions and sanctions, by race, in investigatory stops ($N = 222$–281). *Difference by race of driver is statistically significant ($p < .05$; two-tailed t-test).

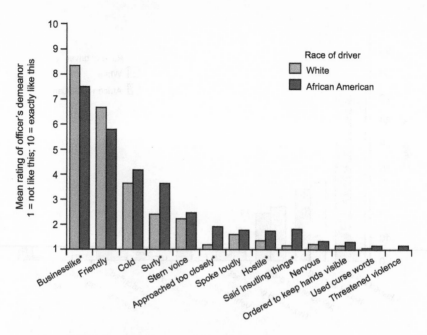

FIGURE 4.3. Officer demeanor, by race of driver, in speeding stops (N = 283–288). *Difference by race of driver is statistically significant (p < .05; two-tailed t-test).

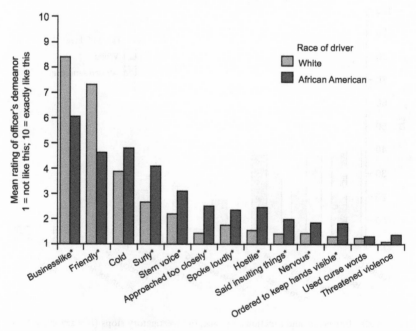

FIGURE 4.4. Officer demeanor, by race of driver, in investigatory stops (N = 216–227). *Difference by race of driver is statistically significant (p < .05; two-tailed t-test).

officers issue citations or warnings; in investigatory stops, these routine sanctions are less common. While the officer's demeanor also differs between these two types of stops, the difference is slight. In both types of stops few drivers report that the officer swore or was insulting. Still, drivers are more likely to characterize the officer as businesslike or even friendly in traffic-safety stops than they are in investigatory stops.

What is striking is how the type of stop alters the treatment of black and white drivers. In traffic-safety stops, race has no significant effect on most types of intrusions and sanctions, but during investigatory stops black drivers are subjected to significantly more threats of arrest, searches, and being handcuffed than whites. To be sure, even in speeding stops, a higher percentage of African Americans than whites—80 percent versus 72 percent—are issued tickets, and higher percentages of African American speeders are subjected to searches. These differences are not statistically meaningful, however. In speeding stops, black drivers receive significantly different treatment than whites on only two dimensions: handcuffing and arrest. The absence of statistically meaningful differences by race in questioning or searches—such probing is the prelude to arrest—indicates that the officers were neither intending nor expecting to arrest black drivers at higher rates than whites during speeding stops.

We turn now to driver perceptions of an officer's demeanor. In traffic-safety stops black drivers rate the officer as less polite than do white drivers, but on most questions the difference is slight and not statistically meaningful. In investigatory stops, African American drivers are more likely than white drivers to describe the officer as acting much more impolitely, and on most questions this gap is wide and statistically meaningful. The impact of the type of stop is striking. For example, in speeding stops, whites and African Americans report similar levels of officer friendliness (the difference is .9 on a 10-point scale), but in investigatory stops the gap on this question grows to 2.7 points on the same scale.

In sum, traffic-safety stops yield unpleasant but thoroughly routine experiences for drivers, indicative of the fact that these stops are made mainly for the purpose of improving traffic safety. Like Keith, drivers are quickly issued a ticket and let go. Investigatory stops are intrusive, interpersonally tense, and sometimes genuinely scary, as when the officer handcuffs the driver; but, in the end, most drivers, like Darrell and his fellow black friends, are let go with no ticket or warning whatsoever. Most investigatory stops yield no evidence of crime.

Before accepting these findings we must ask: are drivers' reports a valid indicator of how the police officer acted? Do these findings reflect peoples' underlying biases toward the police more than the officers' actual behavior? Perhaps a driver who distrusts the police will perceive an officer's words as "surly," when a more trusting driver might interpret the same words differently. Attitudes frame perceptions, but we do not believe that the racial differences reported here are the product of differing degrees of trust in the police. For one thing, the racial differences are especially wide in investigatory stops, suggesting that racial differences in perceived officer disrespect are not fixed, the unchanging product of prior differences in trust, but responsive to officer-initiated actions. For another, in designing our survey questions on how the officer acted, we directed drivers' attention to precise events or behaviors as opposed to more subjective, ungrounded evaluations of the officer. Thus, we asked drivers to report whether the officer issued a ticket or a warning and whether the officer asked why the driver was in the area, handcuffed the driver, threatened the driver with arrest, searched the vehicle or driver, conducted a sobriety test, or arrested the driver. Likewise, with regard to the officer's demeanor, we asked the driver to report specific behaviors rather than broader, ungrounded evaluative opinions, such as whether the officer was polite or respectful.

The crucial question, then, is *why* are African American drivers treated more intrusively and impolitely than white drivers? Is this a product of interactive tit-for-tat escalations or deliberately planned investigatory intrusions? The differences by type of stop illustrated above suggest that the type of stop contributes to these racial disparities. But what can we learn from our data regarding the interactive process during the stop?

The Tit-for-Tat Hypothesis

Although a shared encounter, officers and drivers are not equals; police officers personify the coercive power of the state. In general, officers control the sequence of events. They are trained to stay in control. As an officer approaches the car, he or she is in no rush and pays close attention to the driver's movements. Officers expect most drivers to go into their glove box or reach into a pocket or purse in search of their license and insurance and registration papers. While these actions are typically innocent, officers are alert to the possibility that the driver may be reaching for a weapon. They are attentive to any action that indicates danger or that the driver is hiding something. When speaking with drivers, officers deliberately shape their manner, questions, and actions to keep control over the driver and the stop. Still, the unexpected can happen, and officers are prepared to respond with force. As the traffic officer who told us the following narrative observed, "nothing is ever routine." He had pulled over someone for speeding and then noticed the driver's head drop below the dash board, suggesting that the driver was reaching for something on the car's floor. The officer said he worriedly wondered, "Is this going to be the worst traffic stop I've ever made?"

NARRATIVE 4.3.
Traffic officer, African American male: "Nothing Is Ever Routine"

OFFICER: The thing about all of them, the traffic stops that I make, nothing is ever routine, all of them are different. . . .

I stopped a vehicle for speeding and pulled in behind the vehicle, and the driver basically ducked toward the dashboard area where I couldn't actually see his head. Which made it a little more riskier, but every stop is a high risk, or sometimes high risky stop.

Like I say, nothing is ever routine. You are always looking for things that are just basically predict to yourself that this is going to be the worst traffic stop I've ever made. Every stop you make, you have that type of attitude.

He had his head stuck, you know, under where I actually couldn't see his head, so that brought concern. So as I approached, I just approached towards the passenger's side. . . .

INTERVIEWER: You said you pulled him over for speeding . . . and then he put his head underneath the dash.

OFFICER: Yes, after he stopped and pulled over onto the shoulder, he ducked, basically, as if he was reaching toward the floorboard of the passenger side, which is something really, really risky. It was a nighttime stop, so when you see different things like that is just draws different things to attention, to your attention. . . .

INTERVIEWER: And then when you approached him, did he come up from the dashboard?

OFFICER: Yes, he did. Well, the thing about it is he was expecting that I would probably approach him on the driver's side. So from that position [the passenger's side], I can actually see inside his car. I can actually see his hands, I can see the seat, I can see the floorboard area of his car, before he actually knew I was standing there on the passenger's side. . . .

INTERVIEWER: Do you remember anything in particular about [the driver]?

OFFICER: No, I mean, he just, he dropped, he was bending over, picking up his registration off the floorboard.[22]

This officer was instantly alert to a driver's action that appeared to be furtive—Is the driver reaching for a gun or hiding drugs?—and he approached the car with extra caution, startling the driver. Apprehension and uncertainty infuse police stops, even the most routine ones, and officers address this risk by trying to maintain a calm demeanor and the aura of polite yet firm control over the interaction. So, on the officer's side, there is ample evidence that officers are alert to any sign of threat from the driver and will take steps to maintain control.

But now we come to the first crucial question: if African American drivers are less trusting of the police *are they also more disrespectful and belligerent toward officers*? Are they more likely than whites to act provocatively? At first glance, it seems that they are. In our survey, to examine the level of driver disrespect during the stop we asked three questions: to what extent did you speak to the officer with an angry voice, to what extent did you speak loudly to the officer, and to what extent did you speak sarcastically to the officer? As we will show below, officers do respond significantly more punitively toward drivers who speak disrespectfully in these ways. African Americans speak significantly more disrespectfully than whites toward officers on the first two measures (speaking angrily and loudly) but not the third (speaking sarcastically). For all analyses in this chapter we combined these three measures into an additive index of driver disrespect ($\alpha = .75$).[23] On this index, without taking into account any possible influences other than the driver's race, African Americans spoke significantly more disrespectfully than whites toward officers ($p < .05$, two-tailed t-test).

But this is only part of the story, and a misleading part at that. For one thing, the gap in disrespect between whites and African Americans is quite small (only one-fifth of a standard deviation on the disrespect scale). More importantly, when we take into account factors other than the driver's race, the dominant influence on how disrespectfully the driver acted is not race but the *type* of stop (see column 1 in table 4.1).[24] In fact, among all stops, after taking into account whether the stop was investigatory, African Americans are *not* significantly more disrespectful than white drivers. The key influence on driver disrespect is the type of stop: drivers are significantly more disrespectful toward officers in investigatory stops than traffic-safety stops. This is probably because drivers resent being stopped for very minor violations and then subjected to investigatory intrusions. As the third column in table 4.1 indicates, African Americans do not act more disrespectfully than whites toward

TABLE 4.1. **Extent to which drivers speak disrespectfully to the officer.**

Characteristic	Type of stop		
	All	Speeding	Investigatory
Investigatory stop	0.162**		
	(.078)		
African American	0.061	0.359***	−0.279
	(.084)	(.101)	(.423)
Female	0.053	0.015	0.145
	(.075)	(.085)	(.374)
Age	−0.004	0.002	−0.046***
	(.003)	(.004)	(.017)
Controls			
Education level	−0.029	−0.051*	0.032
	(.024)	(.028)	(.130)
Income	−0.004	0.019	−0.069
	(.014)	(.016)	(.076)
Political conservatism	−0.020	0.003	−0.254**
	(.023)	(.026)	(.123)
Vehicle value (bottom quartile)	0.071	−0.041	0.478
	(.092)	(.117)	(.430)
Vehicle customization	0.138***	0.204****	0.035
	(.051)	(.057)	(.297)
Vehicle damage	0.020	−0.222**	0.053
	(.073)	(.093)	(.334)
Illegal vehicle conditions	−0.068	0.073	−0.461*
	(.060)	(.083)	(.270)
Time driving	0.005	0.019	−0.067
	(.025)	(.029)	(.117)
Rule-abiding driving	−0.083	−0.218*	−0.050
	(.091)	(.116)	(.420)
Extent of speeding	0.006	0.003	0.016
	(.006)	(.007)	(.037)
Number of passengers	0.029	0.012	−0.027
	(.036)	(.041)	(.180)
Number of officers	0.026	0.172***	−0.056
	(.023)	(.051)	(.173)
Constant	−0.535	−0.735	0.327
	(.701)	(.776)	(4.22)
Log pseudolikelihood	−523.36	−163.88	−170.73
LR χ^2 (16)	33.07	54.89	20.84
p	<.01	<.0001	—
N	455	197	165
Left-censored N	1	1	108

Note: Results were obtained using Tobit estimation. Reported results are coefficients, with robust standard errors in parentheses. The dependent variable is an additive index that is not normally distributed. For dependent variables with this characteristic, Tobit is the most appropriate modeling technique (see J. Scott Long, *Regression Models for Categorical and Limited Dependent Variables* [Thousand Oaks, CA: Sage, 1997], 187–216). We have confirmed the results with ordered probit; the results do not differ substantially from those reported here. See the appendix for further discussion.
$*p<.10; **p<.05; ***p<.01; ****p<.001$

officers in investigatory stops, where racial disparities in official intrusions and sanctions are concentrated. Still, while African American drivers are *not* more disrespectful than white drivers in investigatory stops, they *are* somewhat more disrespectful in *speeding* stops (see column 2 of table 4.1). We return to this critical observation in the next chapter, but, for now, the key point is that African Americans appear to be more disrespectful toward the police mainly because they are more subjected to investigatory stops, where disrespect is higher among all drivers.

But these statistical patterns reveal little about drivers' thoughts and emotions. Narratives gathered for this study speak to this crucial question and reveal a key fact that is strikingly at odds with speculations about disrespectful African American drivers. They are especially aware of the possibility of explosive escalations and deliberately act to avoid them. It is true that they view investigatory stops as a violation, but, rather than striking out against this disrespect, black drivers follow a script prescribing quiet acquiescence to police officers' commands and requests in investigatory stops. As Rod Brunson and Ronald Weitzer observed in their rich ethnographic study, deferring to the officers' intrusions in investigatory stops is African American drivers' rational, self-preserving response to the ever-present risk of violent escalation.[25]

Many African American drivers have told us that they do virtually everything to avoid such an escalation: they defer to the officer's commands and requests, avoid any suspicious movements, and keep their mouth shut even when they feel deeply indignant at the officer's intrusions. Occasionally they report that once they lost this careful control and spoke their mind. As Donna put it, "maybe my mouth took it a little further," but then she regained control, and "I stopped myself."[26] But this is rare, and they seem to fear losing this self-control. Billy, an African American, put it this way:

> Like I said I try to, you know, when they approach me, you know try to make it as nonthreatening as possible. Try to, you know, have the information about my car because I know they would want like, driver's license, registration and proof of insurance. Those are the three things that they are going to ask for. And so, myself, I try to make sure to keep up to date all my driver tags and my insurance and also my current driver's license. And, you know, I drive with my seatbelt on and then if they stop me I try to stay nonthreatening as possible, you know, not be pacing around or, you know, looking like, you know. You know, I'm sure they have been schooled and aware of behaviors. So, you

know, try to make myself nonthreatening, that way if the officer ask me questions I try to respond as . . . best I can.[27]

Poignantly, Timothy, a middle-aged black man who scores on our scale of driving habits as a safe driver, put it this way:

> I would really love to say I know that everybody is treated the same. I look for the worst when I'm pulled over by the police. And I know I shouldn't have that mindset, but I really fear the worst. I try not to move; I try not to do anything that it would give them an opportunity to think that I'm gonna try to make a move. And that's a hell of a way to live. That is the truth. That doesn't make any difference whether it's a black policeman or white policeman as far as I'm concerned. . . . I really have a fear of ever being arrested by the police. I never been arrested, so I don't know why I have that fear, but I do have one.[28]

Police officers, too, are especially attentive to the risk of escalation and are trained to forestall it and maintain control so as to avoid drawing a gun and using force. Officers follow a standard script—the officer in the following narrative says he even smiles the same smile so as to avoid confrontation.

NARRATIVE 4.4
Traffic officer, white male: "I Am Kind of Like a Recording"

OFFICER: It was an older, white, female driver, about 45–50 years of age. She was speeding. I believe she was about 55 in a 40. I was running front-moving radar in my car. I noticed her car came up speeding and, of course, confirmed it with my radar gun. . . .

[I] walk up to the car. The first thing out of the lady's mouth is, "Good morning." And I'm like, "Good morning, ma'am."

She asked me what she had done and I explained to her that I needed her driver's license and proof of insurance first. And she gave me her driver's license, so once I had her driver's license, I spoke with her for a few seconds.

I explained the reason I stopped her was her speed, and also she failed to wear a safety belt when she operated her vehicle. And I asked her if everything was current, I always ask, I am kind of like a recording. I ask the same thing, I say: "Is everything currently registered on your motor vehicle?" . . . Then, I will tell them . . . I am going to issue a citation for and explain whatever it is that I am going to give them a ticket for. . . . Then, I go back to either my motorcycle or my car and then I issue the ticket. . . .

When I came back up and I issue the ticket to her, she told me, and this was her exact quote, "This was bullshit," . . . and I should be out catching, you know, murderers and thieves and drug dealers and all of that and shouldn't be messing around with good people.

INTERVIEWER: And how did you respond to her when she said that?

OFFICER: I just smiled. I give the same response to everybody. . . . Most of the time you are going to avoid a confrontation. . . . I have already explained to her what she has needed to know. I leave the car, that way it doesn't cause that person to get even more angered at me, it doesn't cause them to want to get out of the car, it doesn't want to cause them, in my experience, to want to act stupid.[29]

Let's now turn to the other side of the tit-for-tat hypothesis: the possibility that officers act especially punitively toward disrespect when it is expressed by African Americans. There is a long history of whites' indignation against what was once called "uppity" blacks, that is, African Americans who demanded to be treated with equal respect. Our interviews provide some evidence that tit-for-tat escalations develop because officers respond especially punitively toward complaints by *black* drivers, but such instances are rare. We think this is not a primary explanation but acknowledge that some officers sometimes act in this way.

Billy, an African American, described a harrowing experience. He said he had been on his way to a video store in a Kansas City suburb late at night. Along the way, he saw a police officer parked near a stop sign and reported making sure that he stopped fully before proceeding carefully past the officer. But the officer immediately pulled him over. The officer "didn't say anything to me but 'Driver's license, registration, and proof of insurance.'"[30] Billy handed the officer his license but realized his updated insurance papers were back at his home. Billy admits that then he "kind of got upset," and asked the officer why he was being stopped (as we described in the previous chapter, he put the challenge pithily: "because I am a poor man in a ragged car?").[31] As Billy recalls, the officer reacted angrily:

"Show me your hands, show me your hands!" And then I had this paper in my hands, so I just stuck my hands out of the car. Both hands, so he could have both of my hands. He had his pistol pulled out, and I didn't even turn my head, but I could see it out of the peripheral vision of my eye, its barrel, and he pointed it right at my head, you know. That was pretty frightening. You know how sometimes you have, like, an intuition, it was like a voice told me, "you will not die this night." And it was a clear night and as soon as that happened this other police officer . . . pulled around kind of in an almost plain car.[32]

The officer at Billy's side walked away to talk to the new officer, who then approached Billy to talk with him. Billy said: "I asked him, 'Why did that guy pull his weapon on me?' And he said, 'Because you got smart with him.'"[33] The officer pointed his gun at Billy not in reaction to a sign of danger but to punish a complaint.

Donna, an African American woman, told us about a stop in which the officers made frightening threats. The experience started as a simple speeding stop but the officers soon began searching Donna's car. Her narrative does not make clear what justification, if any, the officers used for the search. Although Donna was offended by the search, she was especially frightened by what the officers said:

> I was OK at first, but then when they were like searching [shining the light] in my eyes, then, you know . . . maybe my mouth took it a little further, but I stopped. I was questioning him: "Why do you need to search my car? I was speeding. Can you write me a ticket? You know, here is my insurance, here is my driver's license. So write my ticket so I can go." "Well ma'am, you are getting smart with that." "How am I getting smart?" And I think I cursed, I said a curse word. He was like, "Ma'am, I'm going to take you to jail." And I said, "You don't have any reason to take me to jail." "Oh yes we do." "No, you don't. I know my rights."[34]

Donna said, "He told me that he'll take my kids to the DFS [Missouri Department of Family Services]. It was a horrible experience. I felt that they were harassing me."Later she observed, "My son said once, 'Mom, they are harassing us.' So it was like the ten-year-old could even—that's how bad it was that he realized it."[35]

Mike, an African American man, described a police stop years ago in Chicago in which several officers pulled him over for having unconventional lights on his car.[36] The officers immediately began to look closely at the car's contents, eventually retrieving a thick wire that they used as the justification for a full search of the car. How finding a wire could be used as the legal basis for a search is unclear, although it should be observed that seemingly fabricated justifications for searches are quite common in anecdotal reports of investigatory stops.[37] But this gambit is not the most troubling element of Mike's story. He reported that an officer claimed to find a small pistol in the car. Mike denied ever having seen the pistol. As he tells the story, the officer confronted him with the pistol: "And you know he's like, 'What is this?' I'm like, 'I have no idea.'

And he was like, 'Looks like a gun to me. What do you think?' So he sticks the barrel in my mouth."[38]

Raw, deliberate police bigotry in response to a challenge is not the only possible interpretation of the motivation underlying the officers' actions in these three stories; it is, however, plausible. Mike, Billy, and Donna did not allege that any of the officers used racial slurs, but the officers' actions and words express a palpable animosity, disrespect, and effort at domination that is fairly understood as racial animosity. Mike and Billy were threatened with guns pointed at their heads. Billy and Donna were told to stop "being smart." Donna was threatened with loss of custody of her children. As Jennifer Ritterhouse has powerfully shown in her book *Growing up Jim Crow*, such acts and threats, and particularly the challenge "don't get smart with me," are traditional expressions of white supremacy.[39] Although Billy was arrested, Donna was only given a speeding ticket and Mike was let go with a warning, suggesting that officers in their cases grossly overreached. By comparison, none of the nineteen white drivers in the narrative portion of our study told us of having guns pointed at them. None said that officers warned them to stop being smart. None described officers threatening to take away custody of their children.

*   *   *

In concluding this chapter, we want to emphasize a broader point. The shocking examples of police reaction to disrespect that ended this chapter are rare. To be sure, police stops are interactive encounters and tit-for-tat escalation is always a possibility. Nonetheless, although officers and drivers sometimes feel indignant at the other's words, in most stops officer and driver succeed in avoiding explosive escalations. Officers and African American drivers seem to be especially attentive to the risk of these escalations and work especially hard to avoid them. Thus, officers' intrusions, especially the deep intrusive investigations of African American drivers, are *not* done in reaction to disrespect by these drivers. In the next chapter, we dig deeper into how the type of stop shapes the nature of the police-driver interactions and why these intrusions are made.

How Investigatory Intrusions Are Deliberately Planned (and Racially Based)

I f, as we saw in the previous chapter, investigatory intrusions are not the result of tit-for-tat escalations or frank police bigotry, what is their source? Our research indicates that investigatory intrusions are deliberately planned and racially framed from the start. Although stops are interactive encounters, as we have seen, police officers control the purpose of a stop, and whether this purpose is traffic-safety enforcement or criminal investigation determines the course of the interaction.

In traffic-safety stops, officers seek to issue the citation or warning with as little interpersonal conflict as possible; they hope to finish the official business quickly and move on to the next stop. In investigatory stops, officers may prolong the interaction as long as they feel necessary to scrutinize the visible contents of the passenger compartment and assess whether the driver is being candid or trying to hide something. These questions and intrusions increase the level of conflict between officers and drivers, and thus officers cannot really hope to entirely avoid confrontation as they do in traffic-safety stops. Nonetheless, they are trained to minimize escalations of conflict as much as possible. And, as we will document, when an officer is carrying out an investigatory stop, the driver's race is a principal cue to heightened police suspicion: the driver's race directly shapes how far officers take the investigation.

These intrusions in investigatory stops are not triggered by the driver's disrespect. They unfold in a *rationally planned manner* from the outset of the investigatory stop. This is not unintended escalation: it is planned intrusion. We have already shared several narratives—including Darrell being handcuffed and held on the sidewalk for an hour (4.2) and Joe's experience of two stops done only to check for a warrant for his arrest (1.1)—and will not belabor these examples. The crucial point is that the patterns in those stops, of deliberate intrusion beginning immediately as the officer approaches the vehicle rather than unfolding in response to the driver's words or actions, is typical. Among the sixteen African American drivers participating in our in-depth interviews, twelve told us personal stories of investigatory stops by police officers, and several of these drivers told us more than one such story. More than half of all stories told to us by African American drivers were about investigatory stops, and many of these narratives contained vivid depictions of extremely intrusive investigations by officers in which the investigation began immediately upon the officer's approach to the stopped driver. By contrast, among the nineteen white drivers participating in these interviews, only five reported investigatory stops, and these were generally briefer and considerably less intrusive than those described by African American drivers. These narratives are summarized in tables 5.1 and 5.2.

The vast majority of African Americans' narratives of stops, even of stops that they found offensive, provide no evidence of overt racial animosity on the part of the officers, nor do they provide evidence of a tit-for-tat escalation that grows out of interpersonal tensions. In fact, a striking element of many of the African Americans' stories of intrusive stops is the common observation that the officers were "nice" or "polite"—or, at the very least, not insulting—while carrying out intrusive investigations. Consider Elizabeth's story of an investigatory stop that went no further than the officers' close examination of the visible contents of her car's passenger compartment.

NARRATIVE 5.1
Elizabeth, African American female: "Putting the Spotlight on Me like I Was a Criminal"

ELIZABETH: Well, first I didn't know they were behind me. And then I've just seen the lights so I pulled over, and I asked the police why was he stopping me. He said that I ran a red light. I told him, "I did?" And he said that I was out, like making a left turn, and I was out waiting on traffic to come by so when the last car came by, I went. Okay. There was another policeman that walked up on the passenger side of me and scared me and I said, "It takes two of you to pull me over?" And he said, "Well, I want to see

TABLE 5.1. **A summary of black drivers' narratives of stops, by type of stop.**

Driver	Reason given for stop, by type			Outcome
	Traffic safety	Investigatory	Ambiguous	
Linda	Expired license tag			Ticket
Lisa		No reason given		Followed for 2 weeks; questioned
Mike		Decorative lights		Officer stuck gun in his mouth; arrested
	Speeding			Ticket
	Speeding			Ticket
Douglas	Expired license tag			Warning
Deana		No reason given		Questioned
		No reason given		Questioned
		No reason given		Questioned
Joe		No reason given		Warrant check
		No reason given		Handcuffed; searched; warrant check
Elizabeth	Red light violation			Ticket
Walter		Tags reported stolen		Questioned
Darrell		Investigating old burglary		Handcuffed; held for an hour; released
Billy	Speeding			Ticket
	Speeding			Ticket
		No reason given		Officer pointed gun at his head; ticket
		67 in 65 mph zone		Questioned; searched
		No reason given		Questioned; searched
Nancy			Reason unclear	Unclear
Gary	Speeding			Ticket
Donna	Speeding			Questioned; searched; threatened with arrest and having children taken away
Timothy	Red light violation			Warning; ordered to get out of vehicle
David	Red light violation			Ticket
Kenneth		No reason given		Questioned; held in police car; released
Total (% of all reported)	11 (44)	13 (52)	1 (4)	

Source: Charles R. Epp, Steven Maynard-Moody, and Donald P. Haider-Markel, "Driver Interview Archive," in *Reconstructing Law on the Street: Transcripts of Interviews and Focus Groups* (Lawrence, KS: KU ScholarWorks, 2011), http://hdl.handle.net/1808/8544.

TABLE 5.2. **A summary of white drivers' narratives of stops, by type of stop.**

| Driver | Reason given for stop, by type | | | Outcome |
	Traffic safety	Investigatory	Ambiguous	
James		Speeding		Searched; ticket
John	Speeding			Warning
Linda	Reckless driving			Warning
	Speeding			Ticket
Keith	Speeding			Ticket
Roy			Smoky exhaust	Ticket
Karen	Speeding			Ticket
Bill	Speeding			Ticket
	Speeding			Ticket
Matthew		Headlight out		Handcuffed (tags came up for person with warrant, but ID did not); released
Donald	Speeding			Ticket
		Improper turn		Followed 2 miles; questioned
Mark	Speeding			Ticket
Anthony		Investigation of videotaping		Questioned
	Speeding			Ticket
Helen	Speeding			Ticket
Jeff	Speeding			Ticket
Patrick	Reckless driving			Warning
	Sobriety checkpoint			Questioned
Carl		Excessive noise (stereo)		Warning
Peter	Speeding			Warning
Scott	Speeding			Ticket
	Improper parking			Warning
Todd	Speeding			Ticket
	Speeding			Ticket
	Lights out			Ticket
Laura	Lights out			Warning
	Speeding			Ticket
Total (% of all reported)	22 (79)	5 (18)	1 (4)	

Source: Charles R. Epp, Steven Maynard-Moody, and Donald P. Haider-Markel, "Driver Interview Archive," in *Reconstructing Law on the Street: Transcripts of Interviews and Focus Groups* (Lawrence, KS: KU ScholarWorks, 2011), http://hdl.handle.net/1808/8544.

your driver's license and proof of insurance." And I gave him my driver's license but didn't have proof of insurance, so he went back to his car and then he came back and he said that he wasn't going to write me a ticket for running a red light, which he pulled me over for. And he said he was just going to give me a ticket for not having my insurance card. Well, I felt that I was being racially profiled, I really did. Because he didn't give me the ticket for what he pulled me over for. You know, he was kind of nice about it. He wasn't nasty, no, just kind of nice about it. He went back to his car. I guess he ran my, you know, my plates and whatever. And then he came back and said what I said.

INTERVIEWER: How did the police officer act throughout the stop?

ELIZABETH: Well, the one that stopped me, he was nice. But [not] the one that was on the driver's side and was nosing around and in [my car], flashing, putting the spotlight on me like I was a criminal.[1]

Drivers routinely turn left through a "late yellow" or "early red" light in a busy intersection, yet this "violation" was the justification for Elizabeth's stop: she failed to clear the intersection by the time the light changed. By any reasonable definition, this is a low-level traffic violation and typically not an occasion for a stop. Elizabeth was clearly frustrated, not because of the officer's demeanor—he was "nice"—but because he gave her a ticket for a violation other than the one used to justify the stop. Elizabeth was also upset by the second officer who was "nosing around" with a light on her "like I was a criminal." This appears to be a classic investigatory stop in which officers use a low-level violation to justify a stop and then closely observe the contents of the vehicle and check the driver's identification against computerized records. In this case these initial checks turned up nothing suspicious and so the officers let the driver go relatively quickly.

The vast majority of African American drivers' stories of investigatory stops, like Elizabeth's, describe intrusions by officers that began virtually at the start of the stop and proceed through a cool, polite, and apparently deliberate process controlled by the officers. Consider, for example, Billy's story.

NARRATIVE 5.2.
Billy, African American male: "He Said that I Was Going 67 in a 65-MPH Zone"

And I was stopped once by . . . you know when I was traveling back and forth to Des Moines, I was putting applications out here, resumes, so I was coming down here for a job interview and on the way back to Des Moines before I crossed over to Iowa, a Missouri Highway Patrol stopped me. Boy, he kind of stopped me; I think he just kind of stopped because I passed him. But he was going slower than, at that time I don't if it was 70 miles an hour or 65 or 70; it was 70 miles an hour. And I had set my cruise, and he was following behind this tractor trailer. And I just got in the left lane and rolled past him. Ok, as soon as I rolled past him he turn on his lights. And I had a, at that time I was driving a '79 Cadillac Seville, white, that I was fixing up. You know, I'd been working on restoring it, you know, it was looking pretty good. I had really taken it down to test it out. So he pulled me over and he said, you know, regular procedure "driver's license and registration" and whatever. And he said that I was going 67 in a 65 mile-per-hour zone, or something like a couple miles over the speed limit, that is the reason why stopped me. And I said, "Well, my speedometer said 65." He said, "Well, because you got bigger tires and stuff like that on the car, the car is traveling a lot . . . it travels a lot faster." I think he said then that whatever the speedometer is saying, you are going faster. And he stopped me for that and while he stopped me he was talking to me and he looked in there and I had a cell phone, I had a car phone sitting in there. And then he said, "Do you have any kind of drugs or guns in the car?" And I said, "No." He said, "Do you mind if I search the car?" and I told him, "No, I don't mind." . . . So he told me to go on the front of the car and put your hands on the front of the car. I don't know if he said put your hands on the front of the car, or go stand in front of the car. So I went and stood in front of the car. And I was on the Interstate 35 going north up there. So he went and looked in the car, and looked in my glove box, popped my trunk looked in my trunk and I had some other clothes, and I had my resume, you know, my change of clothes what I was wearing for my interview. So he looked around and everything, and when he got through he came back and he didn't find anything, and he came back and said, "The reason why we checked your car is we've been having problems with people trafficking drugs up and down the highway." So that was that.[2]

A minority of white drivers—5 of 19—told us stories of investigatory stops, but the events described are remarkably benign compared to those of black drivers. No white driver told of facing a gun pointed at him. No white driver reported that an officer stopped her simply to check for outstanding warrants. Although several described talking back to officers, not one said an officer told him to stop being smart or threatened to arrest him for talking back.

One white man, James, was subjected to a vehicle search. He described being stopped for speeding ("43 in a 35," just at our dividing line between real speeding stops and pretextual investigatory stops) and the officer immediately asked for consent to search his car. Like Billy, James said:

Obviously, I said "yes" because I knew if I said "no" there would be, I would be there twice as long. So I let them search the car. They didn't find anything, but I was there for roughly twenty minutes. I mean because they pulled everything out of my car. I mean they went up under seats, they went in ash trays, they went into the glove compartment, they went into my side door compartments. I was finally issued the ticket.[3]

Another white driver, Joseph, was handcuffed during a stop, like two of the African American drivers quoted earlier. In this case, the officer provided a plausible reason: "Your plates come back to someone with a warrant." This turned out to be a mistake, and the officer immediately released Joseph, who told us that he then sharply lectured the officer for making this mistake.[4] Two other white drivers described stops that probably were for purposes of investigation, but in each case these ended quickly and without searches after the officers satisfied their curiosity. (In one of these cases, a white driver was stopped shortly after 9/11, as his visiting mother, a passenger, was videotaping the tall buildings in downtown Kansas City; the officer ended the stop quickly after hearing the explanation.[5])

While black drivers commonly reported being subjected to extended, intrusive investigatory stops that have the flavor of a fishing expedition, complete with vehicle searches based on nothing more than officer curiosity, the few investigatory stops described by white drivers seem brief and based on plausible reasons. James, alone among white drivers, described a full-blown search of his vehicle.

In sharp contrast to investigatory stops, the patterns in traffic-safety stops are different in a way that punctuates the powerful role of the driver's race in investigatory stops. Police officers in traffic-safety stops do not impose significantly greater sanctions on black drivers than white drivers, nor do they commonly convert the stop into an intrusive investigation of black drivers. The accounts of African Americans stopped for speeding are, in most respects, remarkably similar to those of white speeders. In every case, African Americans reported that officers acted in a straightforward manner to issue a speeding ticket. In every case, they reported that the officers acted professionally, if sometimes brusquely. Traffic-safety stops are simply about enforcing the traffic laws.

For example, Mike, an African American man, reported being stopped while "flying" on an interstate through the Kansas City suburbs.[6] He was in the fast lane, following traffic, and was singled out for the speeding stop. Although he wondered why he, and not another, was "snatched over," he did not question the validity of the officer's claim that he was speeding. The officer issued him a ticket and let him go. Billy told stories of two speeding stops. In one, he said that he was stopped while decelerating on an off-ramp of a state highway, and in the other, he was stopped for speeding on an interstate highway.[7] In both cases, the officer issued him a ticket and let him go without further ado.

White drivers' stories of speeding stops are similar to these black drivers' accounts. For one thing, white drivers' stories of speeding stops are brief and uneventful. Mark, for example, reported simply that he was stopped for going "10 over," observed that the officer asked for his ID, took it to the police car, and "when he came back and gave me everything, I didn't say anything. He just handed it [the ticket] to me and walked off."[8] Donald's story conveyed a few more details but remained brief. He reported that the officer "very politely asked me if I knew what the speeding limit was" and how fast he was driving. And then "he told me that he was going to write me a basic speeding ticket . . . and asked me to watch my speed and told me I was free to go."[9] Jeff reported that he was stopped for speeding, that the officer was "cordial," and that he "just told me that the speed limit is 20 and that's the way it goes."[10] Likewise, Todd reported that the officer was "very professional" and "told me how fast I was going."[11] Then, "he wrote me the ticket. . . . And I drove away." James described a stop in which the officer "was nothing but nice. He came up, told me why he pulled me over, and explained to me that I was getting a ticket, and explained to me how it could be paid, and when it could be paid. And the court date. And he says, I'll be right with you. And I was out in 5 minutes."[12]

Racial disparities in officers' intrusions are the product of race-heightened suspicion during investigatory stops. In these stops, officers carry out deliberately planned intrusions that begin from the outset of the stop rather than emerging in response to happenstance discoveries or tit-for-tat escalations. The driver's race appears to be a leading cue that triggers both the decision to stop a driver for an investigatory reason and to pursue an investigatory intrusion during the stop. Drivers pulled over in investigatory stops generally describe the police officers as cool, deliberate, and even polite.

Verifying that Racial Disparities Are Concentrated in Investigatory Stops

The apparent racial disparities illustrated in drivers' narratives are provocative, but are investigatory stops the primary source of these disparities? And if racial disparities are isolated in investigatory stops, are officers' decisions to pursue investigations mainly a response to black drivers' provocations—or, as we claim, do officers pursue these intrusions without regard to how black drivers act?

We developed a statistical model to test these things. Officers' intrusions are measured by an additive index of the actions illustrated in figures 4.1 and 4.2: whether the officer issued a ticket, asked why the driver was in the area, threatened the driver with arrest, searched the driver or vehicle, handcuffed the driver, gave the driver a sobriety test, and/or arrested the driver ($\alpha = .81$). The officer's demeanor toward the driver is measured by an additive index of various dimensions of how the officer spoke or acted to the driver as illustrated in figures 4.3 and 4.4: businesslike, friendly, cold, surly, stern, loudly, hostile, insulting, foul-mouthed, and/or threatening, or approached more closely than comfortable and/or ordered driver to keep hands visible ($\alpha = .88$).[13]

In our statistical models we consider a wide range of possible influences on officer intrusion and demeanor.[14] These include, foremost, the driver's personal characteristics: race, gender, and age. To test whether officers deliberately and primarily pursue deeper intrusions of blacks than whites or instead respond to other elements of the situation, we control for a wide range of factors. One is how respectfully or disrespectfully the driver spoke to the officer. Our measure of this is an additive index of the measures of driver disrespect that we summarized in the previous chapter. We constructed an "interaction variable" (a simple multiplication of the driver's level of disrespect by the driver's race) to test whether officers treat disrespectful African American drivers more intrusively and disrespectfully than similarly disrespectful white drivers. This interaction variable offers a way to test statistically for the tit-for-tat hypothesis.

We control for other possible influences. These include the value of the driver's vehicle, whether the vehicle has had custom modifications (like tinted windows or custom hubcaps), has damage that is in violation of the vehicle code (such as a burned-out headlight), and has damage that is visible but not in violation of the vehicle code (such as rust or unrepaired accident damage). How much, and how, the driver drives are also included in the model. These are measured in terms of how much time the driver spends driving in a typical week, how fast the driver drives, and the extent to which the driver complies with the rules of the road. In addition, we control for the number of passengers (if any), and the number of officers who are present at the stop. The presence of other members of the public (here, passengers) has long been recognized as an influence on police actions.[15] Some earlier research suggests that the number of officers at the scene increases the extent to which the police act intrusively and disrespectfully. The presence of other officers may encourage the police to act more assertively. It is also likely that more officers are assigned or respond to stops they perceive as dangerous. Regardless of cause, the number of officers signals a tenser encounter. We also examine whether the race of the officer has any meaningful impact. Finally, we measure the extent that drivers' level of general distrust in authority colors their perceptions of how intrusively or disrespectfully the officer acted.[16]

To test whether the prominent racial disparities reflect the driver's "race," pure and simple, or a closely analogous style of self-presentation, we also took into account the driver's "personal style," as measured by how closely he or she matches a range of common street styles, such as college student, doctor or lawyer, factory or construction worker, retiree, hip-hop star, or suburban soccer mom, among many others. To our surprise, we find no evidence that this street style had a significant influence on what happens during the stop, and so we do not present these measures in the analysis below.

Controlling for all of these other factors, in investigatory stops (table 5.3, column 2) but not speeding stops (column 1), we find officers subject African Americans to significantly deeper intrusions and more punishing sanctions than whites. Likewise, in speeding stops the driver's gender and age do not much matter, but in investigatory stops officers pursue their intrusions more deeply when the driver is younger or male.

The one key exception to this pattern of biases based on personal characteristics in investigatory stops is the driver's economic class: it has no influence. (It is not statistically significant whether measured as a continuous variable or, as presented here, a dichotomy capturing the difference between the bottom quartile of car values versus others.) The clear unimportance of the driver's economic class is startling, especially in light of the fact that drivers of poor vehicles are more likely to be stopped, as shown in chapter 4.

The general point is crystal clear: in investigatory stops, officers decide how far to pursue investigatory intrusions based on *who* is the driver. Officers act especially intrusively toward African American men, especially young African American men, regardless of their apparent economic class. Middle-class and wealthy African Americans are as subject to these intrusions as are low-income African Americans.

TABLE 5.3. **How the type of stop shapes racial bias**

	Intrusions and sanctions		Officer disrespect	
Characteristic	Speeding stop	Investigatory stop	Speeding stop	Investigatory stop
African American	0.108	0.295**	0.178**	0.314***
	(.072)	(.123)	(.082)	(.094)
Female	−0.113**	−0.452****	−0.068	−0.195**
	(.056)	(.115)	(.064)	(.087)
Age	−0.008***	−0.010**	0.008***	−0.009**
	(.002)	(.004)	(.003)	(.004)
Education level	−0.014	0.002	0.055***	0.031
	(.018)	(.036)	(.020)	(.027)
Vehicle value	0.109	0.210	0.031	0.043
(bottom quartile)	(.077)	(.128)	(.088)	(.098)
Driver disrespect	0.133***	0.185***	0.258****	0.248****
to officer	(.044)	(.060)	(.050)	(.046)
Controls				
Vehicle customization	0.059	0.115	0.081*	0.133**
	(.041)	(.079)	(.046)	(.060)
Vehicle damage	0.084	0.024	−0.012	0.173**
	(.061)	(.103)	(.070)	(.079)
Illegal vehicle	−0.084	0.054	−0.108	−0.081
conditions	(.061)	(.075)	(.066)	(.058)
Domestic luxury car	0.083	−0.338	0.185	−0.417**
	(.159)	(.235)	(.185)	(.179)
Time driving	−0.002	−0.028	0.042**	−0.029
	(.018)	(.041)	(.020)	(.029)
Rule-abiding driving	−0.093	−0.350***	−0.026	0.006
	(.077)	(.123)	(.088)	(.094)
Extent of speeding	−0.009**	−0.002	−0.009*	−0.006
	(.004)	(.011)	(.005)	(.008)
Number of passengers	−0.055**	0.066	−0.047*	−0.022
	(.025)	(.052)	(.028)	(.040)
Number of officers	0.039	0.201****	0.117**	0.128***
	(.052)	(.049)	(.059)	(.058)
Distrust in government	−0.016	0.003	0.065	0.179***
	(.038)	(.076)	(.044)	(.058)
Constant	1.176**	0.150	0.457	0.272
	(.524)	(1.23)	(.596)	(.926)
Log pseudolikelihood	−133.61	−206.74	−159.65	−175.01
LR χ^2 (15)	55.06	83.53	79.39	106.21
p	<.0001	<.0001	<.0001	<.0001
N	236	201	237	201
Left-censored N	45	46	36	1

Note: Results were obtained using Tobit estimation. Reported results are coefficients, with robust standard errors given in parentheses. The dependent variables in these equations are additive indices constructed from the variables reported in figures 4.1 (intrusions and sanction) and 4.2 (officer demeanor) in the previous chapter (the intrusions and sanctions index, Cronbach's α = .81; officer demeanor index, Cronbach's α = .88). The dependent variables are additive indices that are not normally distributed. For dependent variables with this characteristic, Tobit is the most appropriate modeling technique (see J. Scott Long, *Regression Models for Categorical and Limited Dependent Variables* [Thousand Oaks, CA: Sage, 1997], 187–216). We have confirmed the results with ordered probit; the results do not differ substantially from those reported here. See the appendix for further discussion.

*p < .10; **p < .05; ***p < .01; ****p < .001

As expected, driver disrespect contributes to heavier sanctions—but are disrespectful African American drivers treated more harshly than similarly disrespectful white drivers? Table 5.4 addresses this question, reporting the equation modeled in table 5.3 but with the addition of an interaction term measuring the effect of the driver's race and level of disrespect toward the officer (to conserve space, we report only the coefficients of the interaction term and the driver's race and level of disrespect). If officers treat disrespectful African Americans more harshly than similar white drivers, this variable would be positively associated with punitive sanctions and officer disrespect. The results are striking. With one exception, across both traffic-safety and investigatory stops, the interaction term is *negatively* associated with the officer's level of disrespect and the severity of intrusions and sanctions. This pattern suggests that officers may treat disrespectful black drivers *less* punitively than disrespectful white drivers, *especially in investigatory stops*. By

TABLE 5.4. **Are disrespectful black drivers treated more harshly than disrespectful white drivers? The effect of an interaction between the driver's race and disrespect toward the officer.**

Characteristic	Intrusions and sanctions		Officer disrespect	
	Speeding stop	Investigatory stop	Speeding stop	Investigatory stop
African American	0.109	0.335***	0.173**	0.333***
	(.072)	(.123)	(.079)	(.095)
Driver disrespect to officer	0.186***	0.278****	0.106*	0.297****
	(.054)	(.076)	(.059)	(.059)
Interaction: driver race and disrespect	−0.135	−0.221*	0.391****	−0.120
	(.083)	(.115)	(.092)	(.091)
Constant	1.119**	0.150	0.643	0.272
	(.521)	(1.215)	(.575)	(.922)
Log pseudolikelihood	−132.31	−204.93	−150.95	−174.15
LR χ^2 (16)	57.67	87.15	96.78	107.94
p	<.0001	<.0001	<.0001	<.0001
N	236	201	237	201
Left-censored N	45	46	36	1

Note: Results were obtained using Tobit estimation. Reported results are coefficients, with robust standard errors given in parentheses. Control variables (those used in the equation reported in table 5.3: gender, age, education level, vehicle value, whether vehicle is a domestic luxury car, vehicle customization, damage to vehicle, illegal vehicle conditions, time spent driving, rule-abiding driving, extent of speeding, number of passengers, number of officers, and distrust in government) have been omitted for brevity. The dependent variables are additive indices that are not normally distributed. For dependent variables with this characteristic, Tobit is the most appropriate modeling technique (see J. Scott Long, *Regression Models for Categorical and Limited Dependent Variables* [Thousand Oaks, CA: Sage, 1997], 187–216). We have confirmed the results with ordered probit; the results do not differ substantially from those reported here. See the appendix for further discussion. $*p < .10; **p < .05; ***p < .01; ****p < .001$

contrast, with regard to the officer's demeanor, the "driver disrespect–race" interaction variable is positive and significant in traffic-safety stops, suggesting that officers' level of disrespect—but not sanctions—is especially amplified toward disrespectful black drivers in traffic-safety stops. This difference between the two types of stops underscores that officers deliberately maintain a professionally polite demeanor toward African American drivers in investigatory stops, a dynamic that we explored above in the context of drivers' narratives of these stops.

Finally, does the *officer*'s race shape the stop encounter?[17] Are white officers more intrusive toward black drivers than white drivers; are they more punitive and rude? With regard to both the officer's demeanor toward the driver and the officer's investigatory intrusions and sanctions, we find no evidence of a significant interaction between the race of the officer and driver in either investigatory or traffic-safety stops.

Vehicle searches are widely resented, the subject of considerable commentary, and illustrate well how the type of stop affects racial disparities. In investigatory stops African American drivers are five times more likely than white drivers to be subjected to searches of their cars (see table 5.5). We cannot show a comparable multivariate model of the likelihood of being searched in a speeding stop because the number of searches in these stops is so low: while thirty-four drivers reported being searched in an investigatory stop, only nine reported being searched in a speeding stop. But we can provide a simple description of these searches in speeding stops: of these nine searched drivers, six were white and three were black, representing statistically indistinguishable percentages of five percent or less of white and black drivers. For comparison, 26 percent of black drivers in investigatory stops were searched, but only 8.5 percent of white drivers in these stops were searched.

The obvious follow-up question is: Are officers justified in subjecting African Americans to more searches?[18] The hit rate—the rate at which officers discover contraband in a vehicle search—for African American drivers is less than half that for white drivers (11 percent versus 27 percent).[19] This disparity strongly suggests that officers are using looser criteria—they have less reasonable justifications—for selecting African American drivers than white drivers for searches.

Consistent with our discussion of drivers' narratives, the statistical evidence suggests that stop type matters most in explaining racial differences in police stops. In investigatory stops but not traffic-safety stops, officers scrutinize African Americans more intrusively than whites. Ra-

TABLE 5.5. **Likelihood of being searched in an investigatory stop.**

Characteristic	Odds ratio of being searched
African American	5.19***
	(3.26)
Female	0.17***
	(.01)
Age	0.95**
	(.02)
Vehicle value (bottom quartile)	1.46
	(.91)
Log pseudolikelihood	−50.26
LR χ^2 (16)	61.46
p	<.0001
N	200

Note: Results were obtained using logit estimation. Reported results are odds ratios, with robust standard errors given in parentheses. Control variables (those used in the equation reported in table 5.3: whether vehicle is a domestic luxury car, vehicle customization, damage to vehicle, illegal vehicle conditions, time spent driving, rule-abiding driving, extent of speeding, number of passengers, number of officers, and distrust in government) have been omitted for brevity.
*p < .10; **p < .05; ***p < .01; ****p < .001

cial disparities in investigatory intrusions are the product of the investigatory stop.

The Location of the Stop and Its Effect on Intrusions

As described in chapter 1, the African American population in the Kansas City metropolitan area is concentrated in the old urban core, while the suburbs are predominantly white. In these white areas, large proportions of stops of African Americans are made for minor reasons. This pattern is especially great in the inner ring of suburbs that border the old urban core.

Suburban officers are especially likely to carry out investigative intrusions of African American drivers and are much more likely than their urban and exurban counterparts to pursue these investigations in *both* investigatory and traffic-safety stops. We illustrate this pattern with two sets of figures: the incidence of searches of the driver or vehicle (figures 5.1 and 5.2), and whether the officer asked the driver why he or she is in the area (figures 5.3 and 5.4). In the inner-ring suburbs, officers

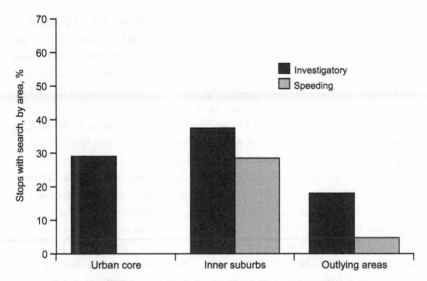

FIGURE 5.1. Searches of African American drivers, by type and location of stop (investigatory stops, 76; speeding stops, 58).

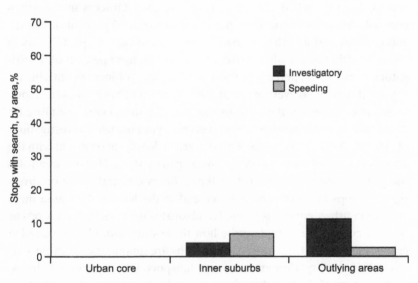

FIGURE 5.2. Searches of white drivers, by type and location of stop (investigatory stops, 133; speeding stops, 225).

conducted searches of African American drivers in over 37 percent of investigatory stops and over 28 percent of traffic-safety stops. In the urban core, officers never conducted a search during traffic-safety stops of African Americans, but did so in nearly 30 percent of all investigatory stops. The pattern in the outlying areas is closer to that of the urban core: officers conducted searches in nearly 19 percent of investigatory stops of African Americans but in less than 5 percent of traffic-safety stops. By contrast, searches of white drivers are exceedingly rare and, in our sample, were never conducted by officers in the urban core.

A similar pattern appears in officers' questions as to why a driver is in the area (figures 5.3 and 5.4): officers are especially likely to ask this question of African American drivers in the inner-ring suburbs. This question is especially demeaning to African Americans and other minorities, because it implies by the asking that they should not be in this area. Officers in the urban core ask, "Why are you in this neighborhood?" of African American drivers mainly in the context of investigatory stops. Officers in the inner suburbs ask this question of a majority of African American drivers in both types of stops and of over two-thirds of these drivers in investigatory stops. White drivers are comparatively less likely to be asked why they are in the area. Officers in the urban core ask this question of white drivers in just over 16 percent of investigatory stops and less than 11 percent in traffic-safety stops. Officers in the inner suburbs ask white drivers this question in 37 percent of investigatory stops and 26 percent of traffic-safety stops; officers in outlying areas ask it of white drivers in about thirty percent of both types of stops.

In sum, officers in the suburbs that ring the urban core are more focused than officers in other areas on carrying out intrusive investigations of African American drivers. This pattern is deeply inconsistent with the stated crime-control rationale for investigatory stops. If crime control is the goal, we might expect to find that officers especially rely on investigatory stops in higher-crime areas, and in the Kansas City area these are in the urban core. For example, advocates for investigatory stops as a crime-control measure describe how these stops should be targeted at crime hotspots, but the inner-ring suburbs are among the wealthiest areas of Kansas City; they are not crime hotspots. Disproportionate investigatory stops of African American drivers in these wealthy suburbs look less like crime control and more like a deliberate effort to keep blacks out. That officers in these suburbs commonly ask black drivers even in

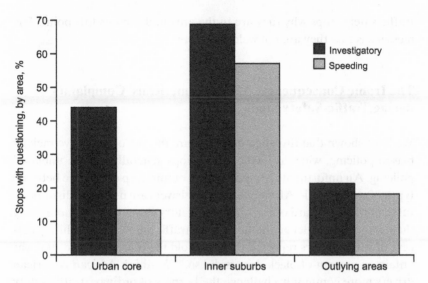

FIGURE 5.3. Incidence of officers' questions as to why African American driver is in the area (investigatory stops, 104; speeding stops, 59).

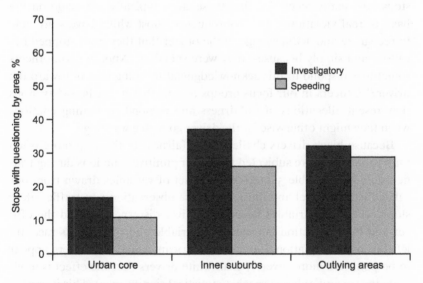

FIGURE 5.4. Incidence of officers' questions as to why white driver is in the area (investigatory stops, 166; speeding stops, 229).

traffic-safety stops why they are in the area underscores this point. The
message is that they are not welcome there.

The Ironic Consequence: African Americans' Complaints during Traffic-Safety Stops

We have shown that investigatory stops are the site of pervasive racially
biased policing, whereas traffic-safety stops generally involve unbiased
policing. An unfortunate irony arises out of this deep difference between
types of stops. While African American drivers are not more disrespectful than whites toward officers in investigatory stops, they *are* more likely
than whites to challenge the fairness of traffic-safety stops: while 7 percent of white drivers reported that they told the officer that the stop was
unfair, 19 percent of black drivers did so.[20] We think African American
drivers more commonly challenge the fairness of ordinary traffic-safety
stops because they are subjected to investigatory stops based on minor
violations. They (and we) view pretext stops as dubious, and this common experience leads them to suspect the fairness and legitimacy of *all*
stops. White drivers, by contrast, are subject primarily to traffic-safety
stops, and many recognize that these stops typically are made on the
basis of real violations. As a consequence, most white drivers are able
to recognize and acknowledge to the officer that they were stopped because—and simply because—they were speeding. And, in turn, officers
sometimes respond to this acknowledgment by being lenient toward the
driver.[21] Officers in our focus groups told us that in traffic-safety stops
they resent allegations of unfairness and respond by issuing citations
when they might otherwise let the driver go with a warning.[22]

Because black drivers challenge the fairness of the stop more often
than whites, they are subjected to greater punitive sanctions during traffic-safety stops. Table 5.6 reports a subset of variables drawn from our
full statistical model and illustrates these observations. In traffic-safety
stops, when the variables measuring driver disrespect toward the officer and the interaction between this variable and the driver's race are
left out of the equation (column 1), African American drivers appear
to be punished more severely than white drivers (but the effect is moderate in size and only approaches statistical significance). This is consistent with the observation of Robin Shepard Engel and Jennifer Calnon
that African American drivers are somewhat more likely than whites to

TABLE 5.6. **Speeding stops: how the race of the driver and disrespect to officer interact to shape sanctions.**

Characteristic	Not controlling for disrespect	Controlling for disrespect
African American	0.141*	0.109
	(.073)	(.072)
Female	−0.109*	−0.109*
	(.058)	(.056)
Age	−0.007***	−0.007***
	(.002)	(.002)
Vehicle value (bottom quartile)	0.108	0.103
	(.078)	(.076)
Driver disrespect toward officer		0.186***
		(.054)
Interaction: driver disrespect and driver race		−0.135
		(.083)
Log pseudolikelihood	−138.18	−132.31
LR χ^2 (14 & 16)	45.91	57.67
p	<.0001	<.0001
N	236	236
Left-censored N	45	45

Note: Results were obtained using Tobit estimation. Robust standard errors are given in parentheses. Control variables (those used in the equation reported in table 5.3: education level, whether vehicle is a domestic luxury car, vehicle customization, damage to vehicle, illegal vehicle conditions, time spent driving, rule-abiding driving, extent of speeding, number of passengers, number of officers, and distrust in government) have been omitted for brevity. The dependent variable is an additive index that is not normally distributed. For dependent variables with this characteristic, Tobit is the most appropriate modeling technique (see J. Scott Long, *Regression Models for Categorical and Limited Dependent Variables* [Thousand Oaks, CA: Sage, 1997], 187–216). We have confirmed the results with ordered probit; the results do not differ substantially from those reported here. See the appendix for further discussion.
*p < .10; **p < .05; ***p < .01; ****p < .001.

be ticketed.[23] But when we control for driver disrespect toward officers (column 2), it becomes clear that African American drivers are punished more severely than white drivers, not because of their race but *because of their complaints*. The results confirm, as we have seen earlier, that drivers who complain are given heavier sanctions in traffic-safety stops. But when controlling for driver disrespect toward officers, African Americans are not sanctioned more heavily than white drivers. By contrast, the independent effect of the driver's gender and age remains unchanged when controlling for the level of driver disrespect. These results strongly suggest that African Americans are more likely to challenge the fairness of traffic-safety stops and that, when they do this, they are less likely to be let off with a warning. White drivers who complain suffer the same fate.

Drivers' experiences support this interpretation. Some white drivers reported getting favorable treatment when acting respectfully toward the officer. John told of being stopped for driving "15 over the limit": "He [the officer] just asked me for my license and insurance. I didn't say a word to him, I just handed it to him. And he said, 'Since most people try to give me excuses and a bunch of other crud, and you didn't, I'm just going to give you a warning.'"[24] Likewise, Keith, another white driver, said that the officer issued a ticket for less than his actual speed after he had acknowledged his fault (narrative 4.1). Laura observed, "A lot of the time, I've gotta be honest with you, I can show my military ID, for example, and I get out of a ticket. But this time he was like, 'No.' . . . And he did write the ticket to where I was doing 65, though, instead of 70. So he did give me a break, as far as that goes."[25] However, white drivers who described complaining were issued a ticket in every instance.

While some white drivers described accepting the legitimacy of a traffic-safety stop, in most African American drivers' descriptions, the driver recalled complaining to the officer that the stop was not fair, and in every one of these cases the officer issued a ticket rather than a warning. Mike, an African American man, told us that he believed that he had been unfairly singled out from among other speeders, and he complained of this to the officer.[26] Likewise, Billy said, "I asked why he stopped me. And he said because I was speeding. And I said, 'Well, how was I speeding?' I said, 'I was decelerating coming off the off-ramp.' And he said, 'Well, you were speeding.' . . . And he came back with a ticket."[27] Similarly, Gary recalled after being told the reason for the stop, "At that point, you know, I was pretty angry about the incident, because I know I wasn't doing 20 over the speed limit. And he just told me, you know, that that is a law, and that I need to pay attention to my speed."[28] We cannot know whether some of these African American drivers would have been let go with a warning (or a ticket for a lower rate of speed) had they not complained to the officer, but, as we noted above, officers told us that complaints ensure a ticket rather than a warning.

*   *   *

Questions, searches, handcuffs, disrespect: these and other elements of criminal investigations are common experiences for African American drivers during police stops. White drivers, by contrast, are largely immune to these experiences. When we asked white and black drivers to tell us accounts of police stops, many white drivers could summon up no more than a few sentences: "He gave me a ticket and left" captures the feel of many white driver stories. In contrast, black drivers poured forth story after story of demeaning stops, often rendered in excruciating detail. "I could see it out of the peripheral vision of my eye, its barrel, and he pointed it right at my head," Billy told us.[29] "They followed me all the way to the house, and I spotted them in the mirror, and I knew I wasn't speeding," Lisa told us. "It took me like fifteen minutes to get home . . . And they did it for about a couple of weeks."[30] Darrell and his friends were held in handcuffs on the side of a residential street in a white neighborhood for an hour and then released. These experiences are concentrated in investigatory stops. In traffic-safety stops the driver's race has little impact on how the officer treats the driver. In investigatory stops the driver's race is the leading influence on how the officer treats the driver: officers impose dramatically greater investigatory intrusions and sanctions on black drivers than on white drivers and also subject black drivers to significantly greater verbal expressions of disrespect.

The cool and deliberate character of officers' investigatory intrusions makes clear that they know exactly what they are doing. The tight correlation between the driver's race and these investigatory intrusions and the clear pattern of officers treating resentful black drivers *more carefully* than mouthy white drivers leads us to infer that officers are fully aware that they are using race as a leading cue in making and carrying out these investigatory stops. The racial disparities observed in this chapter seem clearly not to be a product of something else: African Americans are subjected to deeper investigatory intrusions not because they are poorer, less educated, more disrespectful, or more distrustful of the police than are whites. It is a racial disparity, pure and simple.

CHAPTER SIX

Evaluating the Stop

Looking Beyond Official Politeness

Investigatory stops have gained widespread legitimacy among police professionals, but do these stops have *popular* legitimacy? Are these stops accepted as legitimate by the people targeted in them?

Defenders of investigatory stops claim that people will accept being targeted if the officer making the stop is unfailingly polite and respectful. Thus, William Stuntz declared that "the manner, and the manners, of street stops" are what matter to the people who are stopped, not *whether* they are stopped. He went on to assert that people's perceptions of police discrimination in stops "may have more to do with the way police treat different categories of suspects than with how many people in each category are stopped."[1] As we noted at the outset of this book, Stuntz based this speculation on the theory of procedural justice which posits that people evaluate the legitimacy of official decisions on the basis of whether they believed the process was fair. His view is based particularly on one interpretation of that theory, namely, *that people infer whether a process was fair based on whether the official making the decision showed respect.*[2] As Tom Tyler, the leading scholar of procedural justice, put it, while officers should *be* fair as well as politely respectful, *appearing* to be respectful "is especially advantageous in reducing public dissatisfaction about [racial] profiling."[3]

If this is so, police officers can deploy arbitrary, even race-based, investigatory stops, yet those stopped will accept being targeted so long as the officers maintain a pleasing façade of politeness and respect. Stuntz said as much: officers can "increase the number of *Terry* [investigatory] stops" *and* "substantially reduce complaints of police discrimination" if these stops are "carried out more politely" and suspects are "treated with more dignity."[4] The idea that official politeness lends popular legitimacy to wanton investigatory stops is a key element in the professional legitimacy of these stops and has encouraged their growing use. The leadership of the International Association of Chiefs of Police drew precisely this lesson: they responded to the racial profiling controversy by calling on police departments to train their officers to be respectful and professionally courteous during investigatory stops. Michael Bloomberg, mayor of New York City, has responded to criticism of police stops of pedestrians in that city by saying that "the practice needs to be mended, not ended," in part by getting officers to be more respectful when making these stops.[5]

This chapter addresses two questions. *Do* people accept the legitimacy of a stop if the officer treats them politely? Or do people—at least *some* people—see through a façade of official politeness to the deeper unfairness in investigatory stops? We begin with accounts from two stopped drivers: one white, the other black.

NARRATIVE 6.1.
Jeff, white male: "Maybe I Should Have Gotten Away with It"

JEFF: I've only been pulled over once that I can remember in the last few years. And it was.
. . . I was leaving Lansing Prison, I do volunteer work. And their speed limit there is 20 miles an hour, and when I was leaving the parking lot, I was just a little over 20 going down the street. And I got pulled over; it was Christmas Eve also. And the Lansing Police Department, the officer gave me a ticket, so I wasn't really happy about it. I should've known better.

INTERVIEWER: What did the officer do?

JEFF: Just told me that the speed limit is 20 and that's the way it goes. So I just, you know, I don't know, felt like it was Christmas Eve, doing volunteer work and maybe I should've gotten away with it. But that's the way it works.[6]

NARRATIVE 6.2.
Billy, African American male: "We Didn't Get a Ticket or Anything, But the Officers Searched the Car"

Oh yeah, I also remember . . . it was my wife, and my cousin, and myself—we have driven a rental van . . . and we'd gone to Detroit to pick up my aunt who was gonna come back down to Memphis anyways. Because I had an uncle, at that time, that was terminally ill there. And we've gone, you know, trying to get the family down there.

So we left Kansas City and we got to Windsor, I think, County? If you go from Kansas City out 70 east before you get to St. Peters and St. Charles toward 70. Well, it was kind of raining, and my cousin was driving at that time. And they don't have what they call city police; they have, like, a sheriff, I think, and I'd seen the police over there, you know, parked in the median, and I kind of was telling my cousin, I said, "You got to watch your speed, you know, because the police are out, you know, and they probably are monitoring the highways."

It was raining pretty good that day, and sure enough, as soon as we passed him, they turned on their lights. And one officer, after we pulled over, went to my cousin's side on the driver's side and asked him for ID, which he had a Missouri ID. And then came over to my side looking all in the car, you know. We had luggage all in the back, 'cause we were traveling, you know, we was going to be out for, I think for about four days. . . . So he kind of looked in the car; you know, one officer came on the driver's side and was talking to the driver and then he came over and was trying to talk to me, and he was looking all, leaning inside my car and everything. And then he asked me for my ID.

And I told him that we are driving a rental vehicle and he said, "Do you guys have the rental agreement in the car?" And it was kind of raining, so he took it out there and got it all wet.

But anyway, he looked in there and kept looking around and then he said, "Do you mind if we search your car?"

And I was hoping he wasn't gonna take everything out. . . . Well, we said "no" [meaning, it's OK to do the search] because we didn't want to have to, you know, go through the whole routine. . . . If you say "yes," what are they going to do? Bring dogs and all that? So we say "no."

So he went to the back; they open the back door and I think we give them the key to open the back and everything. They kind of just looked; they moved a bag or two around. And then he comes back, he say, cause they've had problems with people trafficking drugs.

So, that was, I think that was the latest time that happened. . . . We didn't get any tickets. . . . We didn't get a ticket or anything, but the officers searched the car, and then they always tell you it's because they have problems with trafficking drugs. And we felt that we was kind of profiled on that, but you don't know if we were or not.[7]

Our analysis rests on two premises. The first is the procedural justice thesis. We accept its core, that people evaluate official decisions more by whether the process is fair than by whether they get a favorable outcome. For example, drivers accept the legitimacy of a traffic ticket if they think it was fairly imposed. We also accept that in *some* situations people judge the fairness of the process by whether the official was respectful.

But a second premise leads us to doubt that official respectfulness plays this dominant role in shaping drivers'—and, especially, African American drivers'—perceptions of the legitimacy of police stops. The core of this second premise is that a group of people, like African Americans, who are commonly subjected to a punitive process, like police stops, are likely to look for subtler cues to fairness than whether the of-

ficial was polite and respectful. People are especially likely to look beyond respectfulness when, as is true of African Americans, they are a
stigmatized group that is commonly and repeatedly subjected to a process that disproportionately disadvantages members of the stigmatized
group, and the members of this group have developed a shared knowledge of these disparities and of the process that generates them. This
scenario describes the experience of African American drivers, like
Billy, in police stops. They have become sophisticated evaluators of police stops who share knowledge of cues that indicate whether a particular instance of the process is fair or unfair; they see beyond the façade of
professional politeness.

This second premise is based on two bodies of research. One consists
of ethnographic and sociological studies of racial minorities' perceptions
of police stops. These studies show that African Americans and Latinos
have developed and share with each other an extensive body of knowledge about police behavior and police stops.[8] As we saw in the two previous chapters, this shared knowledge provides practical guidance in how
to avoid escalations of tension during these stops. In this chapter we examine how this shared knowledge guides *evaluations* of stops. A second
body of research, from social psychology, suggests that members of stigmatized groups, like African Americans, use their shared knowledge of
"prototypical" discriminatory situations, like police stops, to guide their
assessment of whether they were treated fairly in such a situation.[9] In
these prototypical discriminatory situations, people who are commonly
subjected to discrimination become sophisticated observers: shared stories and knowledge of this type of situation draws their attention to subtle cues as to the presence of discrimination.[10] What members of stigmatized groups look for when evaluating an encounter differs from what
the members of the dominant group look for. As Pamela Johnston Conover observed of attitudes toward public policies more generally, members of different racial groups "are likely to pay attention to different
things; they will evaluate others according to different criteria; and they
will adopt different perspectives in making judgments."[11]

White drivers evaluate stops in relation to whether they were given
a ticket or let off with a warning; they prefer the latter. African American drivers evaluate stops by whether the reason was criminal investigation or traffic-safety enforcement; they regard the latter as more fair
and therefore legitimate. While both white and African American drivers evaluate a stop more positively if the officer is polite and respect-

ful, these other considerations—for whites, the outcome; for blacks, the investigatory intrusion—are equally important. These different perceptual frames are based in different experiences of police stops. They "are not merely a matter of mind," Goffman observed of perceptual framing in general; they grow from and reflect the institutionalized practices of police stops.[12] The range of possibilities in traffic-safety stops experienced by white drivers is narrow: a ticket or being let off with a warning. White drivers, like Jeff, have experienced (or heard of) being let off with a warning when a ticket was deserved, and they hold out hope for this outcome and evaluate stops more positively if they get it. Since they hear of others being let off with a warning, to white drivers "fairness" seems to encompass the possibility of avoiding a ticket.[13] But in the context of a traffic-safety stop, the difference between a ticket and a warning has no broader implications for the driver's standing as a citizen with unencumbered rights. For most white drivers, therefore, a stop is just a stop; it is "normal," even if disliked.

Thus, Jeff focused his evaluation on things other than the officer's demeanor (narrative 6.1). He acknowledged that he had been speeding and thus could not complain of being stopped. But he said he had hoped to be let off with a warning and was frustrated when given a ticket. Ultimately, though, Jeff clearly accepted the stop's legitimacy even though he got an unfavorable outcome.

For black drivers, being let off with a warning is not what matters. By experiencing the difference between traffic-safety and investigatory stops, black drivers see a wider range of possibilities than do most whites: intrusive questions, searches, handcuffing, and threats of violence—but also being let go after an intrusive inquiry and search. Black drivers have directly experienced or have heard stories of investigatory stops. In this context, the distinction that matters is not ticket versus warning but investigatory stop versus traffic-safety stop. African American drivers must constantly wonder: Did he stop me for speeding or because I am black and he wants to check me out? They strive to assess the purpose behind a stop, and when they are certain a stop was truly for traffic-law enforcement they evaluate it significantly more positively; when they think it was an investigatory stop they evaluate it more negatively. For African Americans a stop is never just a stop. If anything about a stop is "normal," it is the constant possibility of intrusive questions and searches, and the implication that the driver looks like a criminal.

To illustrate, consider the prototypical investigatory stop described by Gary, an African American man:

> We are aware that officers need probable cause to pull you over, whether it's speeding or maybe you are swerving between the lines, but they have to have some type of reason for why they can pull you over. And that a lot of time the officers see something that doesn't look right. . . .
>
> So, I think, they, on the spur of the moment, they try to make up a reason. You know, "you turned without a signal," or "you changed lanes without a signal," or "you made an illegal turn," or "your taillight is out." Something so trivial, something so small, it's like, you know, any other time you wouldn't pull someone over for this crap, so why are you pulling me over for it now? Something like that.
>
> I think that they use that type of excuse as probable cause to get you pulled over, so they can find anything. You know, and then they'll have a reason to get you out of the car. "Do you mind if I search the vehicle?" That type of situation, because they already have you pulled over. Apparently, they found something in order to pull you over. So, cops use that as a tool to be able to search the vehicle and try to find something that they suspected is in the car.
>
> I've seen it happen plenty of times. I have friends that, you know, they've had it happen to them. Fortunately, it hasn't happened to me, but I've heard the story about how they did it. . . . It happens, gotta deal with it.[14]

The cues listed by Gary—a minimal justification for the stop, a request to conduct a search—appear frequently in African Americans' narratives of investigatory stops. For example, Billy (narrative 6.2) doubted the legitimacy of his stop even though he never complained of impoliteness or disrespect by the officers. By his description, the officers were professionally courteous. What bothered him was something else: being targeted for an inquisitorial investigation on no apparent basis other than the fact that he and his family were black. There is no mention in the story of a traffic violation, and the officers' inquiries, observations, and ultimate search of the van seem to have begun immediately upon making the stop. Put simply, Billy was frustrated *that he was investigated on no reasonable basis*, not, as Stuntz put it, the "manner" or politeness of the investigation.

Whites and African Americans evaluate police stops based on different frames of reference. We expect that whites' shared knowledge of of-

ficer lenience in traffic-safety stops leads them to hope to be let off with
a warning; when they are not, they regard the stop as less legitimate. African Americans' shared knowledge of investigatory stops leads them to
look carefully for signs that *this* stop is an investigatory stop. When they
infer that it is, they evaluate the stop as deeply unfair—even if the officer
is unfailingly polite. Undoubtedly people like to be treated respectfully
even in this context, but it is common to recognize that a polite, respectful official may nonetheless be acting fundamentally unfairly.

This hypothesis that whites' and African Americans' past experiences and shared knowledge lead to different frames of reference is subtly but importantly different from the standard expectation that African
Americans share a deep and almost unshakable cynicism about the police. Some have suggested that African Americans' distrust of the police reflects "'cognitive landscapes' where crime and deviance are more
or less expected and institutions of criminal justice are mistrusted."[15] We
will call this the "culture of distrust" hypothesis, and it has sometimes
led to the expectation that African Americans are dissatisfied with police stops simply because they are culturally predisposed to distrust the
police.

Let us now turn to our data. The stakes are high. If the appearance of
official respectfulness is, indeed, the main thing that matters, then Stuntz
is correct: polite officers can stop as many black people as they like with
no deleterious consequences for people's sense of fairness. If, however,
people are not fooled by a veneer of official politeness, then Stuntz and
other defenders of investigatory stops have it all tragically wrong.

Shared Knowledge of Police Stops

Drivers widely share an understanding of what happens in police stops.
The experience is common and is the subject of many shared stories.
Past research has suggested that African Americans are more likely
than whites to hear stories of police stops. These studies also suggest
that many of the stories shared by African Americans are of disrespectful behavior by police officers, and it is thought that hearing such stories
leads people to more negatively evaluate police behavior in their own
stops. But these stories also provide information that helps drivers to distinguish fair from unfair stops.

In our sample of Kansas City–area drivers, African Americans are considerably more likely than whites to have heard stories of police disrespect. Just over 37 percent of African Americans have heard such stories, compared to just over 15 percent of whites, a large and statistically significant difference ($p < .001$). This pattern in our survey responses is consistent with the finding of other studies.[16]

Much less is known, however, about how African American and white drivers incorporate what they learn from these stories into their perceptions of police stops. Do they have a mechanical effect on people's evaluations of stops, leading them to more negatively evaluate police behavior in their own stop? Or do these stories shape people's frames of reference? It is more the latter: stories of police disrespect serve to confirm African Americans' own experiences, but for whites, these stories add *new knowledge* and may greatly change perceptions of police stops. As some scholars have speculated, stories of police disrespect represent an accumulation of experience.[17] While few white drivers have personally experienced investigatory stops, a surprising number have heard stories of such stops from African American friends. White drivers who hear such stories seem to become more skeptical of the fairness of police stops. Many African American drivers, by contrast, personally have experienced problematic police stops. These firsthand experiences are the most powerful influences on their level of distrust in the police. When African American drivers hear others' stories of such stops, these stories confirm their own experiences; they have immediate relevance.

Recall, for example, the narrative told by Lisa, an African American woman, who reported that police had followed her home from work every night for two weeks. She described telling her friends at work about this experience, and in turn, hearing similar stories from these friends. It is clear that others' stories confirmed Lisa's experiences. As she put it, "Actually, people at work we all talk about [police stops] . . . if you're in the city, you're not going to be the only one."[18] Likewise, Mike, an African American man, told us that he often heard stories of problematic police stops from his friends and fellow church members. After describing his experiences in two ordinary speeding stops, he commented:

> So those [traffic-safety stops] are not typical of the cases I hear from people that are darker-skinned and are stopped and the cops are just rude to them. . . . Sometimes, they're abusive verbally. Sometimes it's even gone into name-calling. They tell you about blacks being called SOBs or something like that. And sometimes, it does even get physical, 'cause they're going to get searched

when there was not even a reason to get searched. He just pulls them over for speeding, but all of a sudden, now they're searching the car. And for what? I've heard those cases from, like, church members and things like that a lot.[19]

But these stories are not Mike's only source of information about police disrespect; Mike is the driver who told us of a horrific incident in which a Chicago police officer stuck the barrel of a gun in his mouth while questioning him.[20]

While African Americans like Lisa and Mike hear affirmation in others' stories of police intrusions, white drivers experience something else: others' stories of police disrespect are a window into an almost foreign world that contrasts with their personal experience. When we asked Linda, a white woman, whether she thinks the police treat everyone the same, she said, "Well, since I'm a white female, it's pretty easy for me to answer that. I think I'm treated very fairly, but I have a friend that is a black lady, and she gets pulled over quite a bit. So, no, probably not."[21] We probed for her explanation:

No, she never commented, but it seems to me in the same area—we drive similar cars—she gets pulled over an awful lot more than I. I mean, I've only been pulled over once in maybe five years. She's been pulled over at least twice a year in our nice neighborhood. We live in a pretty nice—my neighborhood is a normal, average neighborhood. . . . She's pulled over down at the corner more, and just asked, "Do you live around here?" Which I don't think is a relevant question, but that's just life.[22]

Roy, a white man, similarly told us, "No, I do not believe they treat everyone the same. I know for a fact that they treat minorities differently based from what my friends who are minorities have told me about their experiences."[23] Patrick, another white man, explained,

I have a friend of mine that is a police officer, and I know the things that happen and it's pretty bad. I mean, they do racial profiling and they know it. They look for certain characteristics in certain people. You can't drive certain parts of town with certain types of cars—with certain cars. And if you are white, driving in a certain part of town, you are gonna be profiled. And if you are black, driving in certain parts of town, you are gonna be profiled. Look, it's unfortunate.[24]

Later in this chapter we will statistically test the effect of hearing stories of police disrespect on peoples' evaluations of their own stops, but for now these narratives illustrate an important preliminary point. It is that stories of intrusive police stops are best understood as a source of information about the range of possibilities in a stop. For African Americans, hearing these stories confirms their own personal experience of intrusive stops; but, while acting as confirmation, these stories do not change African Americans' perception that police stops can vary widely from innocuous traffic-safety stops to highly intrusive investigatory stops. For whites, hearing stories of intrusive police stops adds new information; whites who have never experienced an intrusive stop may learn that this is a possibility, and this may lead these previously naïve listeners to view police stops more negatively.

How Background Knowledge Frames Evaluations of the Stop

We turn now to how African Americans' and whites' experiences and background knowledge of different types of police stops frame their evaluations of their own police stops. As we have suggested, whites perceive only a narrow range of possibilities in a police stop: getting a ticket or being let off with a warning. African Americans perceive a broader range of possibilities: being stopped for a traffic-safety violation or an inquisitorial investigation and all of the degrading elements that go along with it. Drivers' narratives illustrate these differences.

Thus, most white drivers' narratives are of typical traffic-safety stops. White drivers never express a fear of the officer demanding to search the vehicle or make an arrest. They evaluate the stop in relation to two considerations: whether they believed they deserved to be stopped and whether they were given a ticket or let off with a warning. Both Keith (narrative 4.1) and John acknowledged speeding and accepted the stop's legitimacy, but in these legitimate speeding stops, these white drivers also focused their evaluation on the sanction.[25] The possibility of being let off with a warning framed each of these white drivers' evaluation of the stop: John was caught going 15 miles per hour over the speed limit yet was let off with a warning and was pleased. Keith, who admitted that he was "caught dead to rights," was given a ticket for less than his admitted speed and accepted that this "didn't suck as bad as it could have."

Laura, who provides the story below, was given a ticket for less than her admitted speed but still expressed resentment that she was not let off with a warning. Notably, Laura, alone among these drivers, also complained about the officer's demeanor.

NARRATIVE 6.3.
Laura, white female: "Military ID"

LAURA: Well, I thought that the speed limit on that time was 65. We were in Missouri, and I live in Kansas and we thought it was 65, of course, you know it's only 55 through there. I was with my mother. He pulled me over.

He was more strict, I guess you would call it. And a lot of times, I've gotta be honest with you, I can show my military ID, for example, and I get out of a ticket. But this time he was like, "No."

And I told him that, you know, I really did think that it was 65 through there and I was doing 70. And he did write the ticket to where I was doing 65, though, instead of 70. Because, of course, it would have been a lot more, you know, a lot higher. So he did give me a break, as far as that goes. He wasn't as pleasant as the first guy, the good-looking guy [in an earlier traffic stop]. But I couldn't get myself out of that one.

INTERVIEWER: I see. What did that officer do when he first pulled you over and got out of the car and came up to you?

LAURA: He asked me if I knew that I was speeding. And I said no I didn't, and I said, "It's 65 through here and I was doing not quite 70."

And he said, "No, it's only 55." And he said, "In Missouri it's only 55 on two-lane highways."

And I didn't know that. And he was kind of hateful on that part but. . . . And he said, "No, you are in Missouri, and it's only 55 on two-lane highways in [state]."

And I said, "I'm sorry, I didn't realize that because I live in Kansas."

INTERVIEWER: Now, you said he was kind of either strict or maybe a little hateful. Was there anything he said or was it something he did or his voice? What conveyed that feeling?

LAURA: Well, when I let him know, you know, I said that "I didn't know that." He said, "Well it is." He wasn't as pleasant as the other gentleman [in her previous narrative].

INTERVIEWER: It was maybe his tone?

LAURA: His tone—yeah! He kind of acted like he . . . I had told him that I didn't realize it was only 55 through there. When I said that, he made the comment, "No, it's 55 on all two-lane highways in [state]." And he kind of said it like that, in an unpleasant way. Yeah. But other than that, he didn't smile or anything. So, yeah. He did enjoy writing that ticket. Not that I thought he shouldn't have given me a ticket, but he could've come across a little . . . oh, well no, you know, "Just try to slow down," you know?[26]

Although many African Americans describe being let go without receiving a ticket, this ostensibly beneficial outcome is not the focus of their evaluation. Instead, African American drivers, like Deana, Billy, and Elizabeth focus on whether or not the stop was really about traffic-

law enforcement or something else. These drivers offer negative evaluations of investigatory stops, whether or not the officer was polite, whether
or not the driver was given a ticket. Deana (narrative 3.1) reported being
"scared" after being stopped twice within a few minutes "for no reason,
just to see where I was going," even though the officers were "nice" and
gave her no tickets. Billy evaluated a stop as "racial profiling," because
the officers, while remaining polite, immediately proceeded to probe
into his vehicle. Elizabeth (narrative 5.1) characterized a stop as "racial
profile" because the officers seemed less interested in the violation they
used to justify the stop—a late turn on a yellow light—than in checking
her out and peering closely into her car.[27]

This pattern of indignation at polite but intrusively inquisitive officers
is common among African Americans' narratives. Lisa told of being followed home from work late at night for two weeks by two police officers who stopped behind her as she came to a stop at her home, ran her
tags, and asked her whether the vehicle was hers (narrative 3.3). Darrell
described being stopped without having violated any traffic law, held in
handcuffs for an hour, and then released (narrative 4.2). Throughout his
interview, he never complained about police disrespect or impoliteness,
but he was clearly indignant at the intrusive investigation.

The narratives offer a corrective in another way, too. Unlike the survey data that are the basis for studies of peoples' perceptions of procedural justice, drivers' narratives describe sequences: how somebody
acted, how another person responded, and how the first person responded to that response. This time-based character speaks to a crucial
element of the respectfulness thesis, which posits that peoples' evaluation of the fairness of the stop is based largely on how respectfully the
officer speaks during the stop.[28] In this view, regardless of the reason or
justification for the stop, if the officer is polite and respectful during the
stop, drivers are likely to evaluate the stop as fair. If the officer is rude
and disrespectful, regardless of the reason or justification for the stop,
drivers are likely to evaluate the stop as unfair.

A small number of narratives follow this "officer talks and then the
driver evaluates the fairness" sequence. The most obvious is Donna's, in
which she describes a tit-for-tat escalation in which officers responded to
her complaints by threatening to arrest her and take her children to the
state child-welfare agency.[29] Her clearly negative evaluation of that stop
seems to have developed in the course of this spiraling escalation. As she
put it, she had been speeding and was "OK with" being stopped for that

reason, but she became increasingly distressed as the officers asked intrusive questions, conducted a search without her consent, and threatened her with arrest and the loss of her children.

More commonly, drivers tell of making evaluations of the fairness of
the stop early in the process, sometimes within a few seconds of realizing they are being stopped and before the officer has spoken a word,
and sometimes immediately upon hearing the officer's justification for
the stop. What they are doing in these first moments is making a quick
"fairness" assessment that focuses on whether they have done anything
justifying a traffic-safety stop. Thus, in many narratives, drivers describe
doing a quick check of their own driving in the space of mere seconds
after first seeing the officer or first seeing the police car's lights behind
them, and making a judgment at this point as to whether they deserve to
be pulled over. As John (a white driver) reported in chapter 3, he looked
at his speedometer immediately upon realizing that he was being pulled
over and, just as immediately, realized that he was going "15 miles over
the speed limit" and deserved to be stopped. Likewise, as Keith put it,
"he had me dead to rights" because he was speeding and knew it (narrative 4.1). These drivers accepted the legitimacy of the stop.

Others, using a similar metric and similarly quick judgment, doubted
the legitimacy of their stop. Joe, the black man who said that he "felt violated" by a stop for the stated purpose of a "warrant check," described
being frustrated with the stop because he felt he had committed no traffic violation and the officer seemed to confirm this by reporting that the
purpose of the stop was to conduct a warrant check (narrative 1.1). Both
Gary and Mike acknowledged speeding, but described quickly comparing their speed against other cars after noticing that they were being
stopped.[30] They reported complaining to the officer as he approached
the vehicle that the stop was unfair because other drivers had been going
just as fast. In all of these cases, and many more, the drivers had decided
the stop was illegitimate before hearing a word from the officer.

Drivers' narratives suggest that while both African American and
white drivers consider officers' demeanor in evaluating the fairness of
a stop, a disrespectful demeanor is not the only important consideration
for either group. Whites' evaluations are framed within the range of typical possibilities in the "normal" traffic-safety stop: ticket versus warning. Blacks' evaluations are framed within a much wider range of possibilities: speeding stop versus intrusive investigation.

How widespread are these differing perspectives? Are the few drivers just quoted representative of broader patterns among many drivers? In a broader population, do these differences in perspective wash out when we take into account whether the officer was polite and respectful and whether the driver is predisposed to distrust the police? We can address these questions with our driver survey data.

To begin, we need a clear understanding of what is meant by accepting the legitimacy of a police stop. The standard definition of "stop legitimacy" is the driver's willingness to accept or challenge the officer's decisions.[31] This understanding of legitimacy dates to early research on the procedural justice thesis. While this definition makes perfect sense in the context of studying why people accept or challenge such official sanctions as traffic tickets and adverse judicial decisions, it is more problematic when applied to police stops. That is because many police stops, especially those that are viewed as problematic by drivers, yield no ultimate "decision" that the driver can plausibly accept or challenge. As revealed by African American drivers' narratives in previous chapters and others we will share below, most investigatory stops end with the officer letting the driver go with no ticket or warning. Thus, Billy was let go without a ticket but viewed the stop as illegitimate. Do drivers like him "accept" the decision to let them go without a ticket? Of course they do. But accepting being let go with no sanction is hardly an indication that the driver found the stop to be legitimate.

For this reason, we adopt a measure of the legitimacy of the stop that more closely fits drivers' narratives. It consists of three parts: in the driver's most recent stop in the past year, to what extent did the officer provide a legitimate reason to make the stop, to what extent did the officer behave properly during the stop, and to what extent was the outcome more severe than the driver felt he or she deserved. For our statistical analyses below, we have combined these three perceptual evaluations into a single index: evaluation of the stop's legitimacy ($\alpha = .75$).[32]

Figure 6.1 reports the mean response to each of these questions by the race and gender of the respondent. African Americans, on average, view their most recent stop as less legitimate on each of these dimensions than do whites. In each of these racial groups, men view their most recent stop as less legitimate than women. These differences between whites and blacks are large and statistically meaningful; the differences by gender are smaller. The pattern is striking and is consistent with the expectation that African Americans are less accepting than whites of the legitimacy of their police stops.

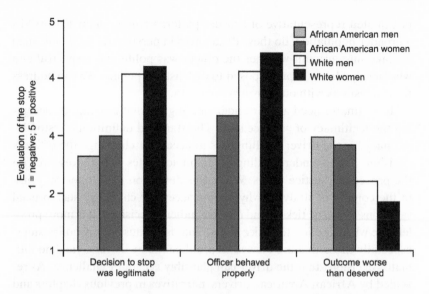

FIGURE 6.1. Evaluations of the legitimacy of the stop, by race and gender of driver (stop legitimacy, 650; officer behavior, 637; severity of outcome, 636). All differences by race are statistically significant ($p < .001$; two-tailed t-test); differences by gender are not statistically significant except for "officer behaved properly" (for both whites and blacks) ($p < .10$; two-tailed t-test), and "outcome more severe than deserved" (for white respondents) ($p < .05$; two-tailed t-test).

We expect that African American drivers' evaluations of their most recent stop are especially influenced by whether the stop was an investigatory stop. Robin S. Engel found that drivers evaluated stops for speeding as more legitimate than other stops.[33] We are fortunate to have two more-direct measures of whether the stop was an investigatory stop, both of which are available to drivers' perceptions. One is our basic measure of whether the officer gave a *de minimis* reason for the stop (such as failure to signal a lane change or having a burned-out license-plate light). We have used this in several previous analyses where we simply called it our "investigatory stop" measure. The other is a cue from the stop experience that is easily available to the driver: whether or not the officer gave the driver a lecture on his or her driving behavior. This is an explicit indication that a stop was for traffic-safety as opposed to investigatory purposes.

By contrast, we expect that whites' evaluations of the stop are influenced by how severe were the sanctions and how much the driver typically violates the rules of the road. Our measure of the severity of the sanctions is the basic measure of the severity of the stop outcome introduced in previous chapters. We use three measures of how much a driver violates the rules of the road: how much the driver reports a tendency to speed and how much he or she reports abiding by other rules of the road (we introduced these in previous chapters), and the number of stops the driver has experienced over his or her lifetime (this is a five-category ordinal variable ranging from 0 to 51 or more). We expect that whites', but not African Americans', evaluations will be influenced by these measures of traffic-law violation, since for white drivers, police stops are recognizably and consistently related to traffic-law violations.

We control for a wide range of other possible influences on the perceived legitimacy of a police stop. Because we have introduced most of these measures in previous chapters we will not repeat the discussion of them here. We have not previously discussed our measures to test the "subculture of distrust" hypothesis. The first measure examines whether the driver has heard stories told by others of disrespectful police behavior in police stops. The second combines two measures of the demographics of the driver's area of residence, specifically the family poverty rate and the black percentage of the population in the driver's area of residence. Both of these controls have been used in past research on peoples' attitudes toward police stops and the police more generally.[34]

Table 6.1 reports the results. In keeping with our expectation that African Americans and whites frame their evaluations in different ways, we analyze these groups separately.[35] What is especially striking about these results is the great divergence between black and white drivers in which elements of the stop experience matter. To be sure, both whites and blacks evaluate the stop more negatively to the extent the officer was impolite. This is a key expectation of the procedural justice theory. Beyond this, however, the rubrics used by black and white drivers diverge; both are concerned about procedural fairness, but use different cues to evaluate whether the stop was fair.

As these results reveal, African Americans base their evaluations of stops on stop type, not stop outcome: they view investigatory stops as significantly less legitimate than traffic-safety stops. White drivers make no similar distinction. Black drivers' evaluations likewise are influenced by whether the officers gave them a lecture on driving safety. Paradoxically, black drivers evaluate stops in which they are lectured as more legitimate than other stops, perhaps precisely because being lectured on

TABLE 6.I. **Drivers' evaluations of the legitimacy of police stops.**

	Drivers, by race	
Characteristic	White	Black
Experiences during the stop		
Investigatory stop	0.003	−0.402**
	(.142)	(.175)
Officer gave lecture on driving safety	−0.019	0.526**
	(.148)	(.236)
Severity of stop sanctions	−0.246**	0.182
	(.119)	(.161)
Officer disrespect	−0.881****	−0.855****
	(.146)	(.124)
Driver's violation of traffic laws		
Extent of speeding	0.026**	0.008
	(.011)	(.014)
Rule-abiding driving	0.302*	0.198
	(.162)	(.202)
Lifetime no. of stops	0.218	−0.328
	(.199)	(.223)
Indirect experiences		
Heard stories of disrespect	−0.001	−0.180
	(.168)	(.176)
Background predispositions		
Political conservatism	0.017	0.001
	(.041)	(.052)
Distrust in authority (local government)	−0.067	−0.174
	(.085)	(.176)
Poverty rate of jurisdiction of residence	0.032	0.002
	(.024)	(.029)
Jurisdiction of residence, % black	−0.002	0.007
	(.008)	(.011)
Female	0.144	−0.025
	(.140)	(.184)
Age	−0.002	−0.002
	(.007)	(.010)
Education	0.028	0.016
	(.044)	(.059)
Income	0.024	−0.036
	(.025)	(.033)
Constant	−2.822**	0.047
	(1.365)	(1.787)
Log pseudo-likelihood	−308.04	−129.55
LR χ^2 (16)	90.56	75.80
p	<.0001	<.0001
N	302	115
Right-censored N	149	28

Note: Results were obtained using Tobit estimation. Data are coefficients, with robust standard errors given in parentheses. The dependent variable is an additive index of the variables illustrated in figure 6.1 and is not normally distributed. For dependent variables with this characteristic, Tobit is the most appropriate modeling technique (see J. Scott Long, *Regression Models for Categorical and Limited Dependent Variables* [Thousand Oaks, CA: Sage, 1997], 187–216). We have confirmed the results with ordered probit; the results do not differ substantially from those reported here. See the appendix for further discussion.

*$p < .10$; **$p < .05$; ***$p < .01$; ****$p < .001$

driving safety is a clear cue that the purpose of the stop was for conventional safety enforcement as opposed to criminal investigation. White drivers' evaluations are not influenced by such lectures, probably because white drivers are not looking for cues as to whether the stop is an investigatory stop.

White drivers' stories, as we have seen, are replete with comments suggesting that they focus on whether "I knew I was speeding and I was in the wrong."[36] These comments suggest that white drivers often accept the legitimacy of a stop when they acknowledge deserving to be stopped, and the statistical results bear out this inference. The more that white drivers acknowledge violating traffic laws by speeding or otherwise violating the rules of the road, the more legitimacy they grant to their most recent stop. Likewise, the more times that white drivers have been stopped prior to the stop they are evaluating, the more legitimacy they grant to the stop (although this relationship is not statistically significant). These factors have this influence because police stops are recognizably related to traffic violations for white drivers. In contrast, for African American drivers, having been stopped frequently in the past is negatively associated with the perceived legitimacy of the most recent stop, although this relationship is not statistically meaningful.

In all, these results suggest that for whites, police stops are recognizably and legitimately a consequence of bad driving. For African Americans the relationship between police stops and actual traffic violations is less clear; a black driver stopped for driving at 10 miles over the speed limit may still wonder whether the reason for the stop was to carry out an investigation. Jacinta Gau and Rod Brunson observe that among young inner-city black men both the law abiding and the law violating were equally subjected to arbitrary police stops, leading both groups to question whether stops are ever truly based on their behavior.[37]

As white drivers' narratives suggest, their evaluations *are* influenced by how severe is the sanction. White drivers hope to be let off with a warning, and they evaluate the stop more negatively if they are given a ticket. This is not so of African American drivers, for whom being let off without a ticket is not a meaningful measure of whether the stop was problematic.

Finally, the results show that drivers' evaluations of the stop are not influenced by their background predispositions. After taking into account the nature of the stop experience, none of the measures of background predispositions—political ideology, distrust in government, level of education, nature of the neighborhood, or age—is significantly related to the driver's evaluation of the most recent stop.[38] Even *indirect* experiences, in the form of hearing stories of police disrespect, have no significant influence on drivers' evaluations of the stop.

How substantial are these effects? Figure 6.2 illustrates the relative magnitude of these effects (using the results of the Clarify procedure).[39] Holding other factors constant, officer disrespect (versus respect) toward the driver alters white and black drivers' evaluations of the stop,

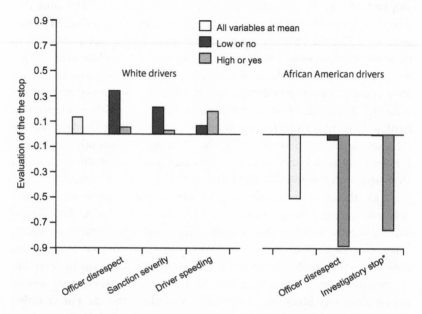

FIGURE 6.2. The impact of various factors on the driver's evaluation of the most recent stop (white drivers, $N = 285$; African American drivers, $N = 108$). Each pair of columns represents the impact of variations in the identified variable on drivers' evaluations of their most recent stop, with all other variables set at their means. The scale covers slightly more than one standard deviation above and below the mean on the dependent variable (drivers' evaluations of the legitimacy of the stop). On the independent variables, "low" represents the twenty-fifth percentile and "high" represents the seventy-fifth percentile on the independent variables except as discussed in the appendix. Results generated using the Clarify procedure in Stata (Gary King, Michael Tomz, and Jason Wittenberg, "Making the Most of Statistical Analysis: Improving Interpretation and Presentation," *American Journal of Political Science* 44, no. 2 [April 2000]: 347–61).

*The measured impact of an investigatory stop represents the impact of a combination of both the objective measure of whether the stop was investigatory and the perceptual cue of whether the officer gave the driver a lecture on driving safety (both variables are dichotomous).

but its impact is similar to other considerations. In addition to officer disrespect, white drivers base their evaluation on the level of sanction. Black drivers respond to the experience of an investigatory stop nearly as strongly as to officer disrespect (note that for black drivers, the column illustrating the effect of being stopped for a non-investigatory reason is very close to the line marking the mean). Even taking into account these influences, white drivers' evaluations of their most recent stops are substantially better than African Americans' evaluations: when all variables are set at their means, the mean evaluation of the stop is substantially higher for whites than African Americans. But this apparent racial difference should not be exaggerated: if an African American experiences a *traffic-safety stop* conducted by a respectful police officer, the driver's evaluation is not substantially worse than the typical white driver's evaluation of his or her most recent stop (which typically is a traffic-safety stop).

What all of this means is that the wide racial gap in people's evaluations of their most recent police stop is largely the product of the different types of stops experienced by whites and African Americans. Were we able to wave a magic wand and turn African Americans' investigatory stops into traffic-safety stops, the racial gap in evaluations of stops would shrink dramatically.

The lesson is clear: African Americans easily recognize investigatory stops and evaluate them far more negatively than traffic-safety stops. It is simply not true that if officers remain professionally respectful they can carry out as many investigatory stops as they wish without causing harm. The problem is not simply the "manner" in which these stops are carried out; the problem is investigatory stops themselves. Investigatory stops are procedurally poisoned at their core.

CHAPTER SEVEN

The Broader Lessons
(and Harms) of Police Stops

So, it's become so commonplace, you know, that I don't trip. It is just a normal thing, or normal for black people anyway. Or black males anyways.[1]

Joe was pulled over by an officer hunting for an arrest. Another officer wanted to see where Deana was going. Lisa was followed home
from work every night for two weeks. Darrell was stopped while driving
through a white neighborhood and then held on the sidewalk in handcuffs for an hour, only to be let go. Billy was stopped and searched, yet
again, while driving to visit a critically ill uncle. How harmful are these
experiences that target African Americans? Do they cause fleeting annoyance or lasting scars? How do they affect one's life, sense of freedom and security, and perceived place in society? Do these experiences
erode faith that the police are fair? Do they affect society more broadly
by contributing to racial divisions and inequalities?

While social scientists are beginning to address these questions, policy makers are not. Judges see only cases in which stops and searches
yield drugs or illegal guns. They typically conclude that the harm to a
driver who is found with illegal drugs was outweighed by the benefits of
reducing crime. Judges do not see the many more stops and searches that
yield no drugs or guns, and they rarely ask whether these stops harm the
innocent, who are subjected to intrusive questions, searches, handcuffing, and worse. Even the police, those closest to the stop, rarely consider
the possibility that investigatory stops may cause deep and lasting harm.
As we have seen, stopped drivers try to remain stoic, and officers may
interpret this as a sign of indifference to the ordeal. Perhaps in the con-

text of the destruction of lives and communities caused by drug and gun crime—conditions police face daily—the brief questioning and incarceration of a fruitless investigatory stop may seem trivial.

An accumulating body of research suggests that intrusive police stops cause deep and lasting harm; they are a form of racial subordination. Bernard Harcourt argues that investigatory stops have a "ratchet effect" with overt and hidden costs.[2] By targeting African Americans, these stops subject this group to pervasive, ongoing surveillance, skew the prison population's racial composition, and reinforce the entrenched stereotype that blacks are criminal and violent. Interview-based studies consistently show that African Americans commonly feel demeaned and even abused by intrusive police stops.[3] Psychological studies demonstrate that African Americans subjected to intrusive police stops experience heightened levels of psychological stress.[4] Much of the research finds that such personal experiences—particularly experiences of police disrespect and frequent subjection to stops—directly erode people's trust in the police.[5] Trust in the police is important because people who do not trust the police are less willing to call the police for help, may be more likely to turn to self-help vigilantism, and may be less willing to cooperate with the police in criminal investigations.[6] The harms may go even deeper: people stopped by the police are less likely to vote.[7] In a society in which voting rates are comparatively low and the poor are among the least likely to vote, the possibility that police stops may further suppress people's willingness to vote is a significant concern.

But many of the just-mentioned studies do not clearly distinguish among types of police stops. What is unclear in many of these studies is whether *any* police stop—or only intrusive investigatory stops—causes these harms. This chapter addresses this crucial question.

Connections between specific experiences and general attitudes are always tenuous. Nonetheless, it is vital to examine if investigatory stops lead individuals to distrust the police, avoid calling them for help, and feel disenfranchised. This chapter is premised on a particular implication of the procedural justice thesis: that people draw broader lessons about their place in society from official treatment.[8] Police stops, the most frequent and visible exercise of public authority over our daily lives, convey an especially powerful message about our place in society. Fairly conducted traffic-safety stops tell a driver that they are an equal member of society and are held to the same rules as everybody else. Racially biased investigatory stops tell a driver that they look like a criminal and people like them are subject to arbitrary control befitting their subordinate status; they are not an equal member of society. Police stops that target minorities communicate to those stopped, and those shielded from such stops, that some citizens are not free to move about as equal members of society. Such stops contribute to whites' sense that they occupy a special, more protected place in the community, while at the same time confirming to African Americans their lower status. Michelle Alexander has powerfully argued that racially based, intrusive police stops carry on the legacy of long-repealed segregationist laws: they exclude African Americans from full and equal membership in the community.[9]

Drivers' Voices

Drivers' comments to us in our post-survey interviews drive home these points. The voices of drivers, black and white, underscore the importance of stops and the stop experience in defining citizenship in mobile America. Even in the absence of personal experience, shared stories contribute to African Americans' understanding that arbitrary, investigatory stops treat them as second-class citizens. Mike, an African American man, told us,

> Yeah, I mean, it's always in the back of your mind. You don't necessarily get in the car expecting it, but you do have it in the back of your mind that the bottom line is that you make sure that you don't have anything in your car. That's the thing, don't have any pipes, don't have anything there that can be construed as a weapon of any sort. Because if they pull you over and they decide, like they can at any given time, that they're going to search your car, then anything that they find can be evidence against you. And they look. I don't believe that they're above planting anything, either.[10]

Donald, a white man who admits that he speeds "all the time," sees police stops from the other side of the racial divide, and his comments suggest how simply observing police stops of others reinforces impressions that blacks are the subjects of police attention. Routinely seeing white violations that are overlooked while blacks are pulled over recreates the stereotypes of black threat and criminality. In answer to our question about whether the police treat everyone the same, he replied by describing an interaction he had with an officer in a recent stop:

No. I mean, you know, I was a white male driving a nice car and I was, like I said, dressed in a kind of uniform [a business shirt with a corporate insignia on its breast]. . . . I just kind of chatted with him. And I just think that by the time he got to the car, he realized that I wasn't that big of a threat, so he was just very polite, and just did his job. [The officer let Donald off with a warning.]

I truly don't believe that that happens in every case. Just driving . . . I would say like 99 percent of the people that I see pulled over on the side of the road are of either African American or Hispanic descent and not the nicest cars. I mean, it's every day. . . . And I always look, because I'm just nosy, and I think we all do, to see who they got instead of you. So, yeah, nine times out of ten, it's going to be a person of color.[11]

The experience from the other side of Donald's window is, of course, quite different. Billy, an African American man, described being held at the front of his car on I-35 while an officer searched the vehicle:

You know, it was a little bit inconvenient, you know, searching my car, me standing in the front of the highway, and you know, I had to stand in front of the car. And, I guess if you're passing by, I do kind of fit that . . . you know, "look." That is how you feel as a person. You know, almost like you look like a criminal. People look as they pass by.[12]

As the officer searched his car and passing drivers gawked, Billy was palpably embarrassed and indignant. He felt that others saw him as dangerous and criminal, that he had that "look." Elizabeth, an African American woman, shared her anger at stops of men like Billy.

I've seen them stop black people, black men, and definitely all I see is everybody being handcuffed, being patted down, handcuffed . . . outside of the car in the back. . . . To me, it's like, you need five or six cars just to stop them? . . . Why do we take, you know, five or six police cars, you know, to stop somebody, especially black people?[13]

In a manner less overt but no less clear than apartheid South Africa's pass laws, these images of stopped, detained, and searched black drivers, so common on the shoulders of our roads, define a diminished version of citizenship for blacks in mobile America. As noted in chapter 6, Timothy, an older African American man, described feeling like less than a citizen in his own community. He had never been arrested, but feared that any encounter with the police could escalate unpredictably.[14] Billy said he also fears for his children. Like the African Americans interviewed by Brunson and Miller and Weitzer, who described teaching their children how to defer to police officers' intrusions, Billy tries to teach his children how to avoid trouble in police stops.[15]

> It's kind of hard, because . . . because I got young kids, . . . young adults and . . . I try to warn my sons about . . . traveling too many in the car . . . The way they dress, . . . the hip-hop style. . . . I tried to . . . show them . . . where they can drive safe, . . . keep your seatbelts on, . . . if the police stops you, . . . like keep your hands on the wheel so they can see them. . . . I try to do things to make them feel nonthreatening.[16]

Although white drivers do not like being stopped by the police, their dislike is fundamentally different than African Americans' fear of investigatory stops and searches, and it has different implications for whites' sense of their place in society. No white driver told us that he feared police stops. No white driver told us that she feared what might transpire during police stops—of searches, handcuffing, and arrest. No white driver told us that he tried to teach his children how to avoid trouble in police stops.

If stops reinforce African Americans' sense of vulnerability, they reaffirm whites' sense of their equality in a community ruled by law and, even, for some white drivers, their authority over the police. Patrick, a white man, described being stopped twice by police officers in separate incidents and proudly told us that in each he had lectured the officers on the law. "I know the police chief very well," he told us, "so I called him and he told me some questions I needed to ask this fellow." So he went back to the site of the stop and confronted the officer.[17] While Patrick's chutzpah is unusual, his sense of influence over police officers is common among white drivers. Laura, a white woman, told us, "I gotta be honest with you, I can show my military ID, for example, and I get out of a ticket." Her husband "has gotten out of many, many, many tickets . . . I would say 90 percent of the time," by using his military ID.[18] Like Patrick, Laura expressed annoyance against an officer who, unlike others, was not influenced by this tactic and actually issued her a ticket.

While African Americans express a simmering outrage over what they see as discriminatory police stops and some whites offer reservations and concern, blacks and whites express a resigned fatalism about the problem. Many studies, from Kristin Bumiller's classic paper to recent psychological research demonstrate that people who face discrimination commonly hesitate to complain, preferring simply to get through the difficult times.[19] The stories told to us by African American drivers fit this pattern. For instance, Lisa said:

> Well, I didn't like it but . . . what can you do? So after a while you know it's kind of dangerous in that area and I just got to the point, well if they're going to escort me home, then I might as well be happy instead of sad. So I looked at them as being escorts.[20]

Surely this is a positive spin on a deeply uncomfortable experience. There is little doubt that Lisa would have preferred not to have this "escort." A police car following you home every night after work—it is difficult to imagine a more powerful message that you are not an equal member of the community.

Verifying the Harms of Investigatory Stops

The drivers we interviewed, black and white, suggested how targeting African Americans for investigatory stops sends unmistakable messages about their lower status. These stops, because they have become so routine, so unremarkable, help define the social meaning of race in contemporary America.[21] Our statistical evidence verifies the harms so evident in these retold experiences.

How Stops Alter Views of Police Fairness

The stop narratives underscore how much African Americans, in comparison to whites, fear and distrust the police. This is a well-established finding.[22] Although men trust the police less than women, and younger people less than older people, these differences pale in comparison to the impact of race. This bedrock fact is illustrated from our driver survey with a simple figure reporting the percentage of drivers, by race, gender, and age who agree or strongly agree with the statement, "The police are out to get people like me" (figure 7.1). The most obvious difference is the dramatic gulf between blacks and whites: blacks are much less

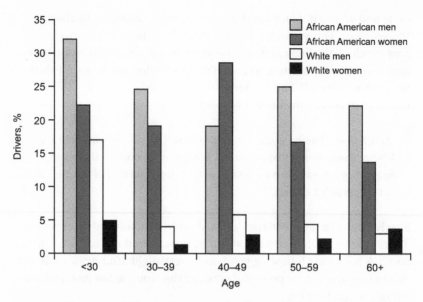

FIGURE 7.1. Percentage of drivers who agree or strongly agree with the statement, "The police are out to get people like me," by race, gender, and age ($N = 2124$). All differences by race are statistically significant ($p < .05$, two-tailed t-test).

trusting of the police than whites. Age matters, too, but mostly for white drivers. As white drivers age, they become more trusting of the police. While increasing age works this magic on white men and women beginning with the symbolic dividing line of age 30, it has no similar effect on black women until age 50. Strikingly, black men age 60 and older distrust the police as much as do black men under age 30. Among both whites and blacks, women are generally more trusting of the police than men, although this difference by gender is not consistent and is not always statistically meaningful.

These patterns are mirrored in drivers' responses to another question, "To what extent would you feel comfortable calling the police if you needed help?" The percentage of drivers by race, gender, and age who agree or strongly disagree that they would feel comfortable calling the police is illustrated in figure 7.2. Nearly one in four African American men under age 30 report feeling uncomfortable calling the police if they need help. Although nearly one in five white men under age 30 share similar qualms, whites' comfort in calling the police increases dramatically with age, while African Americans' does not. Well over one in five African American men in their 40s remain uncomfortable calling the police. By this age the vast majority of whites—nearly nineteen out of twenty—no longer hesitate calling the police. These stunning racial differences suggest a deep problem. At worst, people who are unwilling to call the police may resort to self-help vigilantism to respond to crime; at best they simply take their lumps and move on. Neither is an acceptable pattern in a society claiming that law provides equal protection to all.

Fearing that the police are out to get people like them and feeling uncomfortable calling the police are two dimensions of a broader phenomenon of citizen beliefs in the fundamental fairness of the police and trust in the police. We asked drivers a number of questions regarding their trust in the police. Figure 7.3 illustrates these observations, broken down by race of driver. Blacks, in comparison to whites, have less trust in the police to do the right thing, have less confidence in the police, are less likely to believe the police do not discriminate by race, are less comfortable calling the police if they need help, are more likely to

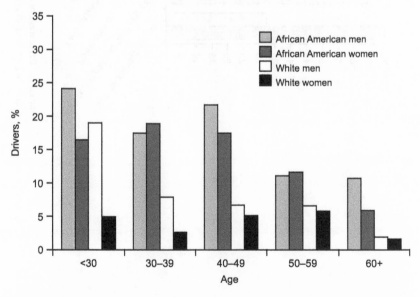

FIGURE 7.2. Percentage of drivers who disagree or strongly disagree that they would feel comfortable calling the police if they needed help ($N = 2144$). All differences by race are statistically significant ($p < .05$), with the exception of male drivers under age 30 and drivers aged 50–59.

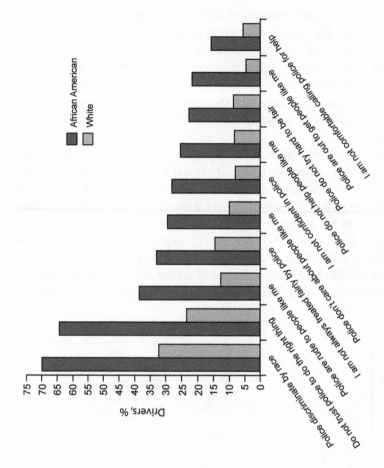

FIGURE 7.3. Percentage of drivers, by race, who report distrusting the police on various dimensions of distrust ($N = 2124–2145$). All differences are statistically significant ($p < .0001$, two-tailed t-test).

disagree that police department does a good job of helping and protecting "people like me," are more likely to agree that the police don't care about "people like me," are less likely to agree that the police are trying hard to be fair even if they make mistakes, are more likely to agree that the police are rude to "people like me," and are more likely to disagree that they have always been treated fairly by the police. We combined these ten questions into an index of the level of distrust of the police ($\alpha = .91$). While these questions seem to consist of two dimensions—trust in the police and perceived fairness of the police—we statistically verified that these two dimensions are functionally equivalent and separating them produces no significant differences in this chapter's observations.[23] Higher values on this index indicate higher levels of distrust of the police.

Do investigatory stops contribute to these vast racial differences in the perceived unfairness and distrust of the police? The results, reported in table 7.1, are clear and striking. Hearing stories of disrespect by the police erodes trust among both blacks and whites, but beyond this commonality, African Americans' distrust is influenced primarily by personal experiences of investigatory stops and the accumulation of stop experiences. Whites' comparatively high level of trust in the police is influenced primarily by background predispositions.[24]

Recent experience of a police stop clearly erodes trust in the police—but the *type* of stop matters. Experiencing a traffic-safety stop has no effect on either whites' or African Americans' trust in the police. By contrast, experiencing an investigatory stop directly and substantially erodes African Americans' trust in the police. Experiencing an investigatory stop also erodes whites' trust in the police, but the impact is less than half that for African Americans.

The accumulation of stop experiences has a profoundly different effect on whites and African Americans. Among African Americans, the more stops the driver has experienced over his or her lifetime, the less they trust the police. The effect is substantial and likely reflects the pattern we have earlier observed: a large proportion of stops of African Americans are investigatory stops and, not surprisingly, the accumulation of experiences of these stops erodes trust in the police. Whites, by contrast, mainly experience traffic-safety stops. The accumulation of experiences of these stops has no effect on whites' trust in the police. More stops of the kind experienced by whites—routine traffic-safety stops or brief, nonpunitive investigatory stops—do not diminish a driver's belief

TABLE 7.1. **Distrust of the police: the effect of investigatory police stops**

Characteristic	All drivers	White	African American
Driver's race and personal experiences			
African American	0.583****		
	(.042)		
Investigatory stop	0.184***	0.136**	0.283**
	(.059)	(.066)	(.115)
Traffic-safety stop	0.054	0.044	0.122
	(.045)	(.048)	(.125)
Stops over lifetime	0.057	0.008	0.260***
	(.068)	(.080)	(.097)
Indirect experiences			
Heard stories of police	0.290****	0.259****	0.362****
disrespect to drivers	(.058)	(.071)	(.064)
Other characteristics			
Female	−0.112***	−0.132***	0.013
	(.039)	(.044)	(.065)
Age	−0.001	−0.001	−0.0047*
	(.002)	(.002)	(.0024)
Education	−0.021**	−0.022**	−0.009
	(.010)	(.011)	(.012)
Income	−0.014**	−0.013*	−0.009
	(.006)	(.007)	(.012)
Political conservatism	−0.050****	−0.058****	−0.014
	(.012)	(.014)	(.017)
Rule-abiding driving	−0.166***	−0.180***	−0.054
	(.058)	(.066)	(.077)
Extent of speeding	0.001	0.004	−0.003
	(.003)	(.004)	(.004)
Poverty rate of	0.012*	0.017**	0.004
jurisdiction	(.007)	(.008)	(.007)
of residence			
Jurisdiction of	−0.003	−.005*	0.0056*
residence,	(.002)	(.003)	(.0033)
% black			
Constant	−0.117	−.266	0.482
	(.400)	(.495)	(.491)
N	1424	889	535
R^2	.31	.20	.21

Note: Results were obtained using ordinary least squares regression. Data are coefficients, with standard errors given in parentheses. Results obtained from Tobit and ordered probit do not differ substantially from those reported here. See the appendix for methodological discussion.
*$p < .10$; **$p < .05$; ***$p < .01$; ****$p < .001$

in the fairness of the police. More such stops may simply confirm to the driver that he or she is a risky driver. But more stops of the kind experienced by African Americans—intrusive investigatory stops that are pursued to searches and sometimes handcuffing—further erode a black driver's belief that the police fairly treat "people like me."

The belief held by whites that the police are fair is influenced by factors disconnected from direct experiences with the police: the driver's gender, education level, time spent driving, risky driving habits, and political attitudes. For example, political conservatives are more positive about the police than liberals, and highly educated people are more positive than those with little education. The predominance of such factors suggests that whites' views of the police are shaped mainly by their background predispositions—their level of education and their political ideology in particular.

Segregation of Neighborhoods

Kenneth, a middle aged black man, told us, "You know, if you saw some young black kid in an old beat up Chevy or something, riding it in Leawood [an affluent white suburb] or somewhere where they have a little money . . . you know the police would stop him and ask him, 'What are you doing out here, boy?'"[25] This pithy comment summarizes another harm of investigatory stops: punishing African Americans for driving in "white" areas.

We asked respondents whether fear of the police influences where they drive and what clothes they wear. African American drivers especially report that police stops regulate where they may drive.[26] Figure 7.4 illustrates the proportion of drivers, by race, gender, and age, who report that they "sometimes" or "often" have "avoided driving in certain areas because of the way police might treat you." In all age groups, the gulf between white and African American drivers is wide. In each of these racial groups, men and women differ, too—but the widest gap is between whites and African Americans. Over 65 percent of African American men—but 40 percent of white men—under age 30 report that they sometimes or often avoid driving in some areas for fear of how the police might treat them. Just under half, 47 percent, of African Americans of both sexes ages 40 to 49—but only 17 percent of white men and 8 percent of white women of this age—report sometimes or often avoiding certain areas for fear of the police. Avoiding certain areas for fear of the police declines by age, but this decline is larger and steadier over time for whites than African Americans. African American men need to reach the age of 50 to feel the same freedom to travel as white men under the age of thirty. Overall, across all age groups, a stunning 40 percent of African Americans, compared to only 12 percent of whites, re-

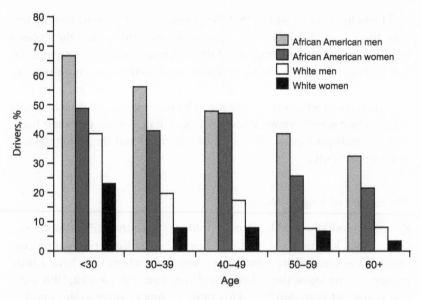

FIGURE 7.4. The percentage of drivers by race, gender, and age who report that they "sometimes" or "often" avoid driving in some areas "because of the way the police might treat me" ($N = 2185$). All differences are statistically significant ($p-.05$), except for the difference between African American men and women aged 40–49.

port that they "sometimes" or "often" avoid driving in certain areas for fear of the police. Likewise, 12 percent of African Americans, but less than 3 percent of whites, report that they sometimes or often are "careful about the clothes I wear because of how the police might treat me."[27]

Using the same control variables employed in the previous analysis, we asked how much the experience of an investigatory stop contributed to people's fear of driving in some areas, and how much the accumulation of police-stop experiences contributed to this fear. The results reported in table 7.2 reveal a now-familiar pattern: investigatory stops and the accumulation of stop experiences especially contribute to African Americans' fear of driving in some areas. Investigatory stops have a lesser effect on whites' fear of driving in some areas. Neither group is affected by the experience of traffic-safety stops.

These differences between white and African American drivers are best understood in light of these groups' different stop experiences. As we have shown in previous chapters, whites are stopped mainly because they have seriously violated traffic-safety laws. The results in table 7.2 suggest that traffic-safety stops do not make white drivers more fearful of how the police might treat them if caught driving in certain areas. African American drivers are also stopped to enforce traffic safety, but a much higher proportion are stopped for questioning or investigation. Accumulating experiences of these investigatory stops, as table 7.2 suggests, powerfully affects African Americans' fear of how the police might treat them for driving in certain areas.

We note, finally, that the location of the driver's most recent stop affects African Americans', but not whites', fear of driving in some areas. African Americans are more fearful of driving in some areas if their most recent stop was in the inner ring of suburbs bordering the core ur-

TABLE 7.2. **Limits to freedom of travel: the effect of investigatory stops.**

Characteristic	All drivers	White	African American
Driver's race and experiences:			
African American	2.833****		
	(.387)		
Investigatory stop	1.386***	0.968*	2.133**
	(.435)	(.520)	(.849)
Traffic-safety stop	−0.240	−0.201	−0.659
	(.425)	(.140)	(.894)
Stops over lifetime	0.374	0.112	2.015**
	(.486)	(.539)	(.784)
Indirect experiences:			
Heard stories of	1.425***	1.208**	2.165****
officer disrespect	(.420)	(.522)	(.509)
Log pseudolikelihood	−1068.16	−868.09	−194.34
F (17)	7.55	3.63	4.73
P	<.0001	<.0001	<.0001
N	1416	886	530
Left-censored N	960	698	262
Right-censored N	216	61	155

Note: Results were obtained using Tobit estimation. Reported results are coefficients, with standard errors given in parentheses. Control variables (sex, age, education level, income level, political attitudes [conservative-to-liberal continuum], extent of speeding, rule-abiding driving, vehicle customization, illegal vehicle conditions, vehicle damage, and the percentage of families in poverty and percentage of population who are black in the respondent's jurisdiction of residence) have been omitted for brevity. Data are weighted to adjust for sampling. The dependent variable is an additive index that is not normally distributed. For dependent variables with this characteristic, Tobit is the most appropriate modeling technique (see J. Scott Long, *Regression Models for Categorical and Limited Dependent Variables* [Thousand Oaks, CA: Sage, 1997], 187–216). We have confirmed the results with ordered probit; the results do not differ substantially from those reported here. See the appendix for further discussion.
*$p<.10$; **$p<.05$; ***$p<.01$; ****$p<.001$

ban areas of the metropolitan area.[28] This perception by African American drivers is consistent with the biased stop patterns in the suburbs that we documented in chapter 3.

Racial Identity

Law and law enforcement reflect racial divisions in society. It is also increasingly clear that they contribute to the ongoing marking of racial identities and maintaining racial divisions. The meaning of "race" itself is a social—and thus partly a legal—construction.[29] While this basic insight is well accepted and the subject of many histories of racial identities, whether law contributes to ongoing racial divisions may seem a more open question. For example, to contemporary Americans it is obvious that the notorious Jim Crow laws requiring racial segregation created racial divisions in an earlier era, but it may seem less obvious how law enforcement may do the same thing today.[30]

Still, a growing number of studies suggest that encounters with the law shape racial identities and, even, racial hierarchies.[31] For example, Andrew Penner and Aliya Saperstein analyzed the National Youth Survey panel and found that respondents who had been incarcerated were more likely to self-identify as "black" and to be perceived by their interviewer as "black."[32] (Unemployment and poverty also increased the identification of a respondent as "black.") In a society in which black people are disproportionately sentenced to prison, imprisonment alters the social meaning of race.

What about investigatory police stops? If they disproportionately target black people, do these stops also subtly mark the people stopped in them as "more" black? One way to address this question is to test how the experience of an investigatory stop affects a person's degree of identification with their race. It is well known that people vary considerably in how much their race is important to their sense of identity and how much they feel loyal to members of their race simply because others are of the same race. Psychological studies have demonstrated that experiencing discrimination increases a person's identification with his or her "race."[33] We asked these two questions of the drivers in our study (how important race is to the respondent's sense of who you are, and how much loyalty the respondent feels to members of his or her race), and we combined them into a simple additive index. As a general matter, African Americans report greater racial identification than whites:

TABLE 7.3. **Racial identification: how investigatory stops affect identification with one's "race."**

Experiences	White	African American
Investigatory stop	−1.138**	1.369**
	(.565)	(.671)
Traffic-safety stop	−.324	−.928
	(.388)	(.674)
Stops over lifetime	0.488	.278
	(.651)	(.611)
Control		
Heard stories of officer disrespect	−.069	0.294
	(.522)	(.415)
Log pseudolikelihood	−3329.64	−367.16
F (9)	4.0	1.93
p	<.001	<.05
N	902	542
Left-censored N	103	0
Right-censored N	98	203

Note: Results were obtained using Tobit estimation. Reported results are coefficients, with standard errors given in parentheses. Control variables (sex, age, education level, income level, and political attitudes [conservative-to-liberal continuum]) have been omitted for brevity. Data are weighted to adjust for sampling. The dependent variable is an additive index that is not normally distributed. For dependent variables with this characteristic, Tobit is the most appropriate modeling technique (see J. Scott Long, *Regression Models for Categorical and Limited Dependent Variables* [Thousand Oaks, CA: Sage, 1997], 187–216). We have confirmed the results with ordered probit; the results do not differ substantially from those reported here. See the appendix for further discussion.
$*p < .10; **p < .05; ***p < .01; ****p < .001$

almost 38 percent reported the highest possible level of racial identification, compared to only 11 percent of whites, a difference that is statistically significant. African Americans, given their experience of racial oppression, have strong feelings of membership in a racial class. Whites, by contrast, are less cognizant of the benefits of being white, or "white privilege." Nonetheless, many whites reported that they do identify with their "race." As might be expected by theories of racial construction, the whites who have the strongest explicit identification with being white are somewhat less educated, have lower incomes, and are more politically conservative than those who claim less racial identification.

How, if at all, does the experience of an investigatory stop shape the strength of racial identity? As shown in table 7.3, enduring an investigatory stop *significantly increases* racial identification among African Americans but *significantly decreases* racial identification among whites. These results are found even after controlling for other possible influences on racial identity: level of education, income, political ideology, gender, age, the racial composition of the respondent's city, and whether the respondent has heard stories of police disrespect. Investigatory police stops, which most commonly target African Americans, influence the ongoing social construction of race in the United States by increasing racial identity among blacks and decreasing racial identity among whites. We can only speculate why whites feel less white after an investigatory stop, but such experiences do, for a moment, remove their privilege and expose them to an experience common to African Americans. Donald, a white man, described being followed by a police car for miles while driving with his black girlfriend.[34] He was eventually pulled over for failure to signal a lane change, and that experience confirmed for him that police engage in racial profiling. He clearly felt some sympathy for the African Americans targeted in similar stops, and the experience seemed to increase his identification with African Americans.

*   *   *

Police stops are a great unifier and divider in American society. At some point virtually every driver is pulled over. But beneath this apparent shared experience, police stops also divide Americans into two groups. On the one side are people for whom police stops are the signal form of surveillance and legalized racial subordination. This group is populated largely by African Americans and other racial minorities. On the other side are people for whom police stops are annoyances that, at worst, yield expensive traffic tickets, but which also reaffirm the driver's place as a full citizen in a rule-regulated society. This group is populated largely by whites.

The dividing line is marked by investigatory police stops. They are the police activity that most directly contributes to the enduring racial dividing line in American society; they help define the meaning of "race." They do so by subtly marking less-than-full membership in the community. Some people in any society have no doubt that they are full members of the community, deserving to be treated with dignity and respect by officials and peers alike. Others feel that that they are not respected as full members of the community; their standing and status are tenuous. Investigatory police stops not only reflect this racial divide but actively affirm and deepen it.

The difference is perhaps best illustrated by two cases. Billy, a middle-aged black man, who reported being stopped a number of times, was subjected to vehicle searches during two stops and an incident in an investigatory stop in which an officer pointed a gun at his head. After telling of these experiences, he summed up his attitude: "So, that's about all the experiences I have. . . . Fortunately, they haven't been really bad for me."[35] By contrast, Laura, a white woman who reported commonly getting only warnings during traffic-safety stops because she showed the officer her military ID, complained that one officer had ignored the ID and had been "rude" and "hateful"—because, in her words, "His tone— yeah! He kind of acted like he . . . I had told him that I didn't realize it was only 55 through there. When I said [that], he made the comment: 'No, it's 55 on all 2 lane highways in Missouri.' And kind of said it like that in an unpleasant way."[36]

The black driver minimized intrusive and even abusive encounters as not "really bad for me," while the white driver expressed visceral annoyance over an exchange of words in which, by her description, the officer uttered no vulgarity, cast no aspersions, and used no derogatory terms but merely used an "unpleasant" tone. The first reflects a worldview in which the predominant form of police stops are investigatory stops; and they invariably control and subordinate. The second reflects a worldview in which the predominant form of police stops are traffic-safety stops; and they reaffirm one's equal citizenship and liberty within the community and, even, authority over the police.

CHAPTER EIGHT

Toward Racial Justice in Police Stops

> Say nothing and it just perpetuates it. And so I'm a minister, my whole thing
> is whatever you see say something about it. Even if it means that eventually
> that we have to start back to marching, sit-ins, whatever we need to do. You
> just have to start to put a stop to some of this stuff. Because if you say nothing
> or do nothing they . . . you're helping the situation and not stopping it.[1]

On December 14, 2010, 21-year-old Marion Denmon was laid to rest,
the victim of yet another apparent gang killing on Kansas City's
troubled east side. During the funeral at the Macedonia Baptist Church
several carfuls of young men drove up and fired more than seventy gun-
shots, apparently as a show of disrespect.[2] Pandemonium broke out and
some mourners rushed to fire shots at the fleeing vehicles. The police
had been told no violence was expected at the funeral and so they had
stayed away. In a neighborhood all too familiar with shootings, nearly
everybody agreed that this one, outside a church and during a funeral,
had crossed the line. People were outraged. Nonetheless, witnesses
stonewalled police efforts to identify the shooters. Nobody talked with
the police, and no shooters were identified, much less caught. It was not
the first time that Kansas City police faced thorough noncooperation
in their investigations. As the mother of a young man shot only a few
months before the funeral incident and only a short distance away observed, "In our community, people are quick to come and tell the family
of the victim things, but they will not tell the police."[3]

If investigatory stops worked as claimed none of this should have happened. Advocates insist that investigatory stops get guns and drugs off
the streets and make cities safer. They also claim that people and neighborhoods subjected to investigatory stops accept the stops and surveil-

lance so long as officers are professional and courteous. East Kansas City is a testing ground for these claims. The Macedonia Baptist Church is in the heart of the area targeted by the Kansas City Gun Experiment, which, in the early 1990s, offered evidence that investigatory stops get guns off the street and dramatically reduce shootings.[4] Sixteen years later, these stops are everyday occurrences, yet guns abound and shootings continue. The Kansas City Police Department is among the more professionalized in the country and has first-rate systems for training and oversight over officers. But after a generation of investigatory stops, neighborhood residents in east Kansas City so distrust the police that they will not cooperate in investigations even when the crime is a gangland shooting at a church funeral.

This book's concluding message is simple: the benefits of investigatory stops are modest and greatly exaggerated, yet their costs are substantial and largely unrecognized. It is time to end this failed practice. Investigatory stops fail because they violate a widely shared norm of fair treatment.[5] This norm requires that people should be treated as equal, respected members of society and not as second-class outsiders, as participants in a common endeavor and not as objects to be controlled and manipulated. When police enforcement activities respect this fundamental norm, as they do in some collaborative, carefully targeted efforts that we will summarize below, members of the community are drawn into cooperation with the police and public safety is enhanced. When police enforcement activities violate this fundamental norm, as they do in investigatory stops, members of the community learn to distrust the police, putting public safety at risk.

Although police widely believe that investigatory stops help fight crime, the evidence supporting this belief is surprisingly thin. To be sure, officers sometimes seize guns and illegal drugs in these stops. But this occurs rarely; most people subjected to these stops are innocent and no weapon or contraband is seized. It is easier to remember the successful stops: Jon Gould and Stephen Mastrofski found that officers unintentionally exaggerate how often they find drugs or guns.[6] In truth, it is extremely rare.

Nor is it clear that investigatory stops help to reduce the crime rate more generally, as the pioneering Kansas City Gun Experiment claimed. In that study, police targeted a neighborhood for widespread investigatory stops and were able to seize more guns than in other neighborhoods. Shootings declined in the targeted neighborhood for a brief period. Sev-

eral attempts to replicate the experiment's findings in other cities, however, yielded unimpressive results. An attempt in Indianapolis compared
two styles of proactive stops, employed in two different neighborhoods.[7]
In one Indianapolis neighborhood the police made widespread investigatory stops of large numbers of drivers, as had been done in Kansas
City; in the other, the police targeted a small number of especially suspicious drivers and pedestrians, and also made home visits to check up
on violent criminal convicts who were on probation. Only in the second
neighborhood, in which targeted enforcement was employed, was there
a reduction in crime. In a second replication, in Pittsburgh, the study authors reported modest crime reduction effects from police stops, but, as
a recent scientific review concluded, these effects were probably exaggerated and police stops in fact may have led to no significant decline in
crime.[8]

But what about New York City? It is widely claimed that investigatory
stops contributed to New York's much publicized success in reducing violent crime—but this, too, is dubious. The most careful analysis of what
has worked in New York, by criminologist Franklin Zimring, concluded
that widespread street stops of pedestrians do little to reduce crime.[9] Instead, reductions in violent crime are due to other, less-publicized police
enforcement efforts that carefully target the actual perpetrators of violent crime.

It is increasingly clear that the most effective kinds of police enforcement are efforts that respect procedural justice norms, as the research of
David M. Kennedy on gang shootings has shown, and as careful meta-
analyses have confirmed.[10] First, police enforcement is most effective
when it carefully targets serious criminals rather than stopping large
numbers of people, many of whom are innocent, in the hope of appre-
hending the few who are guilty. Targeting many to get the few is unjust
and, as we will emphasize below, widely resented. Second, police effectiveness is enhanced when the police work closely with community members and groups to identify serious violators and to bring pressure on
them to cease their predations. Even in low-income, high-crime neighborhoods only a small number of people commit the vast majority of the
crime. Police and community members often know or can find out who
these serious criminals are. Cooperation from community members is
often crucial for identifying criminals and for bringing social pressure
to bear on them in ways that ratify and amplify the efforts of the po-

lice. Community members are more likely to participate in efforts to control serious crime when police treat them as respected participants in a shared effort. Scattershot investigatory stops of people who merely look suspicious are at best a distraction from more focused police efforts. They are not effective.

Cascading Injustice

Scattershot investigatory stops also have serious costs. The most obvious of these is that investigatory stops, even if ostensibly focused on those who look suspicious, target innocent people for highly invasive intrusions aimed at catching the few who are serious criminals. And most of these innocent victims are racial minorities. While trying to prevent a gangland shooting or interdict a major drug shipment, officers day in and day out stop hundreds of innocent people like Deana and Lisa and Joe. As we have shown, African Americans are almost *three times* more likely than whites to be stopped in investigatory police stops. Dennis Rosenbaum observes, and we have confirmed, that "the vast majority of persons who are inconvenienced (if not offended) by these stops are innocent persons of color and limited means."[11] The investigatory stop sacrifices long-term engagement and effectiveness for a short-term "bust."

Racial disparities mar most aspects of U.S. social life from employment to lifespan—but few are as wide as the disparity in who is pulled over in investigatory stops. For example, African Americans suffering from heart disease are about 13 percent less likely than whites to be given angioplasties and about 33 percent less likely to be treated with bypass surgery, disparities that have caused widespread concern.[12] By comparison, African Americans are 270 percent more likely than whites to be subjected to an investigatory stop. This in itself is a deep racial injustice.

The racial disparity in who is stopped is compounded in what happens *during* the investigatory stop. During these stops the police act significantly more intrusively toward African Americans, and especially African American men, than whites. Officers may carry out a range of investigatory intrusions: they may ask drivers probing questions about where they are going and why they are in the neighborhood, may search the driver and the vehicle on the basis of visible evidence of criminality or consent of the driver, may handcuff the driver, may conduct tests for sobriety, and ultimately may arrest the driver. Typically officers proceed further with these intrusions as their suspicions grow after their initial contacts with the driver or passengers. Just as officers are vastly more likely to *stop* African American drivers than whites when carrying out investigatory stops, officers also proceed further with investigatory intrusions during stops of African American drivers. Thus, officers are *five times* more likely to search African Americans than whites, but they are much less likely to find a gun or contraband in searches of African Americans. These deeper intrusions, too, are a racial injustice.

Another cost is that widespread investigatory stops undermine trust in police and willingness to call the police for help. Even after taking into account other factors that contribute to lower levels of trust in the police, among them peoples' distrust of authority, lower levels of education, and higher rates of crime in their community, the experience of an investigatory police stop powerfully erodes peoples' trust in the police. Widespread stops, searches, questioning, and arrests, as Rosenbaum emphasizes, "drive a wedge between the police and the community, as the latter can begin to feel like targets rather than partners."[13] Like people everywhere, residents of low-income, high-crime communities appreciate police enforcement, but they also value freedom from intrusion and fair treatment; they resent being treated like criminals.

Ultimately, as Dennis Rosenbaum concludes, these stops erode peoples' sense of empowerment and "run the risk of further undermining social control and a community's capacity for self-regulation."[14] Worse, they may so embitter neighborhood residents toward the police that people decline to cooperate in police investigations or even come to share a norm, like "no snitching," *against* cooperating with the police.[15] The basic observation of a generation of research is that neighborhood cooperation, both among residents and with the police, is a key condition for reducing the rate of crime. Crime is controlled primarily by communities working with the police, and not the police acting on their own.[16] Addressing persistent poverty and lack of opportunity is critical as well. But even among very poor areas, crime rates are considerably lower where residents share a sense of efficacy, work together to address disorder, call the police to help out with problems, and cooperate with police investigations.[17] Police depend on cooperation to solve crimes. When people are not willing to call the police or cooperate with police investigations the police have very little to go on. The Macedonia Baptist Church shooting remains unsolved simply because people were not willing to talk to the police. Investigatory stops thus rest on the professional illusion that policing can go it alone.

Strikingly, experiencing a traffic-safety stop does *not* erode peoples' trust in the police, and that difference tells us something important. It is simply not the case that every type of experience with the police or even every kind of police enforcement activity erodes trust in the police. *Investigatory* stops erode trust; other stops, which people recognize to be legitimate efforts to enforce the law, do not erode trust. Among African American drivers, in fact, when an officer gives the driver a lecture on driving safety, the driver is considerably more likely to evaluate the stop positively. Getting a driving-safety lecture confirms to the stopped driver that the stop's purpose was legitimate.

Drivers are well aware of the profound racial disparities in police stops, and this awareness shapes perceptions of the police and their own place in society. No one likes to be pulled over, but police stops teach different lessons to African Americans and whites. They teach African Americans that police stops are unpredictable, arbitrary, and a tool of surveillance. They teach whites that police stops are predictable consequences of unsafe driving, and, remarkably, that even well-deserved stops may lead to being let off with a warning if the driver is respectful and polite to the officer. Police stops confirm whites' common assumption that they are full citizens deserving respect and leniency; they teach African Americans that they are targets of suspicion [18] Police stops tell African Americans that they are not free to travel in some areas and may decrease the likelihood of them voting.[19]

As new laws encourage police to hunt for illegal immigrants and the use of investigatory stops expands to target Latinos, these unjust and antidemocratic patterns, unless deliberately checked, are likely to only become more widespread. Police stops to check for immigration documents will be ethnically framed in the way investigatory stops have been racially framed. Persistent stereotypes that undocumented immigrants are mainly from Latin America will lead officers on the street to be more suspicious of people who appear to be Hispanic or Latino and to ask these people for proof of citizenship. The vast majority of the people asked for papers will be citizens or legal residents. These innocent targets of record requests will resent the question and the implication that they look like less than a full, respected member of society.

They will learn to distrust the police and will be less likely to cooperate with the police. Distrust of the police is likely to be even deeper among undocumented immigrants, undermining willingness to call the police even when the need is great. Ethnic framing of records-requests will reproduce and deepen a growing "racialization" of Latino ethnicity. These processes are sadly predictable.

The Supreme Court's decision in *Arizona v. United States* (2012), upholding that state's requirement that local police officers check people's immigration status, is thus likely to cause real, palpable harm for many ordinary people.[20] To be sure, officers' authority to check for documentation is sharply restricted. Arizona law allows officers to check immigration documentation only in the context of a "lawful stop, detention, or arrest" or other "lawful contact," and so it does not authorize officers to stop people only in order to check for documentation. The court's decision adds further restrictions. It struck down a requirement that people carry documentation of their citizenship or immigration status, and it suggested that officers would be acting consistently with the Constitution only if they contacted federal authorities for documentation during an otherwise legal stop and only if they held the driver while waiting for documentation no longer than necessary to write a typical traffic ticket. These requirements will be difficult to follow in practice; police departments will need to carefully train and oversee officers' activities.[21] It is widely expected that federal immigration authorities are unlikely to respond to requests for documentation within the short window allowed. Police errors, such as holding a driver too long, will expose local police agencies to considerable risk of liability, as rights advocacy groups stand ready to bring lawsuits challenging these stops.

Still, technically there are similar legal restrictions on investigatory stops, and these restrictions have not stopped the daily intrusions and violations documented throughout this book. For example, the Supreme Court's decision in *Whren v. United States* authorizes investigatory vehicle stops only when the officer has a lawful justification for making the stop, precisely the Arizona law's requirement.[22] But Joe, the driver in this book's opening narrative, described a stop in which the officer's stated justification was to conduct a "warrant check," which is not a lawful justification. Eighteen percent of black drivers in our survey reported that the officer gave them *no reason* for making the stop. In these stops officers proceeded to ask intrusive questions and often searched the vehicle. Conceivably the officers in these stops had observed the driver make some minor traffic violation but simply did not state it. It is not hard to find a lawful justification to make a stop. The point is that this technical requirement to have a lawful justification for a stop offers no meaningful limitation on officers' authority to make stops. Likewise, there is nothing in the Court's decision in *Arizona v. United States* that will keep officers from stopping drivers on some pretext, calling the federal immigration authorities for documentation, and then, after waiting without response for fifteen minutes, releasing these drivers. Such harassment will be perfectly legal, and many ordinary people will be harmed in the ways we have documented in this book.

Investigatory stops erode individual liberty, undermine democratic equality, and divide local communities by income, race, and ethnicity. They target those who are mainly racial or ethnic minorities for intrusive surveillance and leave others, who are mainly white, free from this intrusion. To be white is to be honored as an equal member of the community and treated fairly; to be African American or Latino is to be disrespected as less than an equal and subject to manipulation by arbitrary inquisitive power.

The core of the problem is not individual racism among a few officers. It is not simply officers' isolated discretionary choices to stop black people and, increasingly, Latinos and other minorities. It is, instead, an institutionally supported practice celebrated by police professional associations, leaders, and local departments. The practice of investigatory stops is itself the engine that racially frames police and public alike.

Our analysis has a broader implication. Racial disparities are widespread in American society, and we challenge scholars to examine whether institutionalized practices contribute to these disparities in areas other than policing. These disparities are well-known in education, health care, employment, and housing, to name but a few. In many of these areas the explanation for racial disparities is undoubtedly complex, and inequality by race in people's wealth is surely a major factor. But too little attention has been paid to the contribution of institutionalized practices, or, as we have described in this book, how accepted ways of carrying out a policy may be racially neutral on their face but racially framed in their deepest structure and implementation. Wherever racial disparities persist over decades, we challenge researchers and policy makers to assume that this is not simply a legacy of the past but an ongoing recreation of deliberate, if often hidden and unrecognized, practice. Studying these practices would require research carefully designed to get closer to the front-line workers who carry out policy and in the process remake it. This sort of research takes time and is not easily done— but there are some emerging models.[23] Importantly, this sort of research may help identify deliberate policy interventions that could make a real and immediate difference.

A Proposal

Our analysis suggests that the most prominent proposals for addressing racial disparities in police stops will not work. The Supreme Court's current solution is to accept investigatory stops, but prohibit officers from deliberately using a driver's race or ethnicity as the key reason for making a stop. Although an ever-present concern, deliberate racism is only a small part of the problem. The current solution of professional policing organizations with regard to racial disparities in stops is to better train officers to be polite and respectful. While professional courtesy is desirable, it is not nearly enough. Critical scholars like Michelle Alexander argue with considerable justification that no piecemeal reform short of ending the war on drugs and the entire punitive crime-control regime will be enough to address the problem.[24] We are sympathetic to this view. Still, emphasizing this overarching quest may lead too easily to a failure to take smaller steps that can make a real difference and which may become key parts of a comprehensive solution.

The immediate task is to change institutionalized practices that have become the taken-for-granted definitions of professionalism, of what it means to do good police work. These practices embody norms and conceptions of good police work as well as particular rules and training protocols. Changing practice requires confronting the norms and ideas that undergird the prominence of investigatory stops in contemporary policing. It requires acknowledging that racial disparities are endemic to these stops and that current police practice contributes to an epidemic of injustice. As servants of state power, the police have an obligation to confront their role in contributing to and reducing this injustice. Bill Bratton, the former police chief of Los Angeles, New York, and Boston, observed, "If we don't solve the race issue, we'll never solve the other issues. The police have traditionally been the flash point for so many of America's racial problems."[25]

Changing norms and practice will also require the leadership of professional policing to frankly acknowledge and actively promote the message that investigatory stops cause harm. They cause harm even when the officer's street-wise hunch draws attention to a driver or pedestrian and when the officer remains courteous and professional throughout the encounter. The current message from leaders that these stops "work" is at best grossly imbalanced, at worst simply false. Every stop of an innocent person causes direct, palpable harm. Every stop justified by a minor violation, every inquisitive question, every light shined in a passenger compartment, every request for consent to search, every search, and every handcuffing of a person only to release them later causes harm. Investigatory stops *are counterproductive to the core crime-fighting mission of policing.* They also divide our communities by race and ethnicity.

To address these deeply entrenched problems, we propose modest pragmatic steps that can be made *tomorrow.* First, police leaders should promote the professional norm of not stopping drivers or pedestrians except when justified by clear evidence of criminal behavior. A new norm of avoiding car and pedestrian stops (except to sanction bad driving) should become a core part of shared professional knowledge within policing. Officers must have more than a pretextual reason for the vast majority of their stops. Professional associations should convey to their members that stops based on hunches or trivial violations is bad practice. Training academies should make it a core part of their curricula. Officers should be taught it in field training. Departments should remind officers of this lesson on an ongoing basis.

Second, to enforce this requirement, police departments should adopt internal guidelines and systems of oversight governing the decision to make a stop and conduct investigatory intrusions that are modeled on how departments regulate uses of force.[26] Thus, departments should prohibit pretextual stops except when justified by an overriding public safety exigency. To oversee this guidance, departments should require officers in every stop to articulate and record their reason for the stop and departments should conduct internal reviews of these reasons. Departments should strive to make pretextual stops the rare exception rather than the common pattern. Further, a computerized search of the person's name in crime records should be allowed only after the legal basis for the stop is reported and recorded. These recording and oversight procedures would severely limit the use of pretext stops in the hunt for crime and deliberately so—but this is an essential step in limiting the racial bias now so evident in investigatory stops.

The essential third step is to prohibit searches unless based on probable cause to believe a crime has been committed. Consent searches authorize unfettered police discretion to search whoever they wish, even though a driver's consent cannot be considered freely given. Drivers told us that they felt they were "incarcerated" when pulled over and that they had no choice but to consent. Training police officers to solicit permission to search cars or persons takes undue advantage of individuals who are psychologically, if not legally, held by the police. Such consent relies on manipulation, as documented in Charles Remsberg's police training manual.[27] Searches should be conducted only after receiving specific authorization by a supervisor and should be allowed on an articulation of probable cause, or, in other words, particularized evidence to believe the person has committed a crime. This evidence should be recorded and evaluated by supervisors.

Although these three steps are far short of ending the war on drugs or punitive crime policy, they may still seem impractical and unlikely to be adopted. While changing well-established and widely accepted practices is difficult, it *is* possible and has precedent,[28] such as the great expansion of professional systems for limiting and regulating officers' uses of force. Forty years ago the police shot black people at dramatically higher rates than whites.[29] Careful study showed that the greatest disparities occurred in the shootings of people suspected of a felony who were fleeing arrest. Racial disparities were much lower in shootings of people who directly threatened the officer (or another person) with a gun or knife. Shooting at suspected felons who were running away was authorized by the "fleeing felon" shooting rule, an age-old, common-law practice. As controversy over the practice grew, police leaders defended the fleeing felon rule as necessary to help police fight crime. If police could not shoot at people running away, it was said, *everybody* would run. Criminals would escape; crime would flourish.

Perhaps the "fleeing felon" shooting rule facilitated arrests. But resentment and controversy over the practice and studies demonstrating how it was a key source of racial disparities in who was shot underscored the practice's troubling costs. Many of the people shot were African American boys, killed when fleeing from the site of tragically minor

crimes: a $10 burglary, a car taken for a joyride. Reform-oriented police
leaders began forbidding their officers from shooting at anybody merely
for running from a felony arrest; a shot was now justified only in order
to defend a life from an imminent threat. This "defense of life" shooting
rule spread among police departments and soon replaced the old "fleeing felon" rule. The Supreme Court endorsed the new approach and con-
demned the old as unconstitutional.[30] As departments trained their officers in the new approach and enforced it with careful oversight, racial
disparities in shootings declined.

The parallels with the current situation are striking. Here, too, racial disparities are the product of a distinct practice, the investigatory
stop. Here, too, police leaders defend this practice as an essential crime-
fighting tool. Here, too, the human costs of the practice are becoming increasingly clear. And here, too, it is increasingly clear that professional
policing can regulate and limit investigatory stops and can develop alternative crime-fighting strategies, strategies that may be *more* effective
than an outmoded practice.

What is needed is motivation to change. Pressure from litigation, the
public, media, and scholars may play a role. This helped to end the practice of shooting at fleeing felons.[31] It makes a difference in police stops,
too. As Patricia Warren and Donald Tomaskovic-Devey have shown, police departments that have come under pressure from media attention
over racial profiling have reduced the level of racial disparities in police
stops in their jurisdictions.[32] It is certainly possible to carry out traffic
stops without disproportionately stopping minorities, as demonstrated
by our finding that traffic-safety stops are not biased.

Changes in law and court rulings, too, are necessary and could provide an enduring foundation for reforms. Although the Supreme Court's
decision striking down the fleeing felon rule came late in the struggle to
end that practice, it contributed to the widespread acceptance of restric-
tive shooting rules and aided in bringing laggard police departments into
line with the new policy. Long before the Supreme Court's decision, litigation and decisions in lower courts had encouraged police departments
to experiment with methods to control officers' uses of force. Especially
as the courts have helped to legitimate the investigatory stop, they have a
responsibility to acknowledge its costs and help to end the practice. But,
at a time when there is little sentiment for stepping back from the war on
drugs and crime, waiting for changes in judicial rulings may condemn
African Americans, Latinos, and others to several more generations of

aggressive and intrusive policing. This is why we have asked police departments to take the lead. But they should know that unless they do, this problem and pressure for change will only grow.

Ultimately higher-court decisions ratifying a prohibition on pretextual stops will probably be necessary to bring recalcitrant departments into line. Even now, without any meaningful reform underway, our data suggest that smaller departments employ investigatory stops in more discriminatory ways than larger ones. If our proposal gains any traction, it is likely to be adopted more thoroughly by leading professionalized police departments than others. Some system for encouraging recalcitrant departments to stop the practice will be necessary. In the absence of a congressional act, something that seems unlikely, enforcement via judicial ruling may be the best that can be hoped for.

Perhaps a necessary step to encourage police reform is an effective alternative. It may be emerging. Some jurisdictions are restricting consent-based searches, and some are developing "targeted" or "focused" enforcement, in the words of David M. Kennedy and James Forman, to replace the "scattershot, stop-lots-of-people-in-the-hope-of-catching-a-few" practice of investigatory stops.[33] Targeted enforcement relies on close police collaboration with neighborhood groups to identify the individuals who engage in serious criminality. It eschews stopping large numbers of people in the hope that some stops will yield contraband or information leading to big busts. As a consequence, arrests are likely to become less numerous but more effective. At the same time, trust with communities is rebuilt, and the social cost of sweeping large numbers of people into the criminal justice system on low-level charges is reduced.

In the context of these changes in organizational norms, rules governing practice, and oversight procedures, improvements in training regarding implicit bias and stereotypes may be extremely valuable. None of us is free of the burden of implicit bias and stereotypes, but police, who carry out the coercive power of the state, have an added responsibility to confront the corrosive influence of implicit stereotypes. Training on implicit bias is likely to be most useful when tied to the implementation of particular rules. For example, training to reduce racial disparities in shootings was most successful when structured by concrete use-of-force rules that allowed shooting only when necessary to save the life of the officer or a third party. In the context of stops, likewise, training might focus on how justifications for making stops should be similar across different racial groups. Unfortunately, the controversy over racial profiling

has had the opposite effect: it has pushed any discussion of race and policing underground. Research and experience reiterate a discouraging
observation: implicit bias resists change largely because it operates outside our conscious awareness. Recognizing the grip of our stereotypes of
black criminality, violence, and lack of credibility helps bring the unconscious to awareness and may loosen their hold on our judgments.

In addition, any effort to complicate peoples' stereotypes by exposing
police and the rest of us to alternative images of African Americans, especially young black men, erodes the foundations of peoples' bias. This
may be one of the most positive aspects of community-engaged policing of the sort proposed by David M. Kennedy and James Forman, since
even the most dangerous urban enclaves—areas seen by outsiders as a
threatening wasteland—are full of honest, nonviolent, trustworthy people just trying to get by. Working directly with these law-abiding citizens
may diminish the likelihood of seeing people like them as the obvious
targets for a stop.

The proposed changes in police practice may in themselves reduce
the hold of negative stereotypes of African Americans. Stereotypes and
bias are not just cultural relics of our racist past; they are continually
re-created by current policies and practices. All too often, the images
of police officers pulling over black drivers or questioning black pedestrians reinforce the stereotype of black criminality. Deliberately changing police practice can, over time, weaken stereotypes by changing the
complexion of who is stopped by the police. Changing who is stopped
may lead to subtle changes in stereotypes of who is *deserving* of being
stopped by the police.

But we also believe that no list of particular reforms will truly address
the problem without a deep change in law, criminal justice policy, and
police priorities. Deeper still, policies are needed to address the underlying conditions that give rise to high crime rates in some urban areas:
concentrated poverty, poor housing, struggling schools, and lack of jobs.
Without broader changes in public policy, and in *police* policy, officers
on the street will continue to make biased choices. The discretionary
choices of individual officers are not, and should not be, fully control-
lable. Even if the recommendations above are implemented, the officer
on the street is likely to sometimes use minor traffic violations as justifications for making stops simply to carry out warrant checks, ask intrusive questions, or try to build a case for a full-blown search. But individual choices that deviate from policy are not at present the problem—the

problem is police policy. If the leadership of American policing can be persuaded that investigatory stops, like shooting people simply for fleeing a felony arrest, are unprofessional, counterproductive, and morally repugnant, then investigatory stops, too, can be reformed, and we can move closer to racial justice in police stops.

Appendix

This methodological appendix provides information on our survey methods and our narrative interview methods. A copy of our survey instrument is archived and available online. The data and accompanying metadata are also available online.[1]

Survey Sampling and Methods Description: Summary

The data reported in this book are drawn from an original telephone survey of a stratified random sample of adult drivers in the Kansas City metro area (with an oversampling of African Americans). The metro area boundaries span six counties in two states (Leavenworth, Wyandotte, Johnson, and Miami in Kansas; and Clay, Jackson, Cass, and Platte in Missouri) and contain forty-four cities. The survey was designed to elicit measures of the variables specified in our hypotheses and was based on the standard victimization survey approach.[2]

Persons under eighteen years of age and nondrivers were not surveyed. African Americans (stopped or not) and white drivers who had been stopped in the last twelve months were oversampled through the use of screening questions on driving and race of respondent. Potential respondents were randomized within households by asking for the driver who was eighteen or older and had the most recent birthday. The sample of telephone numbers was generated for the Kansas City metropolitan area (KCMA).

The telephone survey was conducted between March 2003 and December 2003. During this time no unusual or noteworthy events occurred in the region or metro area regarding police stops or race. The response rate for the survey was 28 percent. The cooperation rate was 40.3 percent, making the refusal rate 59.7 percent.

Survey Sampling and Methods Detailed Description

Our telephone survey of a stratified random sample of adult drivers focused on the six-county KCMA, a racially and economically diverse region that is well suited to examining our research questions. Many of the forty-four cities in the metro area are quite small by geography and population: only eighteen have populations over ten thousand, and only seven have populations over fifty thousand. The metro area contains a wide distribution of population by the standard socioeconomic categories, as noted in chapter one. The KCMA also crosses a state boundary and includes a number of local jurisdictions; the state of Missouri and several local Kansas jurisdictions require their officers to record and report the race of the driver in all police stops.

Sample Design

Our survey sampling design used a multi-phased process designed to generate estimates of the distribution of traffic stops and citations across the general driving population and for conducting robust statistical tests. In order to achieve these goals, we employed a disproportionate stratified sample that oversampled both black drivers and drivers who have been stopped in the past year. Oversampling was achieved through the use of initial screening questions. Stratification was based on two dichotomous variables: race, limited to black or white, and being stopped, whether or not drivers were stopped during the past twelve months. Thus, the four strata were 1) white–not stopped, 2) white–stopped, 3) black–not stopped, and 4) black–stopped.

In the first stage of our data collection, from March to August 2003, we did not screen by race, but we did screen, as we did throughout the survey, for households with drivers. The first survey question asked: "Have you driven a vehicle in Kansas or Missouri at least once in the past month?" If the respondent answered "no," we asked to speak with someone in the household who did. If no one in the household had driven in the past month, we ended the survey. In August 2003 we achieved an adequate subsample of whites who were not stopped ($n = 862$), and we began screening. After August 2003, we continued to ask all respondents questions about racial identification and whether or not they had been stopped by the police in the last twelve months. In the second phase of data collection we screened out whites who had not been stopped. From August to December 2003 we oversampled blacks and anyone who had been stopped. The screening was designed to provide adequate and efficient cross-strata comparisons.

Thus, we collected race and stop data on a very large, random sample of 8,666 KCMA drivers. The proportion of drivers who fell into each of the 4 strata should, therefore, reflect the portion in the population of the KCMA. These proportions are shown in the "P(pop)" column in table A.1. We collected detailed data on a smaller (but still large), disproportionate sample of 2,346 KCMA drivers that overrepresents blacks and drivers who were stopped. The proportion of each group in this sample in each strata are identified in the "P(samp)" column in table A.1. Where we analyze the sample of all drivers we weight the data to adjust for the disproportionate stratified sampling. Where we analyze the subsample of stopped drivers, this is not necessary.

The overall response rate for our survey was 28 percent, and the overall cooperation rate was 58 percent. While these rates appear low, they are consistent with current trends in survey research.[3] Wherever possible we compared our findings to known demographic characteristics. In general our sample reflects the population of the KCMA. Moreover, the sample is large enough to minimize the effects of sample bias.

Perhaps a key question regarding the validity of our results concerns whether the survey reflects significant response bias. We expect, as is standard on surveys, that we undersampled extremely poor people, particularly poor blacks, by telephone. Nonetheless, extremely poor people are also somewhat less likely to drive a vehicle, and so this problem is not fatal to our design.[4] Moreover, the lower response rates among poor blacks are likely to lead to underestimates rather than overestimates of the extent of racial disparities in police-stop practices. The conservative bias that we expect is consistent with the widely accepted social scientific norm of preferring a type I error, or failing to confirm a true hypothesis, to a type II error, or failing to reject a false hypothesis. Nonetheless, both theory and anecdotal evidence on the issue of racial profiling strongly suggests that, to the extent the problem exists, it is not confined to the lower income brackets but affects African Americans of all income levels.[5] Thus, even with lower response rates from poor blacks, we believe our design reliably captures the potential effect of race on stops and ticketing patterns.

In sum, although surveys can have particular threats to validity and reliability, our approach has several key advantages over past studies that relied on official data compiled from officers' citation records. First, our survey method provides a more complete distribution on key variables; by including both "events" and "nonevents" (for instance, we have self-reported data about the driving habits, socioeconomic status, and race of drivers who have been stopped and those who have not been stopped). Official records contain limited information only about individuals who are ticketed. Second, it provides data on both tickets and stops; official records typically contain data only on tickets. And even in jurisdictions that require officers to record the race of drivers who are stopped but not ticketed, officers retain very broad discretion in practice over whether to report a stop and the race of the driver. The lack of reliable official data on traffic stops that do not result in tickets is especially problematic because it is possible that profiling is more prevalent in decisions to make stops than in decisions to issue tickets, particularly if stops are motivated by reasons of harassment or for pretext.[6] Third, our survey provides data on a host of personal characteristics of drivers; official records typically contain information, at best, only on age, race, and sex of drivers, and many jurisdictions do not even record race. Fourth, it provides a more valid measure of a population base against which to compare ticketing patterns, particularly by offering controls for the extent to which drivers are "at risk" of receiving a ticket, such as drivers' time spent on the road, tendency to violate traffic laws, and the like. Most previous studies have relied on general population as a proxy. We believe a survey is the best method for large-scale data collection aimed at hypothesis testing regarding the effects of citizen characteristics on street-level traffic-law enforcement.

Sample Weighting

Because African Americans and drivers who are white were oversampled, analysis of all respondents required weights designed to account for the sampling. We developed weights based on our random draws of respondents from the population of drivers and the characteristics of the general population. Where we analyze the sample of all drivers, we weight the data to adjust for the disproportionate stratified sampling.

TABLE A.I **Sample weights.**

Driver stopped	P (pop)	P (samp)	WF
White, not stopped	0.769	0.387	1.99
White, stopped	0.106	0.223	0.48
African American, not stopped	0.095	0.296	0.32
African American, stopped	0.030	0.095	0.32
	Sum = 1.000	1.001	

Where we analyze the subsample of stopped drivers, this is not necessary. Our weights are listed in table A.I.

Measure of Respondents' Race

We used three measures of the respondents' race. The primary measure in all analyses reported in this book was respondents' answers to the survey question : "If you met someone who did not know you, what race do you think they would think you are?" Response options were: "white or Caucasian," "black or African American," "Asian or Pacific Islander," "American Indian or Native American or Eskimo," "Hispanic or Latino," or "some other race." Respondents were allowed to choose more than one category. We used this measure as our primary measure of race because it best represents the perspective on the driver's race as viewed by a police officer on the street.

A second measure was the standard "race" question used in many surveys: Do you consider yourself white or Caucasian, black or African American, Asian or Pacific Islander, American Indian or Native American or Eskimo, Hispanic or Latino, or some other race? Responses to these two alternative questions regarding respondents' race differed only slightly.

We also extensively tested for the influence of a third measure of respondents' race "street style." We measured this with a series of survey questions using Likert scales in which we asked respondents: "Next I'm going to list several types of people who have different personal styles. Could you tell me how much you look like them." These street styles listed were lawyer or doctor; construction worker; twentysomething single; retiree; suburban parent; hip-hop star or deejay; college student; someone in the military; working person trying to make ends meet; businessperson; street bum; music star; artist or intellectual; professional athlete; and factory worker.

We expected that a respondent's street style—either alone or in conjunction with his or her race, age, or gender—would be associated in some way with whether or how often he or she was stopped by the police or treated by the police during the stop. We were unable to observe any such influence. We tried individual measures of street style; factors extracted from the series of questions; interactions between individual measures and race; and interactions between factors and race. *No measure of street style, either alone or in conjunction with race, age, or gender was significantly associated with any measure of treatment by the police: being stopped, intrusions and sanctions, or officer demeanor.* Simply put, although we tried in various ways, we could not find that the police treated someone who looked like a black doctor differently from someone who looked like a black hip-hop star.

Narrative Methods

We built our sample of respondents for the narratives from among the sample of drivers who reported in our survey that they had been stopped in the past year and whose race is either white or black. In order to recontact respondents for in-depth interviewing, we closed the random sample survey by asking, "Would you be willing to answer additional questions at a future date?" Eighty-seven percent answered "yes"; we asked for the first names of those open to the follow up interview. From this large group we created a purposive sample designed to increase the heterogeneity of respondents, particularly on dimensions that proved significant in our statistical analyses. Based on their survey responses we stratified by race (black or white), sex, driving behavior (risky or safe, on a multi-item additive scale), and age (18–25 vs. 26–49).[7] The pool of possible respondents was 184. Of these, we completed in-depth interviews with 35, of whom 19 were white and 16 were black.[8] Thus, those participating in the in-depth interviews were initially selected randomly. The pool was purposely narrowed based on demographics and not on their description of the stop experience. Accordingly, we are reasonably confident that the narratives reported in this book are not systematically biased with regard to respondents' experience of being stopped by the police.

The narrative interviews were conducted by telephone in 2005 and 2006. Our interviewing protocol was semi-structured and open-ended. After a standard introduction, the interviewer asked the respondent to describe a police traffic stop that the respondent had experienced, from the moment the respondent first was aware of the presence of a police officer to the time he or she was free to drive away. Because our purpose was to elicit how drivers frame and perceive the experience of traffic stops, the interviewer asked the respondent to describe any "memorable" stop that he or she had experienced, thus allowing the driver to select a stop that held some significance. Many respondents described several traffic stops. Although most of the reported experiences occurred within the previous six to seven years, at least one occurred as early as the mid-1970s. After the respondent had finished telling stories of stops, the interviewer asked a series of standard questions focusing particularly on perceptions of whether the police treat everybody fairly, with follow-up probes for bias on the basis of sex, age, and race.

Statistical Methodology Underlying the Reported Observations

The following discussion provides additional methodological information about the procedures underlying key figures and tables, in the order in which they appear by chapter. All equations were run using Stata/SE version 12.0.

Chapter 3: "The Decision to Stop a Driver"

Figure 3.1 shows drivers' responses to survey questions 68 through 90. We coded the following reasons for the stop as *traffic-safety justifications*: speeding ≥ 7 mph over the posted limit, failure to stop at sign or light, dangerous driving, suspicion of impaired driving, roadside check for impairment, failure to turn on lights at night, and a small number of miscellaneous, safety-related reasons. We coded the following reasons for the stop as *investigatory justifications*: no reason given, speeding <7 mph over the posted limit, expired license plate or tag, vehicle equipment violation, failure to signal turn, failure to signal lane change, license plate light out, check of license/registration, driving too slow, warrant check, suspicion of criminal activity, failure to dim high beams, and a small number of miscellaneous, highly discretionary justifications.

Table 3.1 is based on logit regression models that regress various independent variables on three dichotomous dependent variables: whether the driver was stopped in the past twelve months with a) a *speeding* justification, b) a general *traffic-safety* justification (including speeding), or c) an *investigatory* justification. The data are weighted to adjust for sampling. The speeding stops were those in which the officer alleged a speed of ≥7 mph over the posted limit. The traffic-safety stops were those in which the officer alleged any one (or more) of the traffic-safety justifications identified in the discussion of figure 3.1. The investigatory stops were those in which the officer provided a justification identified as an investigatory justification in the discussion of figure 3.1 and *alleged no traffic-safety violation*. The independent variables were drawn from drivers' responses to survey questions. The driver's *race* was based on a respondent's self-report of how a person who does not know the respondent would categorize a respondent's race. The driver's gender was based on the interviewer's coding of the respondent's gender at the close of the interview. The driver's *age* was based on the respondent's self-report. The driver's *car value* was based on the respondent's estimate of the vehicle value. We tested these estimates by comparing a sample to the *Kelley Blue Book* value for each vehicle's make, model, and year; the respondents' estimates and *Blue Book* values were highly correlated (Pearson's $r<.90$). The *time spent driving per week* by the driver was based on an addition of the respondent's self-report of the number of minutes he or she spent driving per weekday and per weekend day. The driver's *extent of speeding* was based on the respondent's self-report of the speed he or she tends to drive under three posted conditions: a 65-mph speed limit, a 55-mph speed limit, and a 30-mph speed limit. We converted these responses to percentages of posted speed (thus, 70 in a 65-mph zone was converted to 1.077), and then calculated the arithmetic mean across the three speed categories. This arithmetic mean percentage is the variable *extent of speeding. Rule-abiding driving* was an additive index of responses to that asked how often the respondent violated common rules of the road: (sped up through yellow lights, forgot to dim headlights when approaching an oncoming vehicle, turned without using a turn signal, changed lanes without using a turn signal, drove after consuming a small amount of alcohol, drove while intoxicated, rolled through a stop sign, raced another auto, changed lanes frequently in order to get ahead of slower-moving vehicles, talked on a cell phone while driving, or did not wear a seat belt). The response options were standard four-item Likert scales. *Car damage* was an additive index of responses to questions that determined the extent to which the vehicle the respondent typically drove had various forms of visible damage (mud or road grime, missing hubcap, unrepaired accident damage, significant rust, or faded or chipped paint). *Vehicle customization* was an additive index of responses to survey questions that elicited the extent to which the vehicle the respondent typically drove had customized features (tinted windows, custom wheels, or a stereo with a subwoofer). *Illegal vehicle conditions* was an additive index of responses to questions that figured the extent to which the vehicle the respondent typically drove had conditions that violate the vehicle code (cracked windshield, expired license plate, a damaged or burned-out headlight, or a damaged or burned-out taillight). *Domestic luxury car* was based on responses to survey questions about the make and model of the vehicle the respondent typically drove. The following vehicles were coded as domestic luxury vehicles: all Cadillacs, Lincolns, and Hummers; Buick Park Avenue; Chevrolet Corvette; Chrysler New Yorker; Chrysler Town and Country; and Chrysler Fifth Avenue. All others were coded as not a domestic luxury vehicle. The following vehicles were coded as *foreign luxury vehicles*: all BMWs, Bugatis, Infinitis, Mercedeses, Lexuses, Saabs, and Volvos. All others were coded as not a foreign luxury vehicle.

Figures 3.2 and **3.3** are based on post-estimation analysis of the respective models reported in table 3.1, using the command prvalue in Stata. Regarding the likelihood of being stopped in an investigatory stop, by race and age, confidence intervals by race are reported in figure A.1.

Figure 3.4 is based on post-estimation analysis of the same model reported in table 3.1, but substituting for the dependent variable a dichotomous dependent variable measuring whether the driver has been stopped more than once in the past year (this variable was constructed from responses to survey question "About how many times have you been stopped by the police in the last 12 months while driving?").

Figure 3.5 is based on post-estimation analysis of the investigatory stop model reported in table 3.1, using the command prvalue in Stata.

Figure 3.6 is based on post-estimation analysis of the investigatory stop model reported in table 3.1, using the command prvalue in Stata.

Figure 3.7 is based on a cross-tabulation of type of stop and responses to the survey questions that elicited information about the location of the most recent stop. We used the survey responses to identify the municipal legal jurisdiction in which the stop occurred.

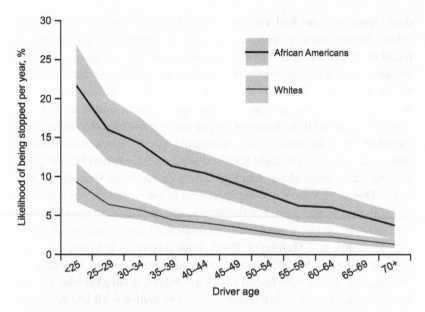

FIGURE A.1. Likelihood of being stopped for an investigatory reason, by race, controlling for all other factors (*N* = 1597). The shaded areas represent the .05 confidence intervals. Estimates generated by post-logit estimation using prvalue (Stata, version 11.)

Chapter 4: "Experiences During the Stop"

Figures 4.1 and **4.2** are based on respondents' answers to survey questions (paraphrased here for brevity): did the officer search your person, frisk you, or pat you down; did the officer search the vehicle; did the officer threaten to arrest you; at any time during the incident were you handcuffed; were you questioned about what you were doing in the area; were you given a verbal warning; were you given a written warning; were you given a traffic ticket or citation; were you tested for drunk or impaired driving; and were you arrested. In these figures, traffic-safety and investigatory stops are distinguished by the measures identified in our discussion of figure 3.1.

Figures 4.3 and **4.4** are based on respondents' answers to survey questions asking to what extent the officer seemed tense or nervous, spoke sternly, spoke loudly, approached the driver more closely than felt comfortable, behaved in an overall hostile manner, said to keep your hands in the open, was friendly, was businesslike, was cold, was surly, said insulting things, used curse words, and threatened the driver physically. Traffic-safety and investigatory stops are distinguished by the measures identified in the discussion of figure 3.1.

Table 4.1 is based on Tobit models of the influence of various factors on the extent to which drivers reported speaking to the officer in ways that we characterized as being disrespectful, by type of stop. The dependent variable, speaking disrespectfully to the officer, is an additive index based on respondents' answers to survey questions: to what extent did you speak with an angry voice to the officer, to what extent did you speak loudly to the officer, and to what extent did you speak sarcastically to the officer, constructed using Stata's alpha command, with variables standardized to mean 0, variance 1 (Cronbach's $\alpha = .75$; factor analysis using the principal factors method indicates that there is one underlying dimension: the eigenvalue of the first factor is 1.38 and of the second factor is −0.05). We used Tobit estimation rather than ordered probit, because the dependent variable is heavily skewed to the low end (most drivers are not openly disrespectful to officers). For this reason, ordered probit is not an appropriate modeling technique, as the core assumption of ordered probit is that the dependent variable is normally distributed. In these conditions, Tobit estimation is preferred.[9]

Chapter 5: "How Investigatory Intrusions are Deliberately Planned (and Racially Based)"

Table 5.3 is based on Tobit models that regress various independent variables on two dependent variables: a) the level of intrusions and sanctions experienced by the driver during the stop, and b) the level of officer disrespect experienced by the driver during the stop.

These dependent variables are additive indices derived from the variables reported in figures 4.1 and 4.2 (intrusions and sanctions) and 4.3 and 4.4 (officer demeanor). These indices were constructed using Stata's alpha command, with variables standardized to mean 0, variance 1 (for the intrusions and sanctions index, Cronbach's $\alpha = .81$; for the officer demeanor index, Cronbach's $\alpha = .88$). Factor analysis using the principal factors method indicates that each of these indices has one primary underlying dimension: for the officer demeanor index, the eigenvalue of the first factor is 5.10 and the second factor is 0.84; for the intrusions and sanctions index, the eigenvalue of the first factor is 3.49 and the second factor is 0.42.

All independent variables are the same as those used in table 3.1, with the addition of three variables: The *number of passengers* in the vehicle at the time of the stop, the *number of officers* present during the stop, and the respondent's *level of distrust in government* (all of which are based on survey answers). We used Tobit estimation rather than ordered probit, because the dependent variables are heavily skewed to the low end (most drivers are let off with low-level sanctions, and most drivers report that the officer was respectful). See figures A.2 and A.3 for histograms of these dependent variables, which show the nonnormal distribution, with cases clustered at the low end of each index. Because of these nonnormal distributions, ordered probit is not an appropriate modeling technique, as the core assumption of ordered probit is that the dependent variable is normally distributed. In these conditions, Tobit estimation is preferred.[10] For the models predicting stop sanctions, the Tobit Akaike information criterion (AIC) = 1.279; the ordered probit AIC = 3.077. For the models predicting officer demeanor, the Tobit AIC = 2.236; the ordered probit AIC = 4.877. The AIC measures indicate that the Tobit models fit the data better than the ordered probit models. As an ancillary check on our results, we reran the models in question using ordered probit, and the results were substantially the same as the reported results using Tobit.

Table 5.4 is based on the same Tobit models as reported in table 5.3, but with two variables added: the level of driver disrespect toward the officer and an interaction term constructed by multiplying the level of

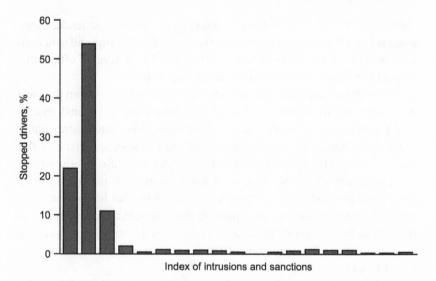

FIGURE A.2. Histogram of the distribution of the index measuring the extent of intrusions and sanctions experienced by stopped drivers ($N = 665$). Lower values on the X axis represent lower levels of intrusions and sanctions.

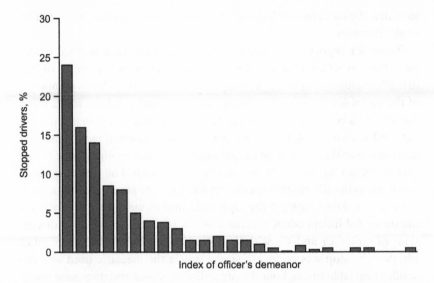

FIGURE A.3. Histogram of the index measuring the officer's demeanor experienced by stopped drivers ($N = 689$). Lower values on the X axis represent a more respectful demeanor.

driver disrespect toward the officer and the driver's race (white = 0; African American = 1). The level of driver disrespect toward the officer is covered in the discussion of table 4.1.

Table 5.5 is based on a logit model in which whether or not the driver was searched is regressed on the full list of independent variables used in the equations reported in tables 5.3 and 5.4. Whether or not the driver was searched is based on the respondents' answers questions regarding the search of person and search of the vehicle.

Figures 5.1 and **5.2** are based on respondents' reports of whether their person or vehicle was searched, by the location of the most recent stop reported by respondents .

Figure 5.3 is based on respondents' reports of whether the officer asked them why they were in the area, by the location of the most recent stop reported by respondents.

Chapter 6: "Evaluating the Stop: Looking Beyond Official Politeness"

Figure 6.1 is based on the respondent's evaluation of the legitimacy of the officer's decision to make the stop, evaluation of the extent to which the officer behaved properly or improperly, and evaluation of the extent to which the outcome of the stop was more severe than the driver felt he or she deserved.

Table 6.1 reports the results of Tobit equations in which we examined the association of independent variables with an index of the driver's evaluation of the legitimacy of the stop. This index is composed of the variables illustrated in figure 6.1. We constructed the index using Stata's alpha command, with variables standardized to mean 0, variance 1 (Cronbach's α = .75; factor analysis using the principal factors method indicates that there is one principal underlying factor: eigenvalue of the first factor is 1.39, and of the second factor is −0.10). The resulting index is not normally distributed (many drivers rate the stop as fair, and thus the index is skewed toward the high end), and so we have used Tobit estimation. All independent variables are as reported in previous discussions of tables 3.1 and 5.3, with the following additions. The measure of whether the stop was an *investigatory stop* is the measure used as a dependent variable throughout the preceding analyses and discussed above under figure 3.1 and Table 3.1. *Officer gave lecture on driving safety* is based on respondents' survey answers. *Severity of stop sanctions* is an index used as a dependent variable in table 5.3 and discussed under that table and figure 4.1. *Officer disrespect* is an index used as a dependent variable in table 5.3 and discussed under that table and figure 4.2. *Lifetime number of stops* is based on respondents' survey answers to the question, "Prior to the past year, how many times in your whole career as a driver would you say you have been pulled over by the police?," divided by the driver's age and multiplied by 10 to bring the coefficients onto the same scale as other independent variables. *Hear stories of disrespect* is based on respondents' answers regarding whether the respondent heard of disrespectful police stops from members of his or her household or others in the past year, transformed into a dichotomous variable coded 1 if the respondent reports hearing from others of a disrespectful police stop and 0 if not. *Political conservatism* is based on respondents' answers to a question that employed a standard Likert scale of the respondent's political attitudes ranging from "strong liberal" to "strong conservative"). *Distrust in authority* is based on respondents' responses to the question, "How much of the time do you think you can trust your local city or county government to do the right thing?" *Poverty rate of jurisdiction* and *black percent of jurisdiction* are the percent of families living below the federal poverty rate and percent of population who are black in the jurisdiction of the respondent's residence; these data were obtained from the 2000 federal census and matched to the jurisdiction of the respondent's reported residence. As the measure of the driver's *economic class* that is most relevant for understanding the driver's evaluation of the stop is his or her *income* level rather than *value of vehicle* (which is the indicator of class that is visible to the officer and thus relevant for understanding officers' decisions), in this equation we used the respondent's *income level* (substituting the value of the respondent's vehicle—the measure of class used in the analyses reported in chapters 3 and 5—does not substantially affect the results; neither measure of class has a statistically significant association with drivers' evaluations of the stop).

Figure 6.3 reports the results of post-regression estimation of the model reported in table 6.1 using the Clarify procedure in Stata. For the independent variables in the figure, "low" represents the twenty-fifth percentile and "high" represents the seventy-fifth percentile, with the following exceptions. "Sanction severity" varies from the minimum on the scale (experienced by some 23 percent of white drivers) to one standard deviation above the mean. "Investigatory stop" estimates the effect of varying from: a) experiencing an investigatory stop on our objective measure of this event the officer *not* giving the driver a lecture on driving safety, to b) not experiencing an investigatory stop and the officer giving the driver a lecture on driving safety (both of these variables are dichotomous). Ordinary least squares regression was used as the estimation technique, because Clarify does not support Tobit estimation. OLS regression is acceptable for this purpose in the present case. The AIC is lower for the OLS model (white drivers, AIC = 550.4; black drivers, AIC = 249.4) than for the Tobit model (white drivers, AIC = 615.8; black drivers, AIC = 278.4), which, in turn are lower than those for the ordered probit model (white drivers, AIC = 1,250.7; black drivers, AIC = 526.5).

Chapter 7: "The Broader Lessons (and Harms) of Police Stops"

Figure 7.1 is based on respondents' answers to the following question: "Tell me how strongly would you agree or disagree with the following statements . . . The local police are out to get people like me."

Figure 7.2 is based on respondents' answers to the following question: "Tell me how strongly would you agree or disagree with the following statements . . . If I needed help I would feel comfortable calling the local police."

Figure 7.3 is based on respondents' answers to the questions and statements: "how much of the time do you think you can trust the local police to do the right thing," "how much confidence do you have in the police in your community," "to what extent do the police in the Kansas City area treat people fairly regardless of race," "if I needed help, I would feel comfortable calling the local police," "the local police department does a good job helping and protecting people like me," "I feel that the local police don't care about people like me," "sometimes police make mistakes, but I believe that they are trying hard to be fair and protect everyone," "the local police are rude to people like me," and "the local police are out to get people like me." For each of these questions, we reported the percentage of drivers by race whose response was on the "distrust" side of the midpoint of each question's Likert scale.

Table 7.1 reports the results of several OLS regression equations that examine the influence of various factors on an index of respondents' distrust in the police. The dependent variable is an additive index of the variables summarized in figure 7.3. The index was constructed using the alpha command in Stata, with variables standardized to mean 0, variance 1 (Cronbach's α = .91; factor analysis using the principal factors method indicates that there is one principal factor: eigenvalue of the first factor is 4.65, and of the second factor is 0.24). All independent variables used in the equations have been summarized above. Although the resulting index is somewhat tilted to the lower end (more respondents tend to report trusting rather than distrusting the police), it is not heavily skewed and is not clearly left-censored. The AIC values for the alternative techniques suggest that the OLS models are fitting the data better than the alternatives, as follows, with one exception: black drivers. All drivers: OLS AIC = 2147.76, Tobit AIC = 2212.97; white drivers: OLS AIC = 1255.12, Tobit AIC = 1816.01; black drivers: OLS AIC = 1078.25, Tobit AIC = 370.78. In the case of black drivers, the AIC scores suggest that the Tobit model fits the data better than the OLS model. But the results of the Tobit and OLS models are virtually identical. In each only three independent variables are significantly associated with the dependent variable: whether the driver's most recent stop was an investigatory stop, the number of stops experienced by the driver over his or her lifetime, and whether the driver has heard stories of disrespectful police behavior during a stop. Further, the coefficients for these three variables are virtually identical. Given these substantial similarities, we opted to report the OLS results rather than report OLS results for all drivers and white drivers and Tobit results for blacks.

Table 7.2 is based on Tobit estimation of the influence of several independent variables on drivers' self-reported tendency to avoid driving in some areas for fear of how the police might treat them. The data are weighted to adjust for sampling. The dependent variable, avoiding driving in some areas, is based on drivers' responses to the question, "To what extent have you avoided driving in some areas because of how the police might treat you?" The responses were on a four-point Likert scale. The response curve was bimodal, with large percentages of responses clustered at the two extremes ("never" and "often"). With such a nonnormally distributed dependent variable, ordered probit is not an appropriate modeling technique, as the core assumption of ordered probit is that the dependent variable is normally distributed. In these conditions, Tobit estimation is preferred.[11] We confirmed the reported Tobit results with two alternative models: one using ordered probit and the other in which the dependent variable was converted to a dichotomy and was analyzed with logit estimation. The results of both alternatives were substantially similar to the reported Tobit results. All independent variables have been described in discussions of earlier equations above.

Table 7.3 is based on Tobit estimation of the influence of several independent variables on drivers' self-reported degree of identification with others of their race. The dependent variable is an additive index constructed from drivers' responses to the questions "We are all members of different ethnic or racial groups. Being a member of my ethnic or racial group is very important to me" and "When someone from outside criticizes my ethnic group, it feels like a personal insult." A seven-point Likert scale was employed; the response curve among all drivers and white drivers was bimodal, with large percentages of responses clustered at the two extremes ("strongly disagree" and "strongly agree"). The response curve among African American drivers was skewed toward the top end, with a large percentage of drivers clustered in the "strongly agree" response. With such a nonnormally distributed dependent variable, ordered probit is not an appropriate modeling technique, as the core assumption of ordered probit is that the dependent variable is normally distributed. In these conditions, Tobit estimation is preferred.[12] We confirmed the reported Tobit results with ordered probit. The results were substantially similar to the reported Tobit results. All independent variables have been described in discussions of earlier equations above.

Notes

Chapter 1

1. Charles R. Epp, Steven Maynard-Moody, and Donald P. Haider-Markel, "Driver Interview Archive," in *Reconstructing Law on the Street: Transcripts of Interviews and Focus Groups* (Lawrence, KS: KU ScholarWorks, 2011), 33, http://hdl.handle.net/1808/8544. All of the names of those interviewed have been changed. For most names, pseudonyms were chosen from lists of the most popular names. For distinctly ethnic names, we chose substitutes from lists of popular ethnic names.

2. Epp et al., "Driver Interview Archive," 30–32.

3. Ibid., 70–78.

4. Ibid., 142–48.

5. Ibid., 64–68.

6. Matthew R. Durose, Erica L. Smith, and Patrick A. Langan, *Contacts Between Police and the Public, 2005*, U.S. Department of Justice, Office of Justice Programs no. NCJ 215243 (Washington DC: Bureau of Justice Statistics, 2007).

7. Richard J. Lundman and Robert L. Kaufman, "Driving while Black: Effects of Race, Ethnicity, and Gender on Citizen Self-Reports of Traffic Stops and Police Actions," *Criminology* 41, no. 1 (2003): 195–220.

8. See, e.g., Robin Shepard Engel and Jennifer M. Calnon, "Examining the Influence of Drivers' Characteristics during Traffic Stops with Police: Results From a National Survey," *Justice Quarterly* 21 (2004): 49–90; our data indicate that the stop rate of African American drivers in the Kansas City area is 24 percent per year (compared to 12 percent for whites).

9. Michael C. Dawson, *Behind the Mule* (Princeton, NJ: Princeton University Press, 1994), 56–58; Michael C. Dawson, *Black Visions* (Chicago: University of Chicago Press, 2002).

10. David A. Harris, *Profiles in Injustice: Why Racial Profiling Cannot Work* (New York: New Press, 2002); Andrew Gelman, Jeffrey A. Fagan, and Alex Kiss,

"An Analysis of the New York City Police Department's 'Stop-and-Frisk' Policy in the Context of Claims of Racial Bias," *Journal of the American Statistical Association* 102: (2007): 813–23. Some studies rely on police citation data. These include Michael R. Smith and Matthew Petrocelli, "Racial Profiling? A Multivariate Analysis of Police Traffic Stop Data," *Police Quarterly* 4 (2001): 4–27; Matthew Petrocelli, Alex R. Piquero, and Michael R. Smith, "Conflict Theory and Racial Profiling: An Empirical Analysis of Police Traffic Stop Data," *Journal of Criminal Justice* 31 (2002): 1–11; Byongook Moona and Charles J. Corley, "Driving across Campus: Assessing the Impact of Driver's Race and Gender on Traffic Enforcement Actions," *Journal of Criminal Justice* 35, no. 1 (2007): 29–37; Gary W. Cordner, G. Williams, and M Zuniga, *San Diego Police Department Vehicle Stop Study: Mid-Year Report* (San Diego, CA: City of San Diego, 2000).; Molly Totman and D. Steward, *Searching for Consent: An Analysis of Racial Profiling Data in Texas* (Austin: Texas Criminal Coalition, 2006); Larry K. Gaines, *An Analysis of Traffic Stop Data in the City of Riverside* (Riverside, CA: City of Riverside, 2003); New York Attorney General's Office, *The New York City Police Department's "Stop and Frisk" Practices* (New York: New York Attorney General's Office, 1999); Alpert Group, *Miami-Dade Police Department Racial Profiling Study* (Fort Lee, NJ: The Alpert Group, 2004); William R. Smith et al., "The North Carolina Highway Traffic Study: Final Report to the National Institute of Justice" (Washington, DC: National Institute of Justice, 2004), https://www.ncjrs.gov/pdffiles1/nij/grants/204021.pdf; Brian L. Withrow, "Driving While Different: A Potential Theoretical Explanation for Race-Based Policing," *Criminal Justice Policy Review* 15, no. 3 (2004): 344–64; Illya D. Lichtenberg, "Driving While Black (DWB): Examining Race as a Tool in the War on Drugs," *Police Practice and Research* 7, no. 1 (2006): 49–60. Other studies conduct observations of driving patterns on particular roadways and compare these to police stop records. These include John L. Lamberth, "Revised Statistical Analysis of the Incidence of Police Stops and Arrests of Black Drivers/Travelers on the New Jersey Turnpike Between Exits or Interchanges 1 and 3 from the Years 1998 Through 1991," in *Report of the Defendant's Expert in State v. Pedro Soto, 734 A 2d 350* (NJ Supr Ct. Law Div., 1996). A handful of studies rely on survey data obtained from drivers. These include Engel and Calnon, "Examining the Influence of Drivers' Characteristics during Traffic Stops";Smith et al., *The North Carolina Highway Traffic Study*; EPIC/MRA, *Standard Enforcement—A Michigan Perspective* (Lansing:, Michigan State Police, n.d.), cited in David A. Harris, *Profiles in Injustice: Why Racial Profiling Cannot Work* (New York: New Press, 2002): 72; Bureau of Justice Statistics, *Contacts between Police and the Public: Findings from the 1999 National Survey* (Washington DC: Department of Justice, Office of Justice Programs, 2001); Durose et al., *Contacts Between Police and the Public*; P. A. Langan et al., *Contacts Between Police and the Public: Findings from the 1999 National Survey* (Washington DC: Department of Justice, 2001); Lundman and Kaufman, "Driving While Black."

11. Both the institutional setting of these stops and the laws governing them differ by type of stop. Highway stops are typically conducted by officers of the state police; these forces employ officers who are specially trained to do one thing: conduct stops (and generally encourage safety) on state and federal highways. As part of the war on drugs, many state police agencies have trained their officers to participate in drug interdiction by looking for illegal drug couriers. Stops of drivers on urban and suburban streets are conducted by officers of city police departments; these forces provide a much broader range of services, including but not limited to traffic-safety enforcement and criminal law enforcement. This broader responsibility has led to the use of vehicle stops not only for drug interdiction, as is more typical of the state police, but also for a wide range of criminal investigation purposes. Stops and frisks of pedestrians are conducted mainly by large urban police departments; these stops share the diverse crime-control and investigation purposes of vehicle stops by urban police departments. The case law authorizing vehicle stops for investigative purposes (e.g., *Whren v. U.S.* 517 U.S. 806, 1996) is distinct from the case law authorizing stops and frisks of pedestrians (e.g., *Terry v. Ohio*, 392 U.S. 1, 1968), but in practice these distinct lines of cases blend together in governing officers' actions, as *Terry* authorizes officer pat-downs of drivers in *Whren*-based vehicle stops (see, e.g., David A. Sklansky, *Traffic Stops, Minority Motorists, and the Future of the Fourth Amendment, Supreme Court Review* [1997]: 271).

12. In addition to the studies cited in note 10 above, see John Knowles, Nicola Persico, and Petra Todd, "Racial Bias in Motor Vehicle Searches: Theory and Evidence," *Journal of Political Economy* 109 (2001) : 203–99; Nicola Persico and D .A. Castleman, "Detecting Bias: Using Statistical Evidence to Establish Intentional Discrimination in Racial Profiling Cases," *University of Chicago Legal Forum* (2005): 217–35; Nicola Persico and Petra Todd, "Generalizing the Hit Rates Test for Racial Bias in Law Enforcement, with an Application to Vehicle Searches in Wichita," *Economic Journal* 116 (2006): F351–57.

13. The research on procedural justice is extensive. The leading studies include Tom R. Tyler, *Why People Obey the Law* (New Haven, CT: Yale University Press, 1990); Tom R. Tyler and Yuen J. Huo, *Trust in the Law: Encouraging Public Cooperation With the Police and Courts* (New York: Russell Sage Foundation, 2002); E. Allen Lind and Tom R. Tyler, *The Social Psychology of Procedural Justice* (New York: Plenum Press, 1988).

14. Jerry L. Mashaw, "Administrative Due Process: The Quest for a Dignitary Theory," *Boston University Law Review* 61 (1981): 885; Laurence H. Tribe, *American Constitutional Law*, 2nd ed. (Mineola, NY: Foundation Press, 1988), 666–76; Rebecca Hollander-Blumoff, "The Psychology of Procedural Justice

in the Federal Courts," *Hastings Law Journal* 63 (2011): 127; John D. Castiglione, "Human Dignity Under the Fourth Amendment," *Wisconsin Law Review* (2008): 665.

15. Tribe, *American Constitutional Law*, 666 (original emphasis).

16. Tom R. Tyler, "Procedural Justice, Legitimacy, and the Effective Rule of Law," *Crime and Justice* 30 (2003): 342.

17. William J. Stuntz, "Local Policing after the Terror," *Yale Law Journal* 111 (2002): 2174.

18. Ibid.

19. Sherry F. Colb, "Innocence, Privacy, and Targeting in Fourth Amendment Jurisprudence," *Columbia Law Review* 96 (1996): 1486.

20. Bernard Harcourt, *Against Prediction: Profiling, Policing and Punishing in an Actuarial Age* (Chicago: University of Chicago Press, 2006).

21. Tyler, "Why People Obey the Law."

22. Eduardo Bonilla-Silva, *Racism without Racists: Color-Blind Racism and the Persistence of Racial Inequality in the United States* (Lanham, MD: Rowman and Littlefield, 2003); Patricia G. Devine, "Stereotypes and Prejudice: Their Automatic and Controlled Components," *Journal of Personality and Social Psychology* 56, no. 1 (1989): 5; John F. Dovidio and Samuel L. Gaertner, "On the Nature of Contemporary Prejudice: The Causes, Consequences, and Challenges of Aversive Racism," in *Confronting Racism: The Problem and the Response*, ed. Jennifer L. Eberhardt and Susan T. Fiske, 3–32 (Thousand Oaks, CA: Sage, 1998); Ian Ayres, *Pervasive Prejudice? Unconventional Evidence of Race and Gender Discrimination* (Chicago: University of Chicago Press, 2001); John Knowles, Nicola Persico, and Petra Todd, "Racial Bias in Motor Vehicle Searches: Theory and Evidence," *Journal of Political Economy* 109 (2001): 203–99; Nicola Persico and D. A. Castleman, "Detecting Bias: Using Statistical Evidence to Establish Intentional Discrimination in Racial Profiling Cases," *University of Chicago Legal Forum* (2005): 217–35; Robin S. Engel, "A Critique of the 'Outcome Test' in Racial Profiling Research," *Justice Quarterly* 25, no. 1 (2008) : 1–36.

23. Kevin R. Johnson, "How Racial Profiling in America Became the Law of the Land: *United States v. Brignoni-Ponce* and *Whren v. United States* and the Need for Truly Rebellious Lawyering," *Georgetown Law Journal* 98 (2010): 1005–77.

24. See, e.g., Nicholas J. G. Winter, *Dangerous Frames: How Ideas About Race & Gender Shape Public Opinion* (Chicago: University of Chicago Press, 2008).

25. Lawrence D. Bobo, "Inequalities That Endure? Racial Ideology, American Politics, and the Peculiar Role of Social Science Changing the Terrain of Race and Ethnicity." In *The Changing Terrain of Race and Ethnicity*, ed. Marcia

Krysan, Amanda T. Lewis and T. Forman, 13–42. (New York: Russel Sage Foundation, 2004), 20.

26. Charles Remsberg, *Tactics for Criminal Patrol: Vehicle Stops, Drug Discovery and Officer Survival* (Northbrook, IL: Calibre Press, 1995), 9.

27. Jon B. Gould and Stephen D. Mastrofski, "Suspect Searches: Assessing Police Behavior under the U.S. Constitution," *Criminology and Public Policy* 3, no. 3 (2004): 315–62.

28. Doris Marie Provine, *Unequal under Law: Race in the War on Drugs* (Chicago: University of Chicago Press, 2007).

29. Glenn C. Loury, *Race, Incarceration, and American Values* (Cambridge, MA: MIT Press, 2008), 4.

30. Jonathan Simon, *Governing through Crime: How the War on Crime Transformed American Democracy and Created a Culture of Fear* (New York: Oxford University Press, 2007); Provine, *Unequal under Law*; Marie Gottschalk, *The Prison and the Gallows: The Politics of Mass Incarceration in America* (New York: Cambridge University Press, 2006).

31. The *Guardian* and London School of Economics and Political Science, *Reading the Riots: Investigating England's Summer of Disorder*, http://s3.documentcloud.org/documents/274239/reading-the-riots.pdf (accessed September 17, 2012); Benjamin Bowling and Coretta Phillips, "Disproportionate and Discriminatory: Reviewing the Evidence on Police Stop and Search," *Modern Law Review* 70, no. 6 (2007): 936–61.

32. Stokely Carmichael and Charles Hamilton, *Black Power: The Politics of Liberation* (New York: Random House, 1967); Louis Knowles and Kenneth Prewitt, eds., *Institutional Racism in America* (Englewood Cliffs, NJ: Prentice-Hall, 1969).

33. See, e.g., Tim Berard, "The Neglected Social Psychology of Institutional Racism," *Sociology Compass* 2, no. 2 (2008): 734–64; Coretta Phillips, "Institutional Racism and Ethnic Inequalities: An Expanded Multilevel Framework," *Journal of Social Policy* 40, no. 1 (2011): 173–92.

34. Provine, *Unequal under Law*.

35. Joe Soss, Richard C. Fording, and Sanford F. Schram, *Disciplining the Poor: Neoliberal Paternalism and the Persistent Power of Race* (Chicago: University of Chicago Press, 2011).

36. Paul J. DiMaggio and Walter W. Powell, "The Iron Cage Revisited: Institutional Isomorphism and Collective Rationality in Organizational Fields," *American Sociological Review* 48 (1983): 147–60; Frank Dobbin and John R. Sutton, "The Strength of a Weak State: The Employment Rights Revolution and the Rise of Human Resources Management Divisions." *American Journal of Sociology* 104 (1998): 441–76; Lauren B. Edelman, "Legal Ambiguity and Symbolic Structures: Organizational Mediation of Civil Rights Law," *American*

Journal of Sociology 97 (1992): 1531–76; Lauren Edelman and Marc C. Suchman, "The Legal Environments of Organizations," *Annual Review of Sociology*
23 (1997): 479; Jeannette A. Coyvas and Stefan Jonsson, "Ubiquity and Legitimacy: Disentangling Diffusion and Institutionalization," *Sociological Theory*
29, no. 1 (2011): 27–53.

37. Philip Selznick, introduction to *Leadership in Administration: A Sociological Interpretation* (Berkeley, CA: University of California Press, 1957).

38. Tim Hallett and Marc J. Ventresca, "Inhabited Institutions: Social Interactions and Organizational Forms in Gouldner's 'Patterns of Industrial Bureaucracy,'" *Theory and Society* 35, no. 2 (April 2006): 213–36; Tim Hallett, "The
Myth Incarnate: Recoupling Processes, Turmoil, and Inhabited Institutions in
an Urban Elementary School," *American Sociological Review* 75, no. 1 (2010):
52–74.

39. Kenneth B. Marshall, "Managing Successful Criminal Patrol Interdiction
Programs," *Police Chief*, July 1999, 30–33; George L. Kelling and William H.
Sousa Jr., *Do Police Matter? An Analysis of the Impact of New York City's Po-
lice Reforms* (New York: Manhattan Institute Center for Civic Innovation 2001);
"It's the Cops, Stupid," editorial, *New York Post*, December 19, 2001; Daniel
Levitas, *The Terrorist Next Door: The Militia Movement and the Radical Right*
(New York: St. Martin's Griffin, 2002); National Highway Traffic Safety Admin-
istration, *Traffic Enforcement: Saving Lives and Combating Crime* (Washington
DC: NHTSA, 1995).

40. Ariz. Rev. Stat. Ann. §11–1051.

41. Survey conducted by Latino Decisions for the Center for American Progress Action Fund and America's Voice. See "Latinos Voice Continued Concerns
about S.B. 1070,"August 3, 2012, http://www.americanprogressaction.org/issues/
immigration/news/2012/08/03/11962/latinos-voice-continued-concerns-about-s-
b-1070/ (accessed October 31, 2012).

42. Sanchez's narrative is one of a number gathered by the Rights Working
Group in a series of community hearings conducted around the country on the
topic of people's experiences in police stops, and published in *Faces of Racial
Profiling: A Report from Communities Across America* (Washington DC: Rights
Working Group, 2010), 43, http://www.rightsworkinggroup.org/sites/default/files/
ReportText.pdf (accessed November 2, 2012).

43. For example, Jim Shee, a U.S. citizen of Chinese and Hispanic descent,
reported the following experience: "It was very vivid April the 6th in 2010, I was
leaving a car wash, and I received a text on my way out and so I pulled over and
was answering my text. A couple minutes later I saw the flashing lights behind
my car, and a Phoenix police officer tapping on my window. So I rolled down my
window and he immediately responds, 'Let me see your papers.' So I produced
my papers. He took them out the window, went to the back of the car, must have
called in by his radio and came back a few minutes later, and he said, 'Well,

you're all clear. You're free to go.' I questioned him and I says, 'Why did you stop me?' And I says, 'Well all I was doing was texting, and which I understand the law says that don't text while you're driving so I'm not driving and I'm checking my text. So you stopped me because I look suspicious.' And he says, 'Yeah, but you're free to go now'" ("SB 1070: 'I Look Suspicious," American Civil Liberties Union, http://www.aclu.org/immigrants-rights/sb-1070-i-look-suspicious; accessed October 31, 2012).

44. Crenshaw, "Mapping the Margins: Intersectionality, Identity Politics, and Violence against Women of Color," *Stanford Law Review* 43, No. 6. (1991): 1241–99.

45. Tom Tyler and E. Allan Lind, "A Relational Model of Authority in Groups," *Advances in Experimental Social Psychology* 25 (1992): 115–91;Tom Tyler et al., "Understanding Why the Justice of Group Procedures Matters: A Test of the Psychological Dynamics of the Group-Value Model," *Journal of Personal and Social Psychology* 70 (1996): 913–30.

46. P. J. Henry, "The Role of Group-Based Status in Job Satisfaction: Workplace Respect Matters More for the Stigmatized," *Social Justice Research* 24 (2011): 231–38.

47. See, e.g., Tribe, *Constitutional Law*, 666–76.

48. Joe Soss, "Lessons of Welfare: Policy Design, Political Learning, and Political Action," *American Political Science Review* 93, no. 2 (1999): 363–80.

49. Suzanne Mettler, "Bringing the State Back in to Civic Engagement: Policy Feedback Effects of the GI Bill for World War II Veterans," *American Political Science Review* 96, no. 2 (2002): 351–65; Andrea L. Campbell, *How Policies Make Citizens: Senior Political Activism and the American Welfare State* (Princeton, NJ: Princeton University Press, 2003).

50. Joe Soss, Jacob S. Hacker, and Suzanne Mettler, eds., *Remaking America: Democracy and Public Policy in an Age of Inequality* (New York: Russell Sage Foundation, 2007).

51. Vesla M. Weaver and Amy E. Lerman, "Political Consequences of the Carceral State," *American Political Science Review* 104, no. 4 (November 2010): 817–33.

52. Carl Milazzo and Ron Hansen, "Race Relations in Police Operations: A Legal and Ethical Perspective," paper presented at the 106th Annual Conference, International Association of Chiefs of Police, Charlotte, North Carolina, Oct. 30–Nov. 3, 1999; updated for the Conference of Arizona Chiefs of Police, Feb. 10, 2000.

53. In these densely populated urban centers, such as New York City, police "stop and frisk" practices are similar to the investigatory traffic stop.

54. John Urry, *Mobilities* (Malden, MA: Policy Press, 2007), 116.

55. Ibid., 130.

56. Hannah Arendt, *The Human Condition* (Chicago: University of Chi-

cago Press, 1958); Jügen Habermas, *The Structural Transformation of the Public Sphere: An Inquiry into a Category of Bourgeois Society* (Cambridge, MA: MIT Press, 1992).

57. Mimi Sheller and John Urry, "The City and the Car," *International Journal of Urban and Regional Research* 24, no. 4 (December 2000): 746.

58. Calculated from Table S0802, "Means of Transportation to Work by Selected Characteristics," U.S. Census Bureau, *American Community Survey Three-Year Estimates 2007–2009*, http://factfinder2.census.gov/faces/tableservices/jsf/pages/productview.xhtml?pid=ACS_11_1YR_S0802&prodType=table.

59. Jeremy Packer, *Mobility without Mayhem: Safety, Cars, and Citizenship* (Durham, NC: Duke University Press, 2008), 5.

60. Thomas J. Sugrue, "Driving While Black: The Car and Race Relations in Modern America," Automobile in American Life and Society website, http://www.autolife.umd.umich.edu/Race/R_Casestudy/R_Casestudy.htm.

61. Ibid.

62. Packer, *Mobility without Mayhem*, 5.

63. Ibid., 196.

64. Sugrue, "Driving While Black."

65. Ben Chappell, *Lowrider Space: Aesthetics and Politics of Mexican American Custom Cars* (Austin: University of Texas Press, 2012).

66. Packer, *Mobility without Mayhem*, 210–211.

67. Sugrue, "Driving While Black."

68. Julia C. Wells, *We Now Demand! The History of Women's Resistance to Pass Laws in South Africa* (Johannesburg, South Africa: Witwatersrand University Press, 2001), 5–6.

69. T. R. Reed and Darryl Fears, "Driver's Licenses Curtailed as Identification," *Washington Post*, Sunday, April 17, 2005.

70. "Immigration Driver's License Restrictions Challenged in Some States," *Immigrants Rights Update* 16, no. 6 (October 21 2002): 13, http://www.nilc.org/2007iru.html#a02.

71. United States General Accounting Office, "Racial Profiling: Limited Data Available on Motorist Stops," in *Report to the Honorable James E. Clyburn, Chairman Congressional Black Caucus* (Washington, DC: General Accounting Office, 2000); David A. Harris, "When Success Breeds Attack: The Coming Backlash Against Racial Profiling Studies," *Michigan Journal of Race & Law* 6 (2001): 265; Samuel Walker, "Searching for the Denominator: Problems with Police Traffic Stop Data and an Early Warning System Solution," *Justice Research and Policy* 3 (2001): 63–95.

72. See later chapters for discussion; see especially Lundman and Kaufman, "Driving While Black; Smith et al. *The North Carolina Highway Traffic Study*; and Engel and Calnon, "Drivers' Characteristics during Traffic Stops." The full

text of our survey of drivers is available in "Kansas City Driving Survey: Selected Items from Questionnaire," *Reconstructing Law on the Street* (Lawrence, KS: KU ScholarWorks, 2011), http://hdl.handle.net/1808/8544.

73. Richard Delgado, "Storytelling for Oppositionists and Others: A Plea for Narrative," *Michigan Law Review* 87 (1989): 2411–41; Mario L. Barnes, "Black Women's Stories and the Criminal Law: Restating the Power of Narrative," *U.C. Davis Law Review* 39 (2006): 941–89.

74. See, e.g., Gary Webb, "DWB: Tracking Unspoken Law Enforcement Racism," *Esquire* April 1, 1999, 118–27.

75. Lundman and Kaufman, "Driving While Black"; Engel and Calnon, "Drivers' Characteristics during Traffic Stops."

76. Michelle Alexander, *The New Jim Crow: Mass Incarceration in the Age of Colorblindness* (New York: New Press, 2010); Michael Tonry, *Punishing Race: A Continuing American Dilemma* (New York: Oxford University Press, 2011); Jerome G. Miller, *Search and Destroy: African American Males in the Criminal Justice System*, 2nd[d] ed. (New York: Cambridge University Press, 2011).

77. United States Census Bureau, "Census 2000, Summary File 3, Table P53, Median Household Income in 1999," (Washington, DC: Census Bureau, 2000). For a full statistical portrait of the Kansas City Metro Area in 2000, see Brookings Institution Center on Urban and Metropolitan Studies, "Kansas City in Focus: A Profile from Census 2000," in *Living Cities: The National Community Development Initiative* (Washington, DC: The Brookings Institution, 2003).

78. Los Angeles: Ian Ayres and Jonathan Borowsky, *A Study of Racially Disparate Outcomes in the Los Angeles Police Department* (Los Angeles: American Civil Liberties Union of Southern California, 2008), http://islandia.law.yale.edu/ayres/Ayres%20LAPD%20Report.pdf; New York City: Andrew Gelman, Jeffrey A. Fagan, and Alex Kiss, "An Analysis of the New York City Police Department's 'Stop-and-Frisk' Policy in the Context of Claims of Racial Bias," *Journal of the American Statistical Association* 102 (2007): 813–23; Wichita, Kansas: Brian L. Withrow, "Race-Based Policing: A Descriptive Analysis of the Wichita Stop Study," *Police Practice and Research* 5, no. 3 (2004): 223–40; St. Louis, Missouri: Jeff Rojek, Richard Rosenfeld, and Scott Decker, "The Influence Of Driver's Race on Traffic Stops in Missouri, *Police Quarterly* 7, no. 1 (2004): 126–47; Boston: Kate Antonovics and Brian G. Knight, "A New Look at Racial Profiling: Evidence from the Boston Police Department," *Review of Economics and Statistics*, 91, no. 1 (2009): 163–77; New Jersey: Peter Verniero and Paul H. Zoubek, "Interim Report of the State Police Review Team Regarding Allegations of Racial Profiling" (Newark: New Jersey Office of the Attorney General, 1999); Louisiana: Jim Ruiz and Matthew Woessner, "Profiling, Cajun Style: Racial and Demographic Profiling in Louisiana's War on Drugs," *International Journal of Police Science & Management* 8, no. 3 (2006): 176–97.

79. Others included Wyoming, Louisiana, Utah, Virginia, and North Carolina, South Dakota, and the provincial police of Ontario, Canada.

80. Other city or county departments included Harrison County, MS; Blackhawk County, IA; Yavapai County, AZ; Baton Rouge, LA; Schoharie County, NY; Lansing, IL; Anson County, NC; Alice, TX; Wildwood, FL; Shaker Heights, OH; Millcreek Township, PA; Milwaukee County, WI; Butts County, GA; Calgary, Alberta, Canada; Ortero County, NM; Orange County, FL; Fairmont, IL; Lake County, FL; Milwaukee, WI; Vancouver, BC, Canada; Sevier County, TN; Coconut Creek, FL; Montgomery County, MD; Dearborn, MI; Los Angeles County, CA; Wauwatosa, WI; Fulton County, GA; and Phelps County, MO.

81. American Anthropological Association, "Statement on 'Race,'" May 17, 1998, http://www.aaanet.org/stmts/racepp.htm; American Sociological Association, *The Importance of Collecting Data and Doing Social Scientific Research on Race* (Washington DC: American Sociological Association, 2003); Laura E. Gómez, "A Tale of Two Genres: On the Real and Ideal Links between Law and Society and Critical Race Theory," in *The Blackwell Companion to Law and Society*, ed. Austin Sarat, 453–70 (Malden, MA: Blackwell Publishing, 2004); Laura E. Gómez, "Understanding Law and Race as Mutually Constitutive: An Invitation to Explore an Emerging Field," *Annual Review of Law and Social Science* 6 (2010): 487–505; Taeku Lee, "Race, Immigration, and the Identity-to-Politics Link," *Annual Review of Political Science* 11 (2008): 457–78; Taeku Lee, "Between Social Theory and Social Science Practice: Toward a New Approach to the Survey Measurement of 'Race,'" in *Measuring Identity: A Guide for Social Scientists*, ed. Rawi Abdelal et al., 113–44 (Cambridge: Cambridge University Press, 2009); Osagie K. Obasogie, "Race in Law and Society: A Critique," in *Race, Law and Society*, ed. Ian Haney López, 445–64 (Burlington, VT: Ashgate, 2007); Aliya Saperstein, "(Re)Modeling Race: Moving from Intrinsic Characteristic to Multidimensional Marker of Status," in *Racism in Post-Race America: New Theories, New Directions*, ed. Charles Gallagher, 335–50 (Chapel Hill, NC: Social Forces Publishing, 2008).

82. Epp et al., "Kansas City Driving Survey."

83. Michael Omi and Howard Winant, *Racial Formation in the United States: from the 1960s to the 1990s*, 2nd ed. (New York: Routledge, 1994).

Chapter 2

1. Mark C. Suchman, "Managing Legitimacy: Strategic and Institutional Approaches," *Academy of Management Review* 20 (1995): 574; see also Philip Selznick, *Leadership in Administration* (New York: Harper and Row, 1957), 17. For a general discussion, see Cathryn Johnson, Timothy J. Dowd, and Cecilia L.

Ridgeway, "Legitimacy as a Social Process," *Annual Review of Sociology* 32 (2006): 53–78.

2. National Advisory Commission on Civil Disorders—Kerner Commission, *Report of the National Advisory Commission on Civil Disorders* (Washington DC: Government Printing Office, 1968).

3. Ibid.

4. Ibid.

5. Robert M. Fogelson, *Big City Police* (Cambridge, MA: Harvard University Press, 1977); Samuel Walker, *A Critical History of Police Reform: The Emergence of Professionalism* (Lexington, MA: Lexington Books, 1977).

6. National Advisory Commission on Civil Disorders—Kerner Commission, *Report of the National Advisory Commission on Civil Disorders*; Harlan Hahn and Judson L. Jeffries, *Urban America and Its Police: From the Post Colonial Era Through the Turbulent 1960s* (Boulder: University Press of Colorado, 2003.

7. David Alan Sklansky, "Not Your Father's Police Department: Making Sense of the New Demographics of Law Enforcement," *Journal of Criminal Law and Criminology* 96, no. 3 (Spring 2006): 1209–243.

8. Wesley Skogan and Susan M. Hartnett, *Community Policing: Chicago Style* (New York: Oxford University Press, 1997); Jack R. Greene, "Community Policing in America: Changing the Nature, Structure, and Function of the Police," in *Policies, Processes, and Decisions of the Criminal Justice System: Criminal Justice*, vol. 3, ed. Juley Horney, 299–370 (Washington, DC: U.S. Department of Justice, 2000); Lori Fridell and M. A. Wycoff, eds., *Community Policing: The Past, Present and Future* (Washington DC: The Annie E. Casey Foundation and the Police Executive Research Forum, 2004).

9. Charles R. Epp, *Making Rights Real: Activists, Bureaucrats, and the Creation of the Legalistic State* (Chicago: University of Chicago Press, 2009); Samuel Walker, *The New World of Police Accountability* (Thousand Oaks, CA: Sage, 2005); Samuel Walker, *Taming the System* (New York: Oxford University Press, 1993).

10. For a fascinating analysis of these dynamics, see Jeannine Bell, *Policing Hatred: Law Enforcement, Civil Rights, and Hate Crime* (New York: New York University Press, 2002).

11. Fogelson, *Big City Police*; Walker, *A Critical History of Police Reform*.

12. Jerome H. Skolnick, *Justice without Trial: Law Enforcement in Democratic Society*, 3rd ed. (New York: MacMillan, 1994); Michael H. Tonry, *Punishing Race: A Continuing American Dilemma* (New York: Oxford University Press, 2011).

13. Skolnick, *Justice without Trial*.

14. Joseph D. Lohman and Gordon E. Misner, *The Police and the Community* (Washington DC: Government Printing Office, 1966), 127–34; Hahn and

Jeffries, *Urban America and Its Police*; Samuel Walker, "Origins of the Contemporary Criminal Justice Paradigm: The American Bar Foundation Survey, 1953–1969," *Justice Quarterly* 9 (1992): 57–58.

15. National Advisory Commission on Civil Disorders—Kerner Commission, *Report of the National Advisory Commission on Civil Disorders*.

16. Angus Campbell and Howard Schuman, "Racial Attitudes in Fifteen American Cities," in *Supplemental Studies for the National Advisory Commission on Civil Disorders*, by the National Advisory Commission on Civil Disorders (Washington DC: Government Printing Office, 1969), table 4.

17. Elijah Anderson, *A Place on the Corner* (Chicago: University of Chicago Press, 1978), 2; see also Terry Williams, *Crackhouse* (Reading, MA: Addison Wesley, 1992).

18. George L. Kelling et al., *The Kansas City Preventive Patrol Experiment: A Summary Report* (Washington DC: Police Foundation, 1974).

19. James Q. Wilson and Barbara Boland, "The Effect of Police on Crime," *Law & Society Review* 12, no. 3 (1978): 370–73.

20. Ibid., 373.

21. Gary W. Cordner, "The Effects of Directed Patrol: A Natural Quasi-Experiment in Pontiac," in *Contemporary Issues in Law Enforcement*, ed. James J. Fyfe (Beverly Hills, CA: Sage, 1981): 40–41, 52; Robert J. Sampson and Jacqueline Cohen, "Deterrent Effects of the Police on Crime: A Replication and Theoretical Extension," *Law and Society Review* 22 (1988): 163–89.

22. George L. Kelling and James Q. Wilson, "Broken Windows: The Police and Neighborhood Safety," *Atlantic*, March 1982, 29–38.

23. James Q. Wilson, "Just Take Away Their Guns," *New York Times Magazine*, March 20, 1994, 1.

24. Lawrence W. Sherman and Dennis P. Rogan, "Effects of Gun Seizures on Gun Violence: 'Hot Spots' Patrol in Kansas City," *Justice Quarterly* 12, no. 4 (1995): 673–93; Lawrence W. Sherman, James W. Shaw, and Dennis P. Rogan, *The Kansas City Gun Experiment* (Washington DC: National Institute of Justice, 1995).

25. Edmund F. McGarrell et al., "Reducing Firearms Violence Through Directed Police Patrol," *Criminology and Public Policy* 1, no. 1 (2001): 119–48.

26. Lawrence W. Sherman, Patrick R. Gartin, and Michael E. Buerger, "Hot Spots of Predatory Crime: Routine Activities and the Criminology of Place," *Criminology* 27 (1989): 27–55. Ronald V. Clarke and David Weisburd, "Diffusion of Crime Control Benefits: Observations on the Reverse of Displacement," *Crime Prevention Studies* 2 (1994): 165–84; Rene Hesseling, "Displacement: A Review of the Empirical Literature," *Crime Prevention Studies* 3 (1994): 197–230; David Weisburd and Lorraine Green Mazerolle, "Crime and Disorder in Drug Hot Spots: Implications for Theory and Practice in Policing," *Police Quarterly* 3 (2000): 331–49.

27. Edmund F. McGarrell, Steven Chermak, and Alexander Weiss, "Reducing Firearms Violence through Directed Patrol: Final Report on the Evaluation of the Indianapolis Police Department's Directed Patrol Project," *Report to the National Institute of Justice, United States Department of Justice* (Indianapolis, IN: Crime Control Policy Center, Hudson Institute, 2000); Edmund F. McGarrell et al., "Reducing Firearms Violence through Directed Police Patrol," *Criminology and Public Policy* 1 (2001): 119–48; Edmund F. McGarrell, Steven Chermak, and Alexander Weiss, "Reducing Gun Violence: Evaluation of the Indianapolis Police Department's Directed Patrol Project," NCJ-188740 (Washington DC: National Institute of Justice, United States Department of Justice, 2002).

28. The Pittsburgh study is reported in Jacqueline Cohen and Jens Ludwig, "Policing Crime Guns," in *Evaluating Gun Policy: Effects on Crime and Violence*, ed. Jens Ludwig and Phillip J. Cook, 217–50 (Washington DC: Brookings Institution Press, 2003); the evaluation is in Christopher S. Koper and Evan Mayo-Wilson, "Police Crackdowns on Illegal Gun Carrying: A Systematic Review of Their Impact on Gun Crime," *Journal of Experimental Criminology* 2 (2006): 227–61.

29. Lawrence W. Sherman et al., *Preventing Crime: What Works, What Doesn't, What's Promising: Report to the U.S. Congress* (Washington DC: National Institute of Justice, 1997), §8:13–15, §8: 30–32.

30. Ibid., §8:20.

31. Ibid., §8:24–25.

32. Doris Marie Provine, *Unequal under Law: Race in the War on Drugs* (Chicago: University of Chicago Press, 2007).

33. Provine, *Unequal under Law*; Craig Reinarman and Harry G. Levine, "Crack in Context: Politics and Media in the Making of a Drug Scare," *Contemporary Drug Problems* 16, no. 4 (1989): 535–78.

34. Harris, *Profiles in Injustice*; Gary Webb, "DWB: Tracking Unspoken Law Enforcement Racism," *Esquire*, April 1, 1999, 118.

35. Harris, *Profiles in Injustice*.

36. Angela Anita Allen-Bell, "The Birth of the Crime: Driving While Black (DWB)," *Southern University Law Review* 25 (1997): 195–225. Harris, *Profiles in Injustice*, 48–51.

37. Scott H. Decker et al., "On the Frontier of Local Law Enforcement: Local Police and Federal Immigration Law," in *Immigration, Crime, and Justice*, ed. William McDonald, 261–78 (New York: Emerald Publishing, 2009): 261–77.

38. Harris, *Profiles in Injustice*, 20–22; Webb, "DWB."

39. Joseph F. Sullivan, "New Jersey Police Are Accused of Minority Arrest Campaign," *New York Times*, February 19, 1990. These reports were confirmed by John L. Lamberth, "Revised Statistical Analysis of the Incident of Police Stops and Arrests of Black Drivers/Travelers on the New Jersey Turnpike Between Exits or Interchanges 1 and 3 from the Years 1998 Through 1991," *Report*

of the Defendant's Expert in State v. Pedro Soto, 734 A 2d 350 (NJ Supr Ct. Law Div., 1996).

40. Sullivan, "New Jersey Police Are Accused."

41. John E. Eck and Edward R. Maguire, "Have Changes in Policing Reduced Violent Crime?," in *The Crime Drop in America*, ed. Alfred Blumstein and Joel Wallman, 207–65 (New York: Cambridge University Press, 2000); Walker and Katz, *Police in America*, 285–87; Katherine Beckett and Steve Herbert, "Dealing with Disorder: Social Control in the Post-Industrial City," *Theoretical Criminology* 12, no. 5 (2008): 5–30.

42. Command-level officer, confidential interview with authors, October 13, 2011 (emphasis added).

43. *Whren et al. v. United States*, 517 U.S. 806 (1996).

44. Ibid., 813.

45. Roy Caldwell Kime, "U.S. Supreme Court Rules on Asset Forfeiture and Traffic Stop Evidence," *Police Chief*, August 1996, 10.

46. Webb, "DWB."

47. Ibid.

48. *Knowles v. Iowa* 525 U.S. 113 (1998).

49. *United States v. Arvizu*, 534 U.S. 266 (2002).

50. Michael J. Whalen, "Supreme Court Rulings Acknowledge Practical Considerations of Law Enforcement," *Police Chief*, April 2002, 11.

51. John S. Ferrell, "Are More Traffic Stops and Fewer Citizen Complaints Mutually Exclusive?," *Police Chief*, July 1999, 35–38.

52. Earl M. Sweeney, "Traffic Enforcement: New Uses for an Old Tool," *Police Chief*, July 1996, 45.

53. Lois Pilant, "Spotlight on Traffic Enforcement," *Police Chief*, June 1995, 23–24; Garrett Morford, Michael Sheehan Jr., and Jack Stuster, "Traffic Enforcement's Role in the War on Crime," *Police Chief*, July 1996, 48; "Top Ten Lies in Traffic Enforcement," *Police Chief*, July 1997, 30; Alexander Weiss and Edmund McGarrell, "Traffic Enforcement & Crime: Another Look," *Police Chief*, July 1999, 25; Kenneth B. Marshall, "Managing Successful Criminal Patrol Interdiction Programs," *Police Chief*, July 1999, 30; Earl M. Sweeney, "Combating Crashes and Crime Through Professional Traffic Stops," *Police Chief*, July 1999, 39; William P. Georges, "Traffic Safety Strategies Yield Tangible Benefits," *Police Chief*, July 2000, 53; Jeffrey W. Runge, "The Role of Traffic Law Enforcement in Homeland Security," *Police Chief*, October 2002, 93; Otis Cox, "Complete Traffic Stops," *Police Chief*, September 2003, 15.

54. International Association of Chiefs of Police Highway Traffic Safety Committee, "Looking Beyond the License Plate Program Underscores Diligent Police Work," *Police Chief*, July 2000, 70–72.

55. Lou Reiter, "Affidavit/Preliminary Expert Report of Lou Reiter," in the

case of *Chavez v. Illinois State Police*, p. 7, http://www.clearinghouse.net/chDocs/public/PN-IL-0003-0002.pdf (accessed May 25, 2012).

56. Charles Remsberg, *Tactics for Criminal Patrol: Vehicle Stops, Drug Discovery and Officer Survival* (Northbrook, IL: Calibre Press, 1995): 9.

57. Ibid.

58. Ibid.

59. *Ligon v. City of New York*, Dist. Court, SD New York, No. 12 Civ. 2274 (SAS) (2013), 131, http://www.clearinghouse.net/chDocs/public/PN-NY-0014-0005.pdf (accessed February 16, 2013).

60. Remsberg, *Tactics for Criminal Patrol*, 45–63.

61. Ibid., 134.

62. Ibid., 134–65; 166.

63. James A. Foster, "Narcotics Enforcement at the Street Level," *Law Enforcement Technology* 19, no. 5 (1992): 20.

64. Ibid.

65. Remsberg, *Tactics of Criminal Patrol*, 217–31.

66. Ibid., 212, 215.

67. Ibid., 214–16.

68. Ibid., 8, 10 (original emphasis).

69. Ibid., 27.

70. Ibid., 25.

71. Ibid., 69.

72. Webb, "DWB," http://www.esquire.com/features/driving-while-black-0499.

73. Remsberg, *Tactics for Criminal Patrol*, 46–47.

74. Michael F. Brown, *Criminal Investigation: Law and Practice*, 2nd ed. (Boston: Butterworth-Heinemann, 2001), 134–35.

75. Remsberg, *Tactics for Criminal Patrol*, 168.

76. Foster, "Narcotics Enforcement," 20.

77. Georges, "Traffic Safety Strategies," 53.

78. Laura E. Gomez, "Looking for Race in All the Wrong Places." *Law & Society Review* 46, no. 2 (2012): 221–46.

79. Erving Goffman, *Frame Analysis: An Essay on the Organization of Experience* (New York: Harper & Row, 1974). See also Nicholas J. G. Winter, *Dangerous Frame: How Ideas about Race & Gender Shape Public Opinion* (Chicago: University of Chicago Press, 2008); Dennis Chong, "How People Think, Reason, and Feel about Rights and Liberties," *American Journal of Political Science* 37 (1993): 867–99; and James N. Druckman and Kjersten R. Nelson, "Framing and Deliberation," *American Journal of Political Science* 47 (2003): 728–44.

80. Jennifer L. Eberhardt, "Imaging Race," *American Psychologist* 60, no. 2 (2005): 187.

81. Howard Schuman, Charlotte Steeh, Lawrence Bobo, and Maria Kryan, *Racial Attitudes in America: Trends and Interpretations* (Cambridge, MA: Harvard University Press, 1997): 39–52.

82. Donald R. Kinder and Lynn M. Sanders, *Divided by Color: Racial Politics and Democratic Ideals* (Chicago: University of Chicago Press, 1996), 124.

83. Eduardo Bonilla-Silva, *Racism without Racists: Color-Blind Racism and the Persistence of Racial Inequality in the United States* (Lanham, MD: Rowman and Littlefield, 2003); Eduardo Bonilla-Silva and David G. Embrick, "Are Blacks Color Blind Too? An Interview-Based Analysis of Black Detroiters' Racial Views," *Race & Society* 4 (2001): 47–67; see also Michelle Alexander, *The New Jim Crow: Mass Incarceration in the Age of Colorblindness* (New York: New Press, 2010).

84. Lawrence D. Bobo and Cybelle Fox, "Race, Racism, and Discrimination: Bridging Problems, Methods, and Theory in Social Psychology Research," *Social Psychology Quarterly* 66, no. 4 (2003): 323. The ongoing African American social and political struggle for equality spans U.S. history from the colonial era through the present. Within this broader struggle, the civil rights era focused on equality under the law and may be thought of as spanning the period from President Truman's 1948 executive order banning racial discrimination in the armed forces and the Fair Housing Act of 1968. The period after 1968 may be thought of as the post–civil rights era. It is marked by ongoing struggle over the meaning of the legal principles established in the civil rights era, growing endorsement by whites of basic civil rights principles, and the emergence of less-explicit forms of racism and racial hierarchy, sometimes called "color-blind" or "laissez-faire" racism.

85. Ibid., 88; Jennifer L. Eberhardt et al., "Seeing Black: Race, Crime, and Visual Processing," *Journal of Personality and Social Psychology* 87, no. 6 (2004): 876.

86. Elijah Anderson, *Streetwise: Race, Class and Change in an Urban Community* (Chicago: University of Chicago Press, 1990), ch. 6. See also William Julius Wilson, *More Than Just Race: Being Black and Poor in the Inner City* (New York: W. W. Norton, 2009).

87. David L. Hamilton and Tina K. Trolier, "Stereotypes and Stereotyping: An Overview of the Cognitive Approach," in *Prejudice, Discrimination, and Racism*, ed. John F. Dovidio and Samuel L. Gaertner, 127–63 (Orlando, FL: Academic Press, 1986), 133. Winter, *Dangerous Frames*, refers to schemas about race and gender in much the same way stereotypes are referenced here.

88. Patricia G. Devine, "Stereotypes and Prejudice: Their Automatic and Controlled Components," *Journal of Personality and Social Psychology* 56, no. 1 (1989): 5.

89. Gordon W. Allport, *Nature of Prejudice* (Cambridge, MA: Addison-Wesley, 1954).

90. Daniel L. Schacter, *The Seven Sins of Memory* (Boston: Houghton Mifflin, 2001), 153. See Also Frederick F. Schauer, *Playing by the Rules: A Philosophical Examination of Rule-Based Decision-Making in Law and Life* (New York: Oxford University Press, 1991), 21–22 and *Profiles, Probabilities, and Stereotypes* (Cambridge, MA: Harvard University Press, 2003).

91. Devine, "Stereotypes and Prejudice," 5.

92. Michael Billig, "Prejudice, Categorization and Particularization: From a Perceptual to a Rhetorical Approach," *European Journal of Social Psychology* 15 (1985): 81.

93. John A. Bargh, "The Cognitive Monster: The Case against the Controllability of Automatic Stereotype Effects," in *Dual Process Theories in Social Psychology*, ed. S. Chaiken and Y. Trop, 361–82 (New York: Guilford, 1999).

94. Irene V. Blair, "Implicit Stereotypes and Prejudice," in *Cognitive Social Psychology: The Princeton Symposium on the Legacy and Future of Social Cognition*, ed. Gordon B. Moskowitz, 359–74 (Mahwah, NJ: Lawrence Erlbaum Associates, Publishers, 2001), 361. See also Mark Chen and John A. Bargh, "Nonconscious Behavioral Confirmation Processes: The Self-Fulfilling Consequences of Automatic Stereotype Activation," *Journal of Experimental Social Psychology* 33 (1997): 541–60; and Amos Tversky and David Kahneman, "Judgment Under Uncertainty; Heuristics and Biases," *Science* 185 (1974): 1124–31.

95. Birt L. Duncan, "Differential Social Perception and Attribution of Intergroup Violence: Testing the Lower Limits of Stereotyping of Blacks," *Journal of Personality and Social Psychology* 43, no. 4 (1976): 590–98.

96. Ibid.

97. Devine, "Stereotypes and Prejudice," 6.

98. Social psychology has developed robust measures of implicit attitudes and bias; for a review see Anthony G. Greenwald et al., "Understanding and Using the Implicit Association Test: Iii. Meta-Analysis of Predictive Validity." *Journal of Personality and Social Psychology* 97, no. 1 (2009): 17–41.

99. Blair, "Implicit Stereotypes and Prejudice," 373.

100. Amanda B. Brodish and Patricia G. Devine, "The Dynamics of Prejudice, Stereotyping and Intergroup Relations: Intrapersonal and Interpersonal Processes," *Social Psychological Review* 71, no. 1 (April 2005): 54–70. See also Lorella Lepore and Rupert Brown, "Category and Stereotype Activation: Is Prejudice Inevitable?" *Journal of Personality and Social Psychology* 72, no. 2 (1997): 275–87.

101. Joshua Correll et al., "The Police Officer's Dilemma: Using Ethnicity to Disambiguate Potentially Threatening Individuals," *Journal of Personality and Social Psychology* 83, no. 6 (2002): 1317.

102. Joshua Correll et al., "Across the Thin Blue Line: Police Officers and Racial Bias in the Decision to Shoot," *Journal of Personality and Social Psychology* 92, no. 6 (2007): 1006–23.

202   NOTES TO PAGES 44–46

103. Dean A. Dabney et al., "The Impact of Implicit Stereotyping on Offender Profiling: Unexpected Results from an Observational Study of Shoplifting," *Criminal Justice and Behavior* 33, no. 5 (October 2006): 646–74.

104. Ibid., 647.

105. Kristin A. Lane, Jerry Kang, and Mahzarin R. Banaji, "Implicit Social Cognition and Law," *Annual Review of Law and Social Science* 3 (2007): 427–51.

106. Milton Heumann and Lance Cassak, *Good Cop, Bad Cop: Racial Profiling and Competing Views of Justice* (New York: Peter Lang Publishing, 2003).

107. Jerome H. Skolnick, *Justice without Trial: Law Enforcement in Democratic Society*, 3rd ed. (New York: MacMillan, 1994).

108. Jerome H. Skolnick, "The Color Line of Punishment," *Michigan Law Review* 96, no. 6 (May 1998): 1479. See also Laurie A. Rudman, "Social Justice in Our Minds, Homes, and Society: The Nature, Causes, and Consequences of Implicit Bias," *Social Justice Research* 17, no. 2 (2004): 129–42.

109. C. L. Ruby and John C. Brigham, "A Criminal Schema: The Role of Chronicity, Race, and Socioeconomic Status in Law Enforcement Officials' Perceptions of Others," *Journal of Applied Social Psychology* 26, no. 2 (1996): 95–112.

110. Justin D. Levinson and Robert J Smith, eds., *Implicit Racial Bias across the Law* (New York: Cambridge University Press, 2012). With regard to prosecutorial discretion, see Robert J Smith and Justin D. Levinson, "The Impact of Implicit Racial Bias on the Exercise of Prosecutorial Discretion," *Seattle Law Journal* 35 (2012): 795–826; With regard to stereotypes of black youth, see Sandra Graham and Brian S. Lowery. "Priming Unconscious Racial Stereotypes about Adolescent Offenders." *Law and Human Behavior* 28, no. 5 (October 2004): 483–504.

111. Eberhardt et al., "Seeing Black," 876.

112. Jennifer L. Eberhardt et al., "Looking Deathworthy: Perceived Stereotypicality of Black Defendants Predicts Capital-Sentencing Outcomes," *Psychological Science* 17, no. 5 (2006): 876–93; see also R. Richard Banks, Jennifer L. Eberhardt, and Lee Ross, "Discrimination and Implicit Bias in a Racially Unequal Society," *California Law Review* 94 (2006): 1172.

113. Tom R. Tyler and Cheryl J. Wakslak, "Profiling and Legitimacy of the Police: Procedural Justice, Attributions of Motive, and Acceptance of Social Authority," *Criminology* 42, no. 2 (2004): 275.

114. Ronald Weitzer, "Racialized Policing: Residents' Perceptions in Three Neighborhoods," *Law & Society Review* 34, no. 1 (2000): 136, 151.

115. Betty Watson, Dionne Jones, and Pat Roberson-Saunders, "Drug Use and African-Americans: Myth versus Reality," *Journal of Alcohol & Drug Education* 40, no. 2 (1995): 19–39.

116. Franklin D. Gilliam and Shanto Iyengar, "Prime Suspects: The Influence of Local Television News on the Viewing Public," *American Journal of Political Science* 44 (2000): 560–73.

117. Robert J. Sampson, "Urban Black Violence: The Effect of Male Joblessness and Family Disruption," *American Journal of Sociology* 93, no. 2 (September 1987): 348–82.

118. Lincoln Quillian and Devah Pager, "Black Neighbors, Higher Crime? The Role of Racial Stereotypes in Evaluations of Neighborhood Crime," *American Journal of Sociology* 107 (2001): 717–67; Ted Chiricos, Michael Hogan, and Marc Gertz, "Racial Composition of Neighborhood and Fear of Crime," *Criminology* 35 (1997): 107–31.

119. Scott A. Akalis, Mahzarin R. Banaji, and Stephen M. Kosslyn. "Crime Alert! How Thinking about a Single Suspect Automatically Shifts Stereotypes toward an Entire Group." *Du Bois Review* 5, no. 2 (2008): 218.

120. Robert J. Sampson and Stephen W. Raudenbush, "Seeing Disorder: Neighborhood Stigma and the Social Construction of 'Broken Windows,'" *Social Psychology Quarterly* 67, no. 4 (2004): 336.

121. Allen Liska and Paul Bellair, "Violent-Crime Rates and Racial Composition," *American Journal of Sociology* 101 (1995): 578–610; John Logan and Brian Stults, "Racial Differences in Exposure to Crime," *Criminology* 37 (1999): 251–76; Pew Center on the States, *One in 100: Behind Bars in America 2008* (Washington DC: The Pew Research Center, 2008.)

122. For recent reviews, see Alice Goffman, "On the Run: Wanted Men in a Philadelphia Ghetto," *American Sociological Review* 74 (June 2009): 339–59; and Naomi Murakawa and Katherine Beckett, "The Penology of Racial Innocence: The Erasure of Racism in the Study and Practice of Punishment," *Law & Society Review* 44, no. 3/4 (2010): 695–730.

123. Robert Sampson and Janet Lauritsen, "Racial and Ethnic Disparities in Crime and Criminal Justice in the United States," in *Crime and Justice*, vol. 22, ed. Michael Tonry, 311–74 (Chicago: University of Chicago Press, 1997).

124. Andrew Gelman, Jeffrey Fagan, and Alex Kiss, "An Analysis of the NYPD's Stop-and-Frisk Policy in the Context of Claims of Racial Bias," *Journal of the American Statistical Association* 102 (2007): 813–23.

125. Timothy Bates, "Driving While Black in Suburban Detroit," *Du Bois Review* 7, no. 1 (2010): 133–50; Patricia Y. Warren and Donald Tomaskovic-Devey, "Racial Profiling and Search: Did the Politics of Racial Profiling Change Police Behavior?" *Criminology & Public Policy* 8, no. 2 (2009): 343–69.

126. Provine, *Unequal under Law*; Katherine Beckett, Kris Nyrop, and Lori Pfingst, "Race, Drugs and Policing: Understanding Disparities in Drug Delivery Arrests," *Criminology* 44, no. 1 (2004): 105–38; Katherine Beckett et al., "Drug Use, Drug Possession Arrests, and the Question of Race: Lessons from Seat-

tle," *Social Problems* 52, no. 3 (2005): 419–41; Robin S. Engel and Rob Tillyer, "Searching for Equilibrium: The Tenuous Nature of the Outcome Test," *Justice Quarterly* 25, no. 1 (2008): 54–71.

127. David Jacobs, "Inequality and Police Strength," *American Sociological Review* 44 (1979): 913–25; Pamela Irving Jackson, *Minority Group Threat, Crime, and Policing* (New York: Praeger, 1989); Allen Liska, Mitchell Chamlin, and Mark Reed, "Testing the Economic Production and Conflict Models of Crime Control," *Social Forces* 64 (1985): 119–38.

128. David Eitle, Stewart J. D'Alessio, and Lisa Stolzenberg, "Racial Threat and Social Control: A Test of the Political, Economic, and Threat of Black Crime Hypotheses," *Social Forces* 81, no. 2 (December 2002): 570.

129. Lee Sigelman and Steven A. Tuch, "Metastereotypes: Blacks' Perceptions of Whites' Stereotypes of Blacks," *Public Opinion Quarterly* 61, no. 1 (Spring 1997): 87–101.

130. Weizer and Tuch, *Race and Policing*, ch. 3.

131. Dennis P. Rosenbaum et al., "Attitudes toward the Police: The Effects of Direct and Vicarious Experience, *Police Quarterly* 8, no. 3 (September 2005): 343–65.

132. Katheryn Russell-Brown, *Underground Codes: Race, Crime, and Related Fires* (New York: New York University Press, 2004): 66.

133. Michael K. Brown et al., *White-Washing Race: The Myth of a Color-Blind Society* (Berkeley: University of California Press, 2003): 51.

134. Robert D. McFadden, "Police Singled Out Black Drivers in Drug Crackdown, Judge Says," *New York Times*, March 10, 1996; Kenneth B. Noble, "Race Issue Rattles Celebrity Haven," *New York Times*, April 23, 1996; Webb, "DWB"; Jim Stewart, "Police Appear to Target Minorities in Efforts to Catch Criminals," *CBS Evening News*, May 22, 1996; Mathew Reilly, "ABC News Program Uses Jamesburg Cops in 'Race-Profiling' Story," *Newark (NJ) Star-Ledger*, October 8, 1996; Paul W. Valentine, "MD Settles Lawsuit Over Racial Profiles: Police Allegedly Targeted Minorities for Searches," *Washington Post*, January 5, 1995; John L. Lamberth, "Report of John Lamberth," (American Civil Liberties Union, 1996); Michael Janofsky, "Maryland Troopers Stop Drivers by Race, Suit Says," *New York Times*, June 5, 1998; Ivar Peterson, "Whitman Says Troopers Used Racial Profiling," *New York Times*, April 20, 1999; David Kocieniewski, "U.S. Will Monitor New Jersey Police on Race Profiling," *New York Times*, December 23, 1999.

135. "Memorandum on Fairness in Law Enforcement," memorandum for the secretary of the treasury, the attorney general, the secretary of the interior, Public papers of the Presidents of the United States, William J. Clinton, June 9, 1999, http://www.gpo.gov/fdsys/pkg/WCPD-1999-06-14/html/WCPD-1999-06-14-Pg1067.htm; Matthew J. Hicklin, "Traffic Stop Data Collection Policies for

State Police, 2004" (Washington DC: U.S. Department of Justice, Bureau of Justice Statistics, 2005).

136. International Association of Chiefs of Police, "Ensuring Professional Traffic Stops: Recommendations from the First IACP Forum on Professional Traffic Stops," *Police Chief*, July 1999, 16.

137. Bobby D. Moody, "Professional Traffic Stops vs. Biased Traffic Stops," *Police Chief*, July 1998, 6.

138. Ronald S. Neubauer, "Untitled Statement Introducing the IACP's Recommendations on Police Stops," *Police Chief*, July 1999, 15.

139. This is based on the work of Tom Tyler and colleagues. See Tom Tyler, *Why People Obey the Law* (New Haven: CT: Yale University Press, 1990); Tom R. Tyler, "Public Trust and Confidence in Legal Authorities: What Do Majority and Minority Groups Members Want from Law and Legal Institutions," *Behavioral Sciences and the Law* 19 (2001): 215–35; and Tom R. Tyler and Yuen J. Huo, *Trust in the Law: Encouraging Public Cooperation with the Police and Courts* (New York: Russell Sage Foundation, 2002).

140. Moody, "Professional Traffic Stops," 6.

141. Ferrell, "More Traffic Stops," 35–38.

142. IACP Highway Safety Committee, "Public Trust," 25.

143. Weiss and McGarrell, "Traffic Enforcement," 25; John S. Farrell, "Are More Traffic Stops and Fewer Citizen Complaints Mutually Exclusive?," *Police Chief*, July 1999, 35–38; IACP, "Ensuring Professional Traffic Stops," 18, 21; J. Wilford Shaw, "Community Policing to Take Guns Off the Street," *Behavioral Sciences and the Law* 11(1993): 361–74.

144. IACP, "Ensuring Professional Traffic Stops," 15.

145. International Association of Chiefs of Police, "Condemning Racial and Ethnic Profiling in Traffic Stops (a Resolution Adopted at the 106th Annual Conference, 3 November 1999)," *Police Chief*, July 2000, 19.

146. Ibid., 30.

147. International Association of Chiefs of Police Highway Safety Committee, "Policies Help Gain Public Trust: Guidance from the IACP Highway Safety Committee," *Police Chief*, July 2000, 26.

Chapter 3

1. Charles R. Epp, Steven Maynard-Moody, and Donald P. Haider-Markel, "Driver Interview Archive," in *Reconstructing Law on the Street: Transcripts of Interviews and Focus Groups* (Lawrence, KS: KU ScholarWorks, 2011), 30, http://hdl.handle.net/1808/8544.

2. Andrew Gelman, Jeffrey A. Fagan, and Alex Kiss, "An Analysis of the

New York City Police Department's "Stop-and-Frisk" Policy in the Context of Claims of Racial Bias," *Journal of the American Statistical Association*, 102: (2007): 813–23; Bureau of Justice Statistics, "Contacts Between Police and the Public: Findings From the 2002 National Survey" (Washington DC: U.S. Department of Justice, 2005); Richard J. Lundman and Robert L. Kaufman, "Driving While Black: Effects of Race, Ethnicity, and Gender on Citizen Self-Reports of Traffic Stops and Police Actions," *Criminology* 41, no. 1 (2003): 195–220; Michael Smith and Matthew Petrocelli, "Racial Profiling? A Multivariate Analysis of Police Traffic Stop Data," *Police Quarterly* 4 (2001): 4–27; William R. Smith et al., "The North Carolina Highway Traffic Study: Final Report to the National Institute of Justice," January 2004, https://www.ncjrs.gov/pdffiles1/nij/grants/204021.pdf; Peter Verniero and Paul H. Zoubek, "Interim Report of the State Police Review Team Regarding Allegations of Racial Profiling" (Newark: New Jersey Office of the Attorney General, 1999); Still, some research finds no evidence of biases in stops; see, e.g., Jeffrey Grogger and Greg Ridgeway, "Testing for Racial Profiling in Traffic Stops from Behind a Veil of Darkness," *Journal of the American Statistical Association*, 101 (2006): 878–87.

3. This observation dates to the pioneering police-discretion studies of the late 1950s and early 1960s. See Joseph Goldstein, "Police Discretion Not to Invoke the Criminal Process: Low-Visibility Decisions in the Administration of Justice," *Yale Law Journal* 69, no. 4 (1960): 543–94; Herman Goldstein, "Police Discretion: The Ideal versus the Real," *Public Administration Review* 23 (1963): 148–56; Jerome H. Skolnick, *Justice without Trial: Law Enforcement in Democratic Society*, 3rd ed. (New York: MacMillan, 1994).

4. Robin Shepard Engel and Jennifer M. Calnon, "Examining the Influence of Drivers' Characteristics during Traffic Stops with Police: Results From a National Survey," *Justice Quarterly 21* (2004): 49–90.

5. Albert J. Meehan and Michael C. Ponder, "Race and Place: The Ecology of Racial Profiling African American Motorists, *Justice Quarterly* 19 (2002): 399–430.

6. See, e.g., in Britain, Robert Reiner, *The Politics of the Police*, 4th ed. (Oxford: Oxford University Press, 2010).

7. Epp et al., "Traffic Officer Interview Archive," 52.

8. Heather MacDonald, "The Racial Profiling Myth Debunked," *City Journal*, Spring 2001, http://www.city-journal.org/html/11_2_the_myth.html.

9. John Lamberth, "Revised Statistical Analysis of the Incidence of Police Stops and Arrests of Black Drivers/Travelers on the New Jersey Turnpike Between Exits or Interchanges 1 and 3 from the Years 1988 through 1991," (unpublished manuscript, 1994).

10. James E. Lange, Kenneth O. Blackman, and Mark B. Johnson, *Speed Violation Survey of the New Jersey Turnpike: Final Report* (Trenton, NJ: Office of the Attorney General, 2001); for discussion, see Robin Shepard Engel and Jenni-

fer M. Calnon, "Comparing Benchmark Methodologies for Police-Citizen Contacts: Traffic Stop Data Collection for the Pennsylvania State Police," *Police Quarterly* 7, no. 1 (2004): 97–125.

11. Donald Tomaskovic-Devey et al., "Self-Reports of Speeding Stops by Race: Results from the North Carolina Reverse Record Check Survey," *Journal of Quantitative Criminology* 22 (2006): 279–97.

12. Rob Tillyer and Robin S. Engel, "Racial Differences in Speeding Patterns: Exploring the Differential Offending Hypothesis," *Journal of Criminal Justice* 40 (2012): 285–95.

13. Epp et al., "Traffic Officer Interview Archive," 72.

14. Thomas J. Sugrue, "Driving While Black: The Car and Race Relations in Modern America," Automobile in American Life and Society website, http://www.autolife.umd.umich.edu/Race/R_Casestudy/R_Casestudy.htm.

15. Charles R. Epp, Steven Maynard-Moody, and Donald P. Haider-Markel, "Police Officer Focus Group Interview," in *Reconstructing Law on the Street: Transcripts of Interviews and Focus Groups* (Lawrence, KS: KU ScholarWorks, 2011), 9, http://hdl.handle.net/1808/8544.

16. Ibid., 4.

17. One gauge is how fast drivers report typically driving in different speed zones—on the assumption that most drivers try to keep their rate of speed below the speed they think may result in a stop. On average, and across different speed zones from 30 to 65 mph, drivers responding to our survey reported driving just below 5 percent over the posted speed limit. Thus, a driver going at this rate would be driving about 68 miles per hour in a 65-mph zone. But this seems low, or a conservative measure of the zone of nonenforcement; drivers probably err on the side of care in avoiding being stopped for speeding. Another gauge for drawing this line is officers' perceptions of the point at which speeding becomes excessive. But officers are hesitant to answer this question, for the obvious reason that it might lead ordinary drivers to increase their speed up to this point. We were able to get officers to tell us at what point a speeding violation becomes a "must stop" (as opposed to a "likely stop"). In one focus group of officers, several reported that speeding 10 or more miles per hour over the posted limit is a "must stop." One gave a number as high as 15 miles per hour over the limit. But these officers also observed that in "rush hour, you'll let a lot of minor infractions go" because "if you make a stop it could cause problems" (Epp et al., "Police Officer Focus Group Interview," 2).

18. The model contains our standard control variables: race, gender, age, income, education, vehicle value, presence of vehicle customization, damage, equipment violations, and self-reported rate of speed, rule-abiding driving, and time driving per week.

19. Epp et al., "Driver Interviews," 156,

20. Ibid., 8.

21. Ibid., 103.

22. Ibid., 52.

23. Ibid., 10–12.

24. Ibid., 73–75.

25. Ibid., 76–77.

26. Ibid., 142–44.

27. Ibid., 54.

28. Ibid.

29. Kevin Fox Gotham, *Race, Real Estate, and Uneven Development: The Kansas City Experience, 1900–2000* (Albany, NY: SUNY Press, 2002). See also Patrick Sharkey, *Stuck in Place: Urban Neighborhoods and the End of Progress Toward Racial Equality* (Chicago: University of Chicago Press, 2013).

30. Albert J. Meehan and Michael C. Ponder, "Race and Place: The Ecology of Racial Profiling African American Motorists, *Justice Quarterly* 19, no. 3 (2002): 399–430.

Chapter 4

1. Charles R. Epp, Steven Maynard-Moody, and Donald P. Haider-Markel, "Driver Interview Archive," in *Reconstructing Law on the Street: Transcripts of Interviews and Focus Groups* (Lawrence, KS: KU ScholarWorks, 2011), 18–19, http://hdl.handle.net/1808/8544.

2. Ibid., 64–66.

3. Cambridge Review Committee, *Missed Opportunities, Shared Responsibilities: Final Report of the Cambridge Review Committee* (Cambridge, MA: City of Cambridge, June 15, 2010), 3, http://www.cambridgema.gov/CityOfCambridge_Content/documents/Cambridge%20Review_FINAL.pdf.

4. Erving Goffman, *Interaction Ritual: Essays in Face-to-Face Behavior* (Chicago: Aldine, 1967).

5. Stanford M. Lyman and Marvin B. Scott, *A Sociology of the Absurd* (Pacific Palisades, CA: Goodyear, 1970): 37–43.

6. Donald J. Black and Albert J. Reiss Jr., "Patterns of Behavior in Police and Citizen Transactions," in *Studies of Crime and Law Enforcement in Major Metropolitan Areas*, vol. 2, ed. Donald J. Black and Albert J. Reiss Jr., 1–139 (Washington DC: Government Printing Office, 1967); Donald Black and Albert J. Reiss Jr., "Police Control of Juveniles," *American Sociological Review* 35 (1970): 63–77; William A. Westley, *Violence and the Police: A Sociological Study of Law, Custom, and Morality* (Cambridge, MA: MIT Press, 1970): 123; Donald Black, "The Social Organization of Arrest," *Stanford Law Review* 23 (1971): 1087–111; John Van Maanen, "The Asshole," in *Policing: A View from the Street*, ed. Peter K. Manning and John Van Maanen, 221–37 (Santa Monica, CA: Goodyear, 1978);

Eric Riksheim and Steven Chermak, "Causes of Police Behavior Revisited," *Journal of Criminal Justice* 21(1993): 353–82; Richard J. Lundman, "Demeanor or Crime? The Midwest City Police-Citizen Encounters Study," *Criminology* 32 (1994): 631–56; Richard J. Lundman, "Demeanor and Arrest: Additional Evidence from Previously Unpublished Data," *Journal of Research in Crime and Delinquency* 33 (1996): 306–23; Richard J. Lundman, "City Police and Drunk Driving: Baseline Data," *Justice Quarterly* 15 (1998): 527–46; Robert E. Worden and Robin L. Shepard, "Demeanor, Crime, and Police Behavior: A Reexamination of the Police Services Study Data," *Criminology* 34 (1996): 83–105; S. Robin, J. J. Sobol, and Robert E. Worden, "Further Exploration of the Demeanor Hypothesis: The Interaction Effects of Suspects' Characteristics and Demeanor on Police Behavior," *Justice Quarterly* 17 (2000): 235–58; C. L. Chambers, "Police Discretion in a Small Town," *Police Practice and Research* 2 (2001): 421–46; Stephen Mastrofski, Michael Reisig, and John McCluskey, "Police Disrespect Toward the Public," *Criminology* 40, no 3 (2002): 519–51; Joseph A. Schafer and Stephen D. Mastrofski, "Police Leniency in Traffic Enforcement Encounters: Exploratory Findings from Observations and Interviews," *Journal of Criminal Justice* 33 (2005): 225–38; Meghan Stroshine, Geoffrey Alpert, and Roger Dunham, "The Influence of 'Working Rules' on Police Suspicion and Discretionary Decision Making," *Police Quarterly* 11, no. 3 (2008): 315–37; Charles R. Epp, Steven Maynard-Moody, and Donald P. Haider-Markel, "Police Officer Focus Group Interview," in *Reconstructing Law on the Street: Transcripts of Interviews and Focus Groups* (Lawrence, KS: KU ScholarWorks, 2011), http://hdl .handle.net/1808/8544.

7. David Weisburd and Rosann Greenspan, *Police Attitudes toward Abuse of Authority: Findings from a National Study* (Washington DC: National Institute of Justice, 2000).

8. On investigatory intrusions, see, e.g., David A. Harris, *Profiles in Injustice: Why Racial Profiling Cannot Work* (New York: New Press, 2002); Matthew R. Durose, Erica L. Smith, and Patrick A. Langan, *Contacts Between Police and the Public, 2005* (Washington DC: Bureau of Justice Statistics, 2007); Robin Shepard Engel and Jennifer M. Calnon, "Examining the Influence of Drivers' Characteristics during Traffic Stops with the Police: Results from a National Survey," *Justice Quarterly* 21 (2004): 49–90; Robert Kane, "The Social Ecology of Police Misconduct," *Criminology* 40 (2002): 867–96; William Terrill and Michael Reisig, "Neighborhood Context and Police Use of Force," *Journal of Research in Crime and Delinquency* 40 (2003): 291–321; Joseph A. Schafer, David L. Carter, Andra Katz-Bannister, "Studying Traffic Stop Encounters," *Journal of Criminal Justice* 32 (2004): 159–70; Alpert Group, *Miami-Dade Police Department Racial Profiling Study* (Fort Lee, NJ: The Alpert Group, 2004), http://www .policeforum.org/library/racially-biased-policing/supplemental-resources/Alpert_ MDPDRacialProfilingStudy%5B1%5D.pdf; Byongook Moona and Charles J.

Corley, "Driving across Campus: Assessing the Impact of Driver's Race and Gender on Traffic Enforcement Actions," *Journal of Criminal Justice* 35, no. 1 (2007): 29–37; Molly Totman and Dwight Steward, *Searching For Consent: An Analysis Of Racial Profiling Data In Texas* (Austin: Texas Criminal Justice Coalition, 2006), http://tppj.org/tppj/report/analysis-racial-profiling-data-texas. On officers' disrespect toward members of the public, see Mastrofski et al., "Police Disrespect"; Rod K. Brunson and Jody Miller, "Young Black Men and Urban Policing in the United States," *British Journal of Criminology* 46 (2006): 623; Jacinta M. Gau and Rod K. Brunson, "Procedural Justice and Order Maintenance Policing: A Study of Inner-City Young Men's Perceptions of Police Legitimacy," *Justice Quarterly* 27, no. 2 (2010): 255–79.

9. Dennis P. Rosenbaum et al., "Attitudes toward the Police: The Effects of Direct and Vicarious Experience," *Police Quarterly* 8, no. 3 (2005): 343–65.

10. Richard Sykes and John Clark, "A Theory of Deference Exchange in Police-Civilian Encounters," *American Journal of Sociology* 81, no. 3 (1976): 584–600.

11. Black, "Organization of Arrest."

12. Rosenbaum et al., "Attitudes toward the Police."

13. Elijah Anderson, *Code of the Street* (New York: Norton, 1999); Elijah Anderson, *Streetwise: Race, Class, and Change in an Urban Community* (Chicago: University of Chicago Press, 1990); Philippe Bourgois, *In Search of Respect: Selling Crack in El Barrio* (New York: Cambridge University Press, 1995).

14. Deanna L. Wilkinson and Jeffrey Fagan, "The Role of Firearms in Violence 'Scripts': The Dynamics of Gun Events among Adolescent Males," *Law and Contemporary Problems* 59, no. 1 (1996): 55–89; Jeffrey Fagan and Deanna L. Wilkinson, "Guns, Youth Violence, and Social Identity in Inner Cities," *Crime and Justice* 24 (1998): 105–88.

15. David F. Luckenbill, "Criminal Homicide as a Situated Transaction," *Social Problems* 25, no. 2 (1977): 176–86.

16. Rod K. Brunson and Ronald Weitzer, "Negotiating Unwelcome Police Encounters: The Intergenerational Transmission of Conduct Norms," *Journal of Contemporary Ethnography* 40, no. 4 (2011): 425–56; Ronald Weitzer and Rod Brunson, "Strategic Responses to the Police Among Inner-City Youth, *Sociological Quarterly* 50 (2009): 235–56.

17. Brunson and Weitzer, "Police Encounters," 448.

18. This amplifies the core observation of Engel and Calnon, "Drivers' Characteristics during Traffic Stops."

19. Schafer and Mastrofski, "Enforcement Encounters"; see also Michael K. Brown, *Working the Streets: Police Discretion and the Dilemmas of Reform* (New York: Russell Sage Foundation, 1981), Robert J. Lundman, "Organizational Norms and Police Discretion: An Observational Study of Police Work with Traffic Law Violators," *Criminology* 17 (1979): 159–71, and Kathryn Schel-

lenberg, "Policing the Police: Surveillance and the Predilection for Leniency," *Criminal Justice and Behavior* 27 (2000): 667–87.

20. Durose et al., "Police and the Public"; Engel and Calnon, "Drivers' Characteristics during Traffic Stops"; Alpert Group, *Miami-Dade Police Department Racial Profiling Study*; Tom R. Tyler and Yuen J. Huo, *Trust in the Law: Encouraging Public Cooperation with the Police and Courts* (New York: Russell Sage Foundation, 2002).

21. Gau and Brunson, "Procedural Justice"; Rod K. Brunson, "'Police Don't Like Black People': African American Young Men's Accumulated Police Experiences," *Criminology & Public Policy* 6 (2007): 71–102; Brunson and Miller, "Young Black Men."

22. Charles R. Epp, Steven Maynard-Moody, and Donald P. Haider-Markel, "Traffic Officer Interview Archive," in *Reconstructing Law on the Street: Transcripts of Interviews and Focus Groups* (Lawrence, KS: KU ScholarWorks, 2011), 25, http://hdl.handle.net/1808/8544.

23. Cronbach's α for the three-item driver disrespect scale is .75; we note, once again, that this is a self-report, but a substantial proportion of stopped drivers acknowledge speaking somewhat disrespectfully to the officer.

24. The models are estimated with Tobit because of the skewed nature of the data—most drivers were not disrespectful toward officers.

25. Weitzer and Brunson, "Strategic Responses to the Police"; Brunson and Weitzer, "Negotiating Unwelcome Police Encounters."

26. Epp et al., "Driver Interview Archive," 100.

27. Ibid., 75.

28. Ibid., 111–12.

29. Epp et al., "Traffic Officer Interviews," 68.

30. Epp et al., Driver Interview Archive, 72.

31. Ibid.

32. Ibid., 71–72.

33. Ibid, 72.

34. Ibid., 99–101.

35. Ibid., 101.

36. Ibid, 21–23.

37. See Gary Webb, "DWB: Tracking Unspoken Law Enforcement Racism," *Esquire*, April 1, 1999, http://www.esquire.com/features/driving-while-black-0499.

38. Epp et al., "Driver Interview Archive," 22.

39. Jennifer Ritterhouse, *Growing Up Jim Crow: How Black and White Southern Children Learned Race* (Chapel Hill: University of North Carolina Press, 2006). See also Steven A. Berrey, "Resistance Begins at Home: The Black Family and Lessons in Survival and Subversion in Jim Crow Mississippi," *Black Women, Gender and Families* 3, no. 1 (2009): 65–90.

Chapter 5

1. Charles R. Epp, Steven Maynard-Moody, and Donald P. Haider-Markel, "Driver Interview Archive," in *Reconstructing Law on the Street: Transcripts of Interviews and Focus Groups* (Lawrence, KS: KU ScholarWorks, 2011), 5–6, http://hdl.handle.net/1808/8544.

2. Ibid., 73–74.

3. Ibid., 2.

4. Ibid., 48.

5. Ibid., 84–86.

6. Ibid., 23–24.

7. Ibid., 70–74.

8. Ibid., 81.

9. Ibid., 52.

10. Ibid., 106–7.

11. Ibid., 149.

12. Ibid., 3.

13. The first two variables (business-like and friendly) are reversed.

14. See Donald J. Black and Albert J. Reiss Jr., "Patterns of Behavior in Police and Citizen Transactions," in *Studies of Crime and Law Enforcement in Major Metropolitan Areas*, vol. 2, ed. Donald J. Black and Albert J. Reiss Jr. (Washington DC: Government Printing Office, 1967); Robin Shepard Engel and Jennifer M. Calnon, "Examining the Influence of Drivers' Characteristics during Traffic Stops with the Police: Results from a National Survey," *Justice Quarterly* 21 (2004): 49–90; Stephen D. Mastrofski, Michael D. Reisig, and John D. McCluskey, "Police Disrespect toward the Public: An Encounter-Based Analysis," *Criminology* 40, no. 3 (2002); Richard L. Lundman and Robert J. Kaufman, "Driving While Black: Effects of Race, Ethnicity, and Gender on Citizen Self-Reports of Traffic Stops and Police Actions," *Criminology* 41, no. 1 (2003): 195–220; Patricia Y. Warren, "Perceptions of Police Disrespect During Vehicle Stops: A Race-Based Analysis." *Crime and Delinquency* 57, no. 3 (2011): 356–76; E. L. Schmitt, P. A. Langan, and M. R. Durose, *Characteristics of Drivers Stopped by the Police, 1999* (Washington DC: Department of Justice, Bureau of Justice Statistics, 2002); William R. Smith et al., *The North Carolina Highway Traffic Study* (Durham, NC: North Carolina Central University, July 21, 2003), http://www.ncjrs.gov/pdffiles1/nij/grants/204021.pdf.

15. Robin S. Engel, J. J. Sobol, and Robert E. Worden, "Further Exploration of the Demeanor Hypothesis: The Interaction Effects of Suspects' Characteristics and Demeanor on Police Behavior," *Justice Quarterly* 17 (2000):235–58; Michael D. Reisig et al., "Suspect Disrespect Toward the Police," *Justice Quarterly* 21, no 2 (2004): 241–68; Eric Riksheim and Steven Chermak, "Causes of Police Behavior Revisited," *Journal of Criminal Justice* 21 (1993): 353–82.

16. For a persuasive analysis of the importance of this control see Warren, "Perceptions of Police Disrespect."

17. In the survey, we asked drivers to indicate the race of the officer (or officers). Officer race is as perceived by the driver.

18. Whether "hit rates"—the relative success of searches of whites and blacks—are a valid measure of racial discrimination in police stops is a matter of considerable debate. We believe that hit rates are of only limited use as a primary indicator of racial discrimination for the simple reason that much of the discrimination we have observed in police stops is found in elements of the stop other than a search. But disparities in hit rates nonetheless illustrate one element of this broader array of racial disparities. On the debate over hit rates, see John Knowles, Nicola Persico, and Petra Todd, "Racial Bias in Motor Vehicle Searches: Theory and Evidence," *Journal of Political Economy* 109 (2001): 203–99; Ian Ayres, *Pervasive Prejudice? Unconventional Evidence of Racial and Gender Discrimination* (Chicago: University of Chicago Press, 2001), 404–18; Nicola Persico and D. A. Castleman, "Detecting Bias: Using Statistical Evidence to Establish Intentional Discrimination in Racial Profiling Cases," *University of Chicago Legal Forum* (2005): 217–35; Nicola Persico and Petra Todd, "Generalizing the Hit Rates Test for Racial Bias in Law Enforcement, with an Application to Vehicle Searches in Wichita," *Economic Journal* 116 (2006): F351–57; Robin S. Engel, "A Critique of the 'Outcome Test' in Racial Profiling Research," *Justice Quarterly* 25, no. 1 (2008): 1–36.

19. Hit rates calculated from drivers' reports of whether the officer took any items as a result of the search.

20. This difference is statistically significant ($t = 2.62$, $p = .01$, two-tailed t-test) and not attributable to a difference by race of driver in the rate at which the driver was caught speeding because there is no significant difference by race.

21. For observational results consistent with this analysis, see Joseph A. Schafer and Stephen D. Mastrofski, "Police Leniency in Traffic Enforcement Encounters: Exploratory Findings from Observations and Interviews," *Journal of Criminal Justice* 33 (2005): 231.

22. Charles R. Epp, Steven Maynard-Moody, and Donald P. Haider-Markel, "Police Officer Focus Group Interview," in *Reconstructing Law on the Street: Transcripts of Interviews and Focus Groups* (Lawrence, KS: KU ScholarWorks, 2011), http://hdl.handle.net/1808/8544.

23. Engel and Calnon, "Drivers' Characteristics during Traffic Stops," 71.

24. Epp et al., "Driver Interview Archive," 8.

25. Ibid., 157.

26. Ibid., 23–26.

27. Ibid., 170.

28. Ibid., 92.

29. Ibid., 72.
30. Ibid., 11.

Chapter 6

1. William J. Stuntz, "Local Policing after the Terror," *Yale Law Journal* 111, no. 8 (2002): 2173.
2. Tom R. Tyler, "Public Trust and Confidence in Legal Authorities: What do Minority and Majority Group Members Want from the Law and Legal Institutions?" *Behavioral Sciences and the Law* 19 (2001): 215–35; Tom R. Tyler and Yuen J. Huo, *Trust in the Law: Encouraging Public Cooperation with the Police and Courts* (New York: Russell Sage Foundation, 2002); Tom R. Tyler, "Procedural Justice, Legitimacy, and the Effective Rule of Law," *Crime and Justice* 30 (2003): 283–357; Tom R. Tyler and Cheryl J. Wakslak, "Profiling and Legitimacy of the Police: Procedural Justice, Attributions of Motive, and Acceptance of Social Authority," *Criminology* 42, no. 2 (2004): 253–81. Tyler's emphasis on procedural fairness departs from earlier research that found that drivers' evaluations are based on both the severity of the outcome and the demeanor of the officer. See Ben Brown and William Benedict, "Perceptions of the Police: Past Findings, Methodological Issues, Conceptual Issues and Policy Implications," *Policing* 25, no. 3 (2002): 543–80; Michael D. Reisig and Mark E. Correia, "Public Evaluations of Police Performance: An Analysis across Three Levels of Policing," *Policing* 20, no. 2 (1997): 311–25.
3. Tyler, "Procedural Justice," 342.
4. Stuntz, "Local Policing," 2174.
5. Kate Taylor, "Stop-and-Frisk Policy 'Saves Lives,' Mayor Tells Black Congregation," *New York Times* June 10, 2012; see also Wendy Ruderman, "Rude or Polite, City's Officers Leave Raw Feeling in Stops," *New York Times*, June 26, 2012.
6. Charles R. Epp, Steven Maynard-Moody, and Donald P. Haider-Markel, "Driver Interview Archive," in *Reconstructing Law on the Street: Transcripts of Interviews and Focus Groups* (Lawrence, KS: KU ScholarWorks, 2011), 106, http://hdl.handle.net/1808/8544.
7. Ibid., 76–77.
8. Rod K. Brunson and Ronald Weitzer, "Negotiating Unwelcome Police Encounters: The Intergenerational Transmission of Conduct Norms," *Journal of Contemporary Ethnography* 40, no 4 (2011): 425–56; Ronald Weitzer and Rod Brunson, "Strategic Responses to the Police Among Inner-City Youth, *Sociological Quarterly* 50 (2009): 235–56. See also Robert J. Sampson and Dawn Jeglum Bartusch, "Legal Cynicism and (Subcultural?) Tolerance of Deviance: The Neighborhood Context of Racial Differences," *Law & Society Review* 32, no. 4 (1998): 801; Steven G. Brandl et al., "Global and Specific Attitudes toward

the Police: Disentangling the Relationship," *Justice Quarterly* 11 (1994): 119–34; Dennis P. Rosenbaum et al., "Attitudes toward the Police: The Effects of Direct and Vicarious Experience," *Police Quarterly* 8, no. 3 (2005): 343–65; Ronald Weitzer and Steven A. Tuch, *Race and Policing in America: Conflict and Reform* (New York: Cambridge University Press, 2006); Jim Sidanius and Felicia Pratto, *Social Dominance: An Intergroup Theory of Social Hierarchy and Oppression* (New York: Cambridge University Press, 1999).

9. Mary L. Inman and Robert S. Baron, "Influence of Prototypes on Perceptions of Prejudice," *Journal of Personality and Social Psychology* 70 (1996): 727–39; James M. Flournoy Jr., Steven Prentice-Dunn, and Mark R. Klinger, "The Role of Prototypical Situations in the Perceptions of Prejudice of African Americans," *Journal of Applied Social Psychology* 32, no. 2 (2002): 406–23; Joe R. Feagin, "The Continuing Significance of Race: Anti-Black Discrimination in Public Places," *American Sociological Review* 56 (1991): 101–16; Susan T. Fiske and Shelley E. Taylor, *Social Cognition* (New York: McGraw-Hill, 1991).

10. Inman and Baron, "Influence of Prototypes"; L. Feldman-Barrett and J. K. Swim, "Appraisals of Prejudice and Discrimination," in *Prejudice: The Target's Perspective*, ed. J. K. Swim and C. Stangor, 11–36 (San Diego: Academic Press, 1998); M. S. Bynum, E. T. Burton, and C. Best, "Racism Experiences and Psychological Functioning in African American College Students: Is Racial Socialization a Buffer?" *Cultural Diversity and Ethnic Minority Psychology* 13 (2007): 64–71.

11. Pamela Johnston Conover, "The Influence of Group Identification on Political Perception and Evaluation," *Journal of Politics* 46, no. 3 (1984): 763.

12. Erving Goffman, *Frame Analysis: An Essay on the Organization of Experience* (New York: Harper & Row, 1974).

13. Our analysis thus confirms an old observation, much neglected in the procedural justice literature, that for some drivers what matters is whether they get a ticket or are let off with a warning. See Brown and Benedict, "Perceptions of the Police"; Reisig and Correia, "Police Performance."

14. Epp, et al., "Driver Interview Archive," 96.

15. Sampson and Bartusch, "Tolerance of Deviance"; See also James Frank et al., "Reassessing the Impact of Race on Citizens' Attitudes toward the Police: A Research Note," *Justice Quarterly* 13 (1994): 321–34; Brandl et al., "Attitudes toward the Police"; Rosenbaum et al., "Attitudes toward the Police"; Weitzer and Tuch, *Race and Policing in America*; Sidanius and Pratto, *Social Dominance*.

16. Weitzer and Tuch, *Race and Policing in America*; Patricia Y. Warren, "Perceptions of Police Disrespect During Vehicle Stops: A Raced-Based Analysis," *Crime & Delinquency* 57, no. 3 (2011): 356–76.

17. Weitzer and Tuch, *Race and Policing in America*; Warren, "Perceptions of Police Disrespect."

18. Epp et al., "Driver Interview Archive," 11.

19. Ibid., 25.

20. Ibid., 21.

21. Ibid., 14.

22. Ibid., 15.

23. Ibid., 39.

24. Ibid., 116.

25. Ibid., 8–9.

26. Ibid., 157–59.

27. Ibid., 56–59.

28. Tyler and Huo, *Trust in the Law*; Tyler and Wakslak, "Profiling and Legitimacy of the Police."

29. Epp et al., "Driver Interview Archive," 99–101.

30. Ibid., 92, 21.

31. See Tyler and Wakslak, "Profiling and Legitimacy of the Police," 256.

32. Cronbach's α for this index is .75. Higher values on the index indicate greater perceived legitimacy of the stop.

33. Robin Shepard Engel, "Citizens' Perceptions of Distributive and Procedural Injustice During Traffic Stops with Police," *Journal of Research in Crime and Delinquency* 42, no. 4 (November 2005): 445–81.

34. Weitzer and Tuch, *Race and Policing in America*; Warren, "Perceptions of Police Disrespect."

35. As Weitzer and Tuch observe, "analyses of pooled samples may mask important race-specific determinants of perceptions" (*Race and Policing in America*, 6).

36. Narrative of Donald, white male, in Epp et al., "Driver Interview Archive," 53.

37. Jacinta M. Gau and Rod K. Brunson, "Procedural Justice and Order Maintenance Policing: A Study of Inner-City Young Men's Perceptions of Police Legitimacy," *Justice Quarterly* 27, no. 2 (2010): 255–79.

38. As noted earlier, some of these variables have been found to have a significant influence on evaluations of the police in past studies. See, e.g., Peggy Sullivan, Roger G. Dunham, and Geoffrey P. Alpert, "Attitude Structure of Different Ethnic and Age Groups Concerning the Police," *Journal of Criminal Law & Criminology* 78 (1987): 177–96. For instance, at least two studies have found that among African Americans, level of income is negatively correlated with evaluations of the police: the wealthier the person, the more skeptical he or she is of the police. John Hagan and Celeste Albonetti, "Race, Class, and the Perceptions of Criminal Injustice in America," *American Journal of Sociology* 88 (1982): 329–55; Weitzer and Tuch, *Perceptions of Racial Profiling*; Warren, "Perceptions of Police Disrespect."

39. Gary King, Michael Tomz, and Jason Wittenberg, "Making the Most of

Statistical Analysis: Improving Interpretation and Presentation," *American Journal of Political Science* 44, no. 2 (April 2000): 347–61.

Chapter 7

1. Narrative of Kenneth, African American man, in Charles R. Epp, Steven Maynard-Moody, and Donald P. Haider-Markel, "Driver Interview Archive," in *Reconstructing Law on the Street: Transcripts of Interviews and Focus Groups* (Lawrence, KS: KU ScholarWorks, 2011), 143, http://hdl.handle.net/1808/8544.

2. Bernard E. Harcourt, *Against Prediction: Profiling, Policing and Punishing in an Actuarial Age* (Chicago: University of Chicago Press, 2006).

3. Rod K. Brunson and Jody Miller, "Young Black Men and Urban Policing in the United States," *British Journal of Criminology* 46, no 4. (2006): 613–40. See also Jacinta M. Gau and Rod K. Brunson, "Procedural Justice and Order Maintenance Policing: A Study of Inner-City Young Men's Perceptions of Police Legitimacy," *Justice Quarterly* 27, no. 2 (2010): 255–79.

4. Amber J. Landers et al., "Police Contacts and Stress among African American College Students," *American Journal of Orthopsychiatry* 81, no. 1 (2011): 72–81; on the psychological harms from experiencing discrimination more generally, see N. B. Anderson, M. McNeilly, and H. F. Myers, "A Biopsychosocial Model of Race Differences in Vascular Reactivity," in *Cardiovascular Reactivity to Psychological Stress and Disease*, ed. J. J. Flascovich and E. S. Katkin, 83–108 (Washington DC: American Psychological Association, 1993); N. Krieger and S. Sidney, "Racial Discrimination and Blood Pressure: The CARDIA Study of Young Black and White Adults," *American Journal of Public Health*, 86 (1996): 1370–78; R. Clark et al., "Racism as a Stressor for African Americans: A Biopsychological Model," *American Psychologist* 54 (1999): 805–16; R. J. Contrada et al., "Ethnicity-Related Sources of Stress and their Effects on Well-Being," *Current Directions in Psychological Science* 9 (2000): 136–39; R. A. Launier, "Stress Balance and Emotional Life Complexes in Students in a Historically African American College," *Journal of Psychology* 131 (1997): 175–86.

5. Tom Tyler, *Why People Obey the Law* (New Haven: CT: Yale University Press, 1990); Tom R. Tyler and Yuen J. Huo, *Trust in the Law: Encouraging Public Cooperation with the Police and Courts* (New York: Russell Sage Foundation, 2002); Tom R. Tyler and Cheryl J. Wakslak, "Profiling and Legitimacy of the Police: Procedural Justice, Attributions of Motive, and Acceptance of Social Authority," *Criminology* 42, no. 2 (2004): 253–81; Ben Bradford, Jonathan Jackson, and Elizabeth Stanko, "Contact and Confidence: Revisiting the Impact of Public Encounters with the Police," *Policing and Society* 19, no. 1 (2009): 20–46; Jacinta M. Gau, "A Longitudinal Analysis of Citizens' Attitudes about Police,"

Policing 33, no. 2 (2010): 236–52; Michael Leiber, Mahesh Nalla, and Margaret Farnsworth, "Explaining Juveniles' Attitudes toward the Police," *Justice Quarterly* 15 (1998): 151–73; Richard Scaglion and Richard Condon, "Determinants of Attitudes toward City Police," *Criminology* 17 (1980): 485–94; Wesley Skogan, "Citizen Satisfaction with Police Encounters," *Police Quarterly* 8 (2005): 298–321; Paul Smith and Richard Hawkins, "Victimization, Types of Citizen-Police Contacts, and Attitudes toward the Police," *Law and Society Review* 8 (1973): 135–52; Ronald Weitzer and Steven A. Tuch, *Race and Policing in America: Conflict and Reform* (New York: Cambridge University Press, 2006).

6. Chris L. Gibson et al., "The Impact of Traffic Stops on Calling the Police for Help," *Criminal Justice Policy Review* 21, no.2 (2010): 139–59.

7. Vesla M. Weaver and Amy E. Lerman, "Political Consequences of the Carceral State," *American Political Science Review* 104, no. 4 (November 2010): 817–33.

8. E. Allan Lind and Tom R. Tyler, *The Social Psychology of Procedural Justice* (New York: Plenum, 1988); Tom Tyler and E. Allan Lind, "Intrinsic Versus Community-Based Justice Models: When Does Group Membership Matter?," *Journal of Social Issues* 46 (1990): 83–94; Tom Tyler and E. Allan Lind, "A Relational Model of Authority in Groups," in *Advances in Experimental Social Psychology*, ed. M. P. Zanna, 115–91 (San Diego, CA: Academic, 1992).

9. Michelle Alexander, *The New Jim Crow: Mass Incarceration in the Age of Colorblindness* (New York: New Press, 2010).

10. Epp et al., "Driver Interview Archive," 25.

11. Ibid., 53–54.

12. Ibid., 79.

13. Ibid., 57–58.

14. Ibid., 111.

15. Brunson and Miller, "Young Black Men and Urban Policing"; Ronald Weitzer, "Racialized Policing: Residents' Perceptions in Three Neighborhoods." *Law & Society Review* 34, no. 1 (2000): 129–56.

16. Epp et al., "Driver Interview Archive," 75.

17. Ibid., 136.

18. Ibid., 157, 158.

19. Kristin Bumiller, *The Civil Rights Society: The Social Construction of Victims* (Baltimore, MD: Johns Hopkins University Press, 1988). The psychological studies are summarized in Cheryl R. Kaiser and Brenda Major, "A Social Psychological Perspective on Perceiving and Reporting Discrimination," *Law & Social Inquiry* 31, no. 4 (2006): 801–30.

20. Epp et al., "Driver Interview Archive," 11.

21. For a broader discussion, see Laura E. Gomez, "Looking for Race in All the Wrong Places," *Law & Society Review* 46, no. 2 (2012): 221–46.

22. Weitzer and Tuch, *Race and Policing in America*; Brunson and Miller,

"Young Black Men and Urban Policing"; Gau and Brunson, "Procedural Justice and Order Maintenance Policing"; Jon Hurwitz and Mark Peffley, "Explaining the Great Racial Divide: Perceptions of Fairness in the U.S. Criminal Justice System," *Journal of Politics* 67, no. 3 (2005): 762–83.

23. Factor analysis confirms that a single factor underlies these items (the first factor has an eigenvalue of 4.57, while the second factor has an eigenvalue of .18); if separated into two indices, with one composed of the "trust"-related questions and the other composed of the "fairness"-related questions, the two indices are highly correlated (Pearson's $r = .78$); and substituting either of these separate indices for the combined index in the multivariate models reported below produces no significant difference in the substance of the results.

24. The dependent variable, drivers' level of perceived unfairness of the police, is not normally distributed. Responses are somewhat but not greatly skewed toward the low end of the index, indicating that drivers tended to report somewhat greater trust than distrust in the police. Because of this departure from a normal distribution, we have checked the OLS results against those obtained using Tobit analysis with lower censoring. The results are nearly identical in every respect; because OLS is a more efficient estimator and the results are more readily interpretable, here we only report the OLS results. See Lawrence C. Hamilton, *Regression with Graphics* (Pacific Grove, CA: Brooks/Cole, 1992); and C. R. Rao et al., *Linear Models: Least Squares and Alternatives* (New York: Springer Series in Statistics, 1999).

25. Epp et al., "Driver Interview Archive," 146.

26. Timothy Bates, "Driving While Black in Suburban Detroit," *Du Bois Review* 7, no. 1 (2010):133–50.

27. The difference between whites and blacks in their worry about the clothes they wear when they drive is highly statistically significant ($t = -9.23; p < .0001$).

28. This result is obtained by introducing in the above model dummy variables for stop locations (in place of type of stop; the type of stop variables are collinear with stop location variables).

29. Michael C. Dawson, *Behind the Mule* (Princeton, NJ: Princeton University Press, 1994); Michael C. Dawson, *Black Visions* (Chicago: University of Chicago Press, 2002); Ian F. Haney Lopez, *White by Law: The Legal Construction of Race* (New York: New York University Press, 1996); Laura E. Gomez, "Understanding Law and Race as Mutually Constitutive: An Invitation to Explore an Emerging Field," *Annual Review of Law and Social Science* 6 (2010): 487–505.

30. Alexander, *The New Jim Crow*.

31. See, e.g., Michael Omi and Howard Winant, *Racial Formation in the United States: from the 1960s to the 1990s*, 2nd ed. (New York: Routledge, 1994).

32. Andrew Penner and Aliya Saperstein, "How Social Status Shapes Race," *Proceedings of the National Academy of Sciences of the United States of America* 105 (2008): 19628–30.

33. Kenneth L. Dion and Brian M. Earn, "The Phenomenology of Being a Target of Prejudice," *Journal of Personality and Social Psychology* 32 (1975): 944–50; Patricia Gurin and Aloen Townsend, "Properties of Gender Identity and Their Implications for Gender Consciousness," *British Journal of Social Psychology* 25 (1986): 139–48.

34. Epp et al., "Driver Interview Archive," 52–55.

35. Ibid., 78.

36. Ibid., 157–58.

Chapter 8

1. Mike, an African American driver commenting on police stops, in Charles R. Epp, Steven Maynard-Moody, and Donald P. Haider-Markel, "Driver Interview Archive," in *Reconstructing Law on the Street: Transcripts of Interviews and Focus Groups* (Lawrence, KS: KU ScholarWorks, 2011), 26–27, http://hdl.handle.net/1808/8544.

2. Najahe Sherman, "Pastors and Community Leaders Gather to Express Outrage over Church Shooting," 41 Action News, December 15, 2010, http://www.kshb.com/dpp/news/local_news/pastors-and-community-leaders-gather-to-express-outrage-over-church-shooting#ixzz1yoKtT8AE.

3. Eric L. Wesson, "Unsolved Homicides: What Can Be Done?" *Call* (Kansas City) December 10–16, 2010.

4. Lawrence W. Sherman, James W. Shaw, and Dennis P. Rogan, "The Kansas City Gun Experiment," *Research in Brief*, January 1995, 1–11.

5. See Tom R. Tyler, *Why People Obey the Law?* (New Haven, CT: Yale University Press, 1990), and our discussion in chapter 1.

6. Jon B. Gould and Stephen D. Mastrofski, "Suspect Searches: Assessing Police Behavior under the Constitution," *Criminology and Public Policy* 3 (2004): 316–62.

7. Edmund F. McGarrell, Steven Chermak, and Alexander Weiss, "Reducing Firearms Violence Through Directed Patrol: Final Report on the Evaluation of the Indianapolis Police Department's Directed Patrol Project," *Report to the National Institute of Justice*, (Indianapolis, IN: Crime Control Policy Center, Hudson Institute, 2000); Edmund F. McGarrell, Steven Chermak, Alexander Weiss, and Jeremy Wilson, "Reducing Firearms Violence through Directed Police Patrol," *Criminology and Public Policy* 1 (2001): 119–48; Edmund F. McGarrell, Steven Chermak, and Alexander Weiss, "Reducing Gun Violence: Evaluation of the Indianapolis Police Department's Directed Patrol Project," NCJ-188740 (Washington DC: National Institute of Justice, United States Department of Justice, 2002).

8. The Pittsburgh study is reported in Jacqueline Cohen and Jens Ludwig,

"Policing Crime Guns," in *Evaluating Gun Policy: Effects on Crime and Violence*, ed. Jens Ludwig and Phillip J. Cook, 217–50 (Washington DC: Brookings Institution Press, 2003); the evaluation is in Christopher S. Koper and Evan Mayo-Wilson, "Police Crackdowns on Illegal Gun Carrying: A Systematic Review of Their Impact on Gun Crime," *Journal of Experimental Criminology* 2 (2006): 227–61.

9. Franklin E. Zimring, *The City That Became Safe: New York's Lessons for Urban Crime and Its Control* (New York: Oxford University Press, 2011).

10. Anthony A. Braga et al., "Problem-Oriented Policing, Deterrence, and Youth Violence: An Evaluation of Boston's Operation Ceasefire," *Journal of Research in Crime and Delinquency* 38 (2001): 195–225; David M. Kennedy, *Don't Shoot: One Man, A Street Fellowship, and the End of Violence in Inner-City America* (New York: Bloomsbury, 2012); Anthony A. Braga and David L. Weisburd, "The Effects of Focused Deterrence Strategies on Crime: A Systematic Review and Meta-Analysis of the Empirical Evidence," *Journal of Research in Crime and Delinquency* 49, no. 3 (2012): 323–58.

11. Dennis P. Rosenbaum, "The Limits of Hot Spots Policing," In *Police Innovation: Contrasting Perspectives*, edited by David Weisburd and A. A. Braga, 245–63 (Cambridge: Cambridge University Press, 2006), 255.

12. "Addressing Racial and Ethnic Disparities in Health Care: Fact Sheet," Agency for Healthcare Research and Quality, http://www.ahrq.gov/research/findings/factsheets/minority/disparit/.

13. Rosenbaum, "The Limits of Hot Spots Policing," 253.

14. Ibid., 257.

15. For general discussion of "stop snitching," see Delores Jones-Brown, "Forever the Symbolic Assailant: The More Things Change, the More they Remain the Same," *Criminology and Public Policy* 6, no. 1 (2007): 113–14.

16. David H. Bayley, *Police for the Future* (New York: Oxford University Press, 1994); Robert J. Sampson, Stephen W. Raudenbush, and Felton Earls. "Neighborhoods and Violent Crime: A Multilevel Study of Collective Efficacy," *Science* 277 (1997): 918–24; John E. Eck and William Spelman, "Problem-Solving: Problem-Oriented Policing in Newport News," (Washington DC: Police Executive Research Forum, 1987).

17. Robert J. Sampson and Stephen W. Raudenbush, "Systematic Social Observation of Public Spaces: A New Look at Disorder in Urban Neighborhoods," *American Journal of Sociology* 105, no. 3 (1999): 603–51.

18. This is the view reported in our survey by 20 percent of African American men under age 35.

19. Vesla M. Weaver and Amy E. Lerman, "Political Consequences of the Carceral State." *American Political Science Review* 104, no. 4 (November 2010): 817–33.

20. *Arizona v. United States* 567 U.S. 11–182 (2012).

21. See, e.g., Margaret Stock, "Online Symposium: The Court Throws Arizona a Tough Bone to Chew," *SCOTUSblog*, June 27, 2012, http://www.scotusblog .com/2012/06/online-symposium-the-court-throws-arizona-a-tough-bone-to -chew/ (accessed November 15, 2012).

22. *Whren v. United States* 517 U.S. 806 (1996).

23. Brian D. Smedley, Adrienne Y. Stith, and Alan R. Nelson, eds. *Unequal Treatment: Confronting Racial and Ethnic Disparities in Health Care* (Washington DC: National Academy Press, 2003).

24. Michelle Alexander, *The New Jim Crow: Mass Incarceration in the Age of Colorblindness* (New York: New Press, 2010).

25. Quoted in Tracey Meares, "The Legitimacy of Police among Young African-American Men," *Marquette Law Review* 92, no. 4 (2009): 562.

26. See, e.g., Samuel Walker, *The New World of Police Accountability* (Thousand Oaks, CA: Sage, 2005); Charles R. Epp, *Making Rights Real: Activists, Bureaucrats, and the Creation of the Legalistic State* (Chicago: University of Chicago Press, 2009).

27. Charles Remsberg, *Tactics for Criminal Patrol: Vehicle Stops, Drug Discovery and Officer Survival* (Northbrook, IL: Calibre Press, 1995), 214–16.

28. A useful catalog of possible reforms is found in David A. Harris, *Profiles in Injustice: Why Racial Profiling Cannot Work* (New York: New Press, 2002), 145–207.

29. On reform of racial disparities in police shootings see Samuel Walker, *Taming the System* (New York: Oxford University Press, 1993) and Epp, *Making Rights Real.*

30. *Tennessee v. Garner,* 471 U.S. 1 (1985)

31. Epp, *Making Rights Real.*

32. Patricia Y. Warren and Donald Tomaskovic-Devey, "Racial Profiling and Searches: Did the Politics of Racial Profiling Change Police Behavior?" *Criminology & Public Policy* 8, no. 2 (2009): 343–69.

33. See Kennedy, *Don't Shoot*; and Braga and Weisburg, "Focused Deterrence." James Forman Jr. and Trevor Stutz, "Beyond Stop and Frisk," *New York Times*, April 19, 2012, summarizes studies of several cities written under the auspices of the Innovations in Policing Clinic, Yale Law School.

Appendix

1. Charles R. Epp, Steven Maynard-Moody, and Donald P. Haider-Markel, "Kansas City Driving Survey: Selected Items from Questionnaire" and ""Dataset and Meta-Data," in *Reconstructing Law on the Street* (Lawrence, KS: KU

ScholarWorks, 2011), http://hdl.handle.net/1808/8544. This material will be available after February 1, 2016.

2. Robert Groves et al., *Survey Methodology.* 2nd ed. (Hoboken, NJ: John Wiley & Sons, 2009), 52–56.

3. Andrew Kohut, Scott Keeter, Carol Doherty, Michael Dimock, and Leah Christian. *Assessing the Representativeness of Public Opinion Surveys* (Washington, DC: Pew Research Center for the People and the Press, 2012), http://www.people-press.org/files/legacy-pdf/Assessing%20the%20Representativeness%20Of%20Public%20Opinion%20Surveys.pdf.

4. Robert Bullard and Glenn S. Johnson, "Environmental and Economic Justice: Implications for Public Policy," *Journal of Public Management & Social Policy* 4 (1998): 137–48.

5. David A. Harris *Profiles in Injustice: Why Racial Profiling Cannot Work* (New York: New Press, 2002).

6. Ibid.

7. The observed rate of stops declined significantly with age; among our subsample of drivers age fifty and older, the number of drivers who were stopped is sufficiently small that we decided against seeking to expand variation in age into these age categories.

8. Contacting and interviewing drivers proved to be a very time-consuming process. We developed a "priority" list for calls to respondents without regard to their responses on our survey items, and stopped seeking additional driver interviews from among the initial sample of 184 when we determined that additional interviews were beginning to yield results sufficiently similar to those already obtained such that further interviews did not merit the additional effort.

9. See, e.g., Scott Long's classic discussion of limited dependent variables and the use of Tobit to address them: *Regression Models for Categorical and Limited Dependent Variables* (Thousand Oaks, CA: Sage, 1997), 187–216.

10. Ibid.

11. Ibid.

12. Ibid.

Bibliography

"Addressing Racial and Ethnic Disparities in Health Care: Fact Sheet." Agency for Healthcare Research and Quality, U.S. Department of Health and Human Services. http://www.ahrq.gov/research/findings/factsheets/minority/disparit/.

Akalis, Scott A., Mahzarin R. Banaji, and Stephen M. Kosslyn. "Crime Alert! How Thinking about a Single Suspect Automatically Shifts Stereotypes toward an Entire Group." *Du Bois Review* 5, no. 2 (2008): 217–33.

Allen-Bell, and Angela Anita. "The Birth of the Crime: Driving While Black (DWB)." *Southern University Law Review* 25 (1997): 195–225.

Allport, Gordon W. *Nature of Prejudice*. Cambridge, MA: Addison-Wesley, 1954.

Alpert Group. *"Miami-Dade Police Department Racial Profiling Study*. Fort Lee, NJ: The Alpert Group, 2004.

Anderson, Elijah. *Code of the Street*. New York: Norton, 1999.

———. *A Place on the Corner*. Chicago: University of Chicago Press, 1978.

———. *Streetwise: Race, Class, and Change in an Urban Community*. Chicago: University of Chicago Press, 1990.

American Anthropological Association. "Statement on 'Race,'" May 17, 1998, http://www.aaanet.org/stmts/racepp.htm.

American Sociological Association. *The Importance of Collecting Data and Doing Social Scientific Research on Race*. Washington, DC: American Sociological Association, 2003.

Anderson, Norman B., Maya McNeilly, and Hector F. Myers. "A Biopsychosocial Model of Race Differences in Vascular Reactivity." In *Cardiovascular Reactivity to Psychological Stress and Disease*, edited by James J. Flascovich and Edward S. Katkin. 83–108. Washington, DC: American Psychological Association, 1993.

Antonovics, Kate, and Brian G. Knight. "A New Look at Racial Profiling: Evidence from the Boston Police Department." *Review of Economics and Statistics* 91, no. 1 (2009): 163–77.

Arendt, Hannah. *The Human Condition*. Chicago: University of Chicago Press, 1958.

Ayres, Ian. *Pervasive Prejudice? Unconventional Evidence of Race and Gender Discrimination*. Chicago: University of Chicago Press, 2001.

Ayres, Ian, and Jonathan Borowsky. *A Study of Racially Disparate Outcomes in the Los Angeles Police Department*. Los Angeles: American Civil Liberties Union of Southern California, 2008.

Banks, R. Richard, Jennifer L. Eberhardt, and Lee Ross. "Discrimination and Implicit Bias in a Racially Unequal Society." *California Law Review* 94 (2006): 1169–90.

Bargh, John A. "The Cognitive Monster: The Case against the Controllability of Automatic Stereotype Effects." In *Dual Process Theories in Social Psychology*, edited by Shelly Chaiken and Yaacov Trop, 361–82. New York: Guilford, 1999.

Barnes, Mario L. "Black Women's Stories and the Criminal Law: Restating the Power of Narrative." *UC Davis Law Review* 36 (2006): 941–89.

Bates, Timothy. "Driving while Black in Suburban Detroit." *Du Bois Review* 7, no. 1 (2010): 133–50.

Bayley, David F. *Police for the Future*. New York: Oxford University Press, 1994.

Beckett, Katherine, and Steve Herbert. "Dealing with Disorder: Social Control in the Post-Industrial City." *Theoretical Criminology* 12, no. 5 (2008): 5–30.

Beckett, Katherine, Kris Nyrop, Lori Pfingst, and Melissa Bowen. "Drug Use, Drug Possession Arrests, and the Question of Race: Lessons from Seattle." *Social Problems* 52, no. 3 (2005): 419–41.

Bell, Jeannine. *Policing Hatred: Law Enforcement, Civil Rights, and Hate Crimes*. New York: New York University Press, 2002.

Berard, Tim. "The Neglected Social Psychology of Institutional Racism." *Sociology Compass* 2, no. 2 (2008): 734–64.

Berrey, Steven A. "Resistance Begins at Home: The Black Family and Lessons in Survival and Subversion in Jim Crow Mississippi." *Black Women, Gender and Families* 3, no. 1 (2009): 65–90.

Billig, Michael. "Prejudice, Categorization and Particularization: From a Perceptual to a Rhetorical Approach." *European Journal of Social Psychology* 15 (1985): 79–103.

Black, Donald J. "The Social Organization of Arrest." *Stanford Law Review* 23 (1971): 1087–111.

Black, Donald J., and Albert J. Reiss Jr. "Patterns of Behavior in Police and Citizen Transactions." In *Studies of Crime and Law Enforcement in Major Metropolitan Areas*, vol. 2, edited by Donald J. Black and Albert J. Reiss Jr., 1–139. Washington, DC: Government Printing Office, 1967.

——. "Police Control of Juveniles." *American Sociological Review* 35 (1970): 63–77.

Blair, Irene V. "Implicit Stereotypes and Prejudice." In *Cognitive Social Psychology: The Princeton Symposium on the Legacy and Future of Social Cognition*, edited by E. Moskowitz and B. Gordon, 359–74. Mahwah, NJ: Lawrence Erlbaum Associates, 2001.

Bobo, Lawrence D. "Inequalities that Endure? Racial Ideology, American Politics, and the Peculiar Role of Social Science Changing the Terrain of Race and Ethnicity." In *The Changing Terrain of Race and Ethnicity*, edited by Marcia Krysan, Amanda T. Lewis, and T. Forman, 13–42. New York: Russell Sage Foundation, 2004.

Bobo, Lawrence D., and Cybelle Fox. "Race, Racism, and Discrimination: Bridging Problems, Methods, and Theory in Social Psychology Research." *Social Psychology Quarterly* 66, no. 4 (2003): 319–32.

Bonilla-Silva, Eduardo. *Racism without Racists: Color-Blind Racism and the Persistence of Racial Inequality in the United States*. Lanham, MD: Rowman and Littlefield, 2003.

Bonilla-Silva, Eduardo, and David G. Embrick. "Are Blacks Color Blind Too? An Interview-Based Analysis of Black Detroiters' Racial Views." *Race & Society* 4 (2001): 47–67.

Bourgois, Philippe. *In Search of Respect: Selling Crack in El Barrio*. New York: Cambridge University Press, 1995.

Bowling, Benjamin, and Coretta Phillips. "Disproportionate and Discriminatory: Reviewing the Evidence on Police Stop and Search." *Modern Law Review* 70, no. 6 (2007): 936–61.

Bradford, Ben, Jonathan Jackson, and Elizabeth Stanko. "Contact and Confidence: Revisiting the Impact of Public Encounters with the Police." *Policing and Society* 19, no. 1 (2009): 20–46.

Braga, Anthony A., David M. Kennedy, Elin J. Waring, and Anne Morrison Riehl. "Problem-Oriented Policing, Deterrence, and Youth Violence: An Evaluation of Boston's Operation Ceasefire." *Journal of Research in Crime and Delinquency* 38 (2001): 195–225.

Braga, Anthony A., and David Weisburd. "The Effects of Focused Deterrence Strategies on Crime: A Systematic Review and Meta-Analysis of the Empirical Evidence." *Journal of Research in Crime and Delinquency* 49, no. 3 (2012): 323–58.

Brandl, Steven G., J. Frank, R. E. Worden, and T. S. Bynum. "Global and Specific Attitudes toward the Police: Disentangling the Relationship." *Justice Quarterly* 11 (1994): 119–34.

Brodish, Amanda B., and Patricia G. Devine. "The Dynamics of Prejudice, Stereotyping and Intergroup Relations: Intrapersonal and Interpersonal Processes." *Social Psychological Review* 71, no. 1 (April 2005): 54–70.

Brookings Institution Center on Urban and Metropolitan Studies. "Kansas City in Focus: A Profile from Census 2000." In *Living Cities: The National Community Development Initiative*. Washington, DC: The Brookings Institution, 2003.

Brown, Ben, and William R. Benedict. "Perceptions of the Police: Past Findings, Methodological Issues, Conceptual Issues, and Policy Implications." *Policing* 20, no. 2 (2002): 543–80.

Brown, Michael F. *Criminal Investigation: Law and Practice*. 2nd ed. Boston: Butterworth-Heinemann, 2001.

Brown, Michael K. *Working the Street: Police Discretion and the Dilemmas of Reform*. New York: Russell Sage Foundation, 1981.

Brown, Michael K., Martin Carnoy, Elliott Currie, Troy Duster, David B. Oppenheimer, Marjorie M. Shultz, and David Wellman. *Whitewashing Race: The Myth of a Color-Blind Society*. Berkeley: University of California Press, 2003.

Brunson, Rod K. "'Police Don't Like Black People': African American Young Men's Accumulated Police Experiences." *Criminology & Public Policy* 6 (2007): 71–102.

Brunson, Rod K., and Jody Miller. "Young Black Men and Urban Policing in the United States." *British Journal of Criminology* 46, no. 4 (2006): 613–40.

Brunson, Rod K., and Ronald Weitzer. "Negotiating Unwelcome Police Encounters: The Intergenerational Transmission of Conduct Norms." *Journal of Contemporary Ethnography* 40, no. 4 (2011): 176–86.

Bullard, Robert, and G. S. Johnson. "Environmental and Economic Justice: Implications for Policy." *Journal of Public Management & Social Policy* 4 (1998): 137–48.

Bumiller, Kristin. *The Civil Rights Society: The Social Construction of Victims*. Baltimore, MD: Johns Hopkins University Press, 1988.

Bureau of Justice Statistics. *Contacts between Police and the Public: Findings from the 1999 National Survey*. Washington, DC: Department of Justice, Office of Justice Programs, 2001.

Burston, Betty Watson, Dionne Jones, and Pat Roberson-Saunders. "Drug Use and African-Americans: Myth versus Reality." *Journal of Alcohol & Drug Education* 40, no. 2 (1995): 19–39.

Bynum, M. S., E. T. Burton, and C. Best. "Racism Experiences and Psychological Functioning in African American College Students: Is Racial Socialization a Buffer?" *Cultural Diversity and Ethnic Minority Psychology* 13 (2007): 64–71.

Campbell, Angus, and Howard Schuman. "Racial Attitudes in Fifteen American Cities." In *Supplemental Studies for the National Advisory Commission on Civil Disorders*, by the National Advisory Commission on Civil Disorders, 1–67. Washington, DC: Government Printing Office, 1968.

Campbell, Andrea L. *How Policies Make Citizens: Senior Political Activism and the American Welfare State.* Princeton, NJ: Princeton University Press, 2003.

Cambridge Review Committee. *Missed Opportunities, Shared Responsibilities: Final Report of the Cambridge Review Committee.* Cambridge, MA: City of Cambridge, June 15, 2010. http://www.cambridgema.gov/CityOfCambridge _Content/documents/Cambridge%20Review_FINAL.pdf.

Carmichael, Stokely, and Charles Hamilton. *Black Power: The Politics of Liberation.* New York: Random House, 1967.

Castiglione, John D. "Human Dignity under the Fourth Amendment." *Wisconsin Law Review* 665 (2008): 101–56.

Chambers, C. L. "Police Discretion in a Small Town." *Police Practice and Research* 2 (2001): 421–46.

Chen, Mark, and John A. Bargh. "Nonconscious Behavioral Confirmation Processes: The Self-Fulfilling Consequences of Automatic Stereotype Activation." *Journal of Experimental Social Psychology* 33 (1997): 541–60.

Chiricos, Ted, Michael Hogan, and Marc Gertz. "Racial Composition of Neighborhood and Fear of Crime." *Criminology* 35 (1997): 107–31.

Chong, Dennis. "How People Think, Reason, and Feel About Rights and Liberties." *American Journal of Political Science* 37 (1993): 867–99.

Clark, R., N. B. Anderson, V. R. Clark, and D. R. Williams. "Racism as a Stressor for African Americans: A Biopsychological Model." *American Psychologist* 54 (1999): 805–16.

Clarke, Ronald V., and David Weisburd. "Diffusion of Crime Control Benefits: Observations on the Reverse of Displacement." *Crime Prevention Studies* 2 (1994): 165–84.

Cohen, Jacqueline, and Jens Ludwig. "Policing Crime Guns." In *Evaluating Gun Policy: Effects on Crime and Violence,* edited by Jens Ludwig and Phillip J. Cook, 217–50. Washington, DC: Brookings Institution Press, 2003.

Colb, Sherry F. "Innocence, Privacy, and Targeting in Fourth Amendment Jurisprudence." *Columbia Law Review* 96 (1996): 1486.

Conover, Pamela Johnston. "The Influence of Group Identification on Political Perception and Evaluation." *Journal of Politics* 46, no. 3 (1984): 763.

Contrada, R. J., R. D. Ashmore, M. L. Gary, E. Coups, J. D. Egeth, A. Sewell, K. Ewell, T. Goyal, and V. Chasse. " Ethnicity-Related Sources of Stress and Their Effects on Well-Being." *Current Directions in Psychological Science* 9 (2000): 136–39.

Cordner, Gary W. "The Effects of Directed Patrol: A Natural Quasi-Experiment in Pontiac." In *Contemporary Issues in Law Enforcement,* edited by James J. Fyfe, 37–58. Beverly Hills, CA: Sage, 1981.

Cordner, Gary W., G. Williams, and M. Zuniga. "San Diego Police Department Vehicle Stop Study: Mid-Year Report." San Diego, CA: City of San Diego, 2000.

Correll, Joshua, Bernadette Park, Charles M. Judd, and Bernd Wittenbrink. "The Police Officer's Dilemma: Using Ethnicity to Disambiguate Potentially Threatening Individuals." *Journal of Personality and Social Psychology* 83, no. 6 (2002): 1314–29.

Correll, Joshua, Bernadette Park, Charles M. Judd, Bernd Wittenbrink, and Tracie Keesee. "Across the Thin Blue Line: Police Officers and Racial Bias in the Decision to Shoot." *Journal of Personality and Social Psychology* 92, no. 6 (2007): 1006–23.

Cox, Otis. "Complete Traffic Stops." *Police Chief*, September 2003, 15.

Coyvas, Jeannette A., and Stefan Jonsson. "Ubiquity and Legitimacy: Disentangling Diffusion and Institutionalization." *Sociological Forces* 29, no. 1 (2011): 27–53.

Crenshaw, Kimberlé W. "Mapping the Margins: Intersectionality, Identity Politics, and Violence against Women of Color," *Stanford Law Review* 43, no. 6 (1991): 1241–99.

Dabney, Dean A., Laura Dugan, Volkan Topalli, and Richard C. Hollinger. "The Impact of Implicit Stereotyping on Offender Profiling: Unexpected Results from an Observational Study of Shoplifting." *Criminal Justice and Behavior* 33, no. 5 (October 2006): 646–74.

Dawson, Michael. *Behind the Mule.* Princeton, NJ: Princeton University Press, 1994.

———. *Black Visions.* Chicago: University of Chicago Press, 2002.

Decker, Scott H., Paul G. Lewis, Doris Marie Provine, and Monica W. Varsanyi. "On the Frontier of Local Law Enforcement: Local Police and Federal Immigration Law." In *Immigration, Crime, and Justice*, edited by William McDonald. 261–78. New York: Emerald Publishing, 2009.

Delgado, Richard. "Storytelling for Oppositionists and Others: A Plea for Narrative." *Michigan Law Review* 87 (1989): 2411–41.

Devine, Patricia G. "Stereotypes and Prejudice: Their Automatic and Controlled Components." *Journal of Personality and Social Psychology* 56, no. 1 (1989): 5–18.

DiMaggio, Paul J., and Walter W. Powell. "The Iron Cage Revisited: Institutional Isomorphism and Collective Rationality in Organizational Fields." *American Sociological Review* 48 (1983): 147–60.

Dion, Kenneth L., and Brian M. Earn. "The Phenomenology of Being a Target of Prejudice." *Journal of Personality and Social Psychology* 32 (1975): 944–50.

Dobbin, Frank, and John R. Sutton. "The Strength of a Weak State: The Employment Rights Revolution and the Rise of Human Resources Management Divisions." *American Journal of Sociology* 104 (1998): 441–76.

Dovidio, John F., and Samuel L. Gaertner. "On the Nature of Contemporary Prejudice: The Causes, Consequences, and Challenges of Aversion Racism."

In *Confronting Racism: The Problem and the Response*, edited by Jennifer L. Eberhardt and Susan T. Fiske 3–32. Thousand Oaks, CA: Sage, 1998.

Druckman, James N., and Kjersten R. Nelson. "Framing and Deliberation." *American Journal of Political Science* 47 (2003): 728–44.

Duncan, Birt L. "Differential Social Perception and Attribution of Intergroup Violence: Testing the Lower Limits of Stereotyping of Blacks." *Journal of Personality and Social Psychology* 43, no. 4 (1976): 590–98.

Durose, Matthew R., Erica L. Smith, and Patrick A. Langan. *Contacts between Police and the Public, 2005*. Washington, DC: Bureau of Justice Statistics, 2007.

Eberhardt, Jennifer L. "Imaging Race." *American Psychologist* 60, no. 2 (2005): 181–90.

Eberhardt, Jennifer L., Paul G. Davies, Valerie J. Purdie-Vaughns, and Sheri Lynn Johnson. "Looking Deathworthy: Perceived Stereotypicality of Black Defendants Predicts Capital-Sentencing Outcomes." *Psychological Science* 17, no. 5 (2006): 383–86.

Eberhardt, Jennifer L., Phillip Atiba Goff, Valerie J. Purdie, and Paul G. Davies. "Seeing Black: Race, Crime, and Visual Processing." *Journal of Personality and Social Psychology* 87, no. 6 (2004): 876–93.

Eck, John E., and Edward R. Maguire. "Have Changes in Policing Reduced Violent Crime?" In *The Crime Drop in America*, edited by Alfred Blumstein and Joel Wallman 207–65. New York: Cambridge University Press, 2000.

Eck, John E., and William Spelman. *Problem-Solving: Problem-Oriented Policing in Newport News*. Washington, DC: Police Executive Research Forum, 1987.

Edelman, Lauren B. "Legal Ambiguity and Symbolic Structures: Organizational Mediation of Civil Rights Law." *American Journal of Sociology* 97 (1992): 1531–76.

Eitle, David, Stewart J. D'Alessio, and Lisa Stolzenberg. "Racial Threat and Social Control: A Test of the Political, Economic, and Threat of Black Crime Hypotheses." *Social Forces* 81, no. 2 (2002): 557–76.

Engel, Robin Shepard. "A Critique of the 'Outcome Test' in Racial Profiling Research." *Justice Quarterly* 1 (2008): 1–36.

Engel, Robin Shepard, and Jennifer M. Calnon. "Examining the Influence of Drivers' Characteristics during Traffic Stops with Police: Results from a National Survey." *Justice Quarterly* 21 (2004): 49–90.

Engel, Robin Shepard, J. J. Sobol, and Robert E. Worden. "Further Exploration of the Demeanor Hypothesis: The Interaction Effects of Suspects' Characteristics and Demeanor on Police Behavior." *Justice Quarterly* 17 (2000): 235–58.

Engel, Robin Shepard, and Rob Tillyer. "Searching for Equilibrium: The Tenuous Nature of the Outcome Test." *Justice Quarterly* 25, no. 1 (2008): 54–71.

EPIC-MRA. *Standard Enforcement—A Michigan Perspective.* Lansing: Michigan State Police, n.d.

Epp, Charles R. *Making Rights Real: Activists, Bureaucrats, and the Creation of the Legalistic State.* Chicago: University of Chicago Press, 2009.

Epp, Charles R., Steven Maynard-Moody, and Donald P. Haider-Markel. "Driver Interview Archive." In *Reconstructing Law on the Street: Transcripts of Interviews and Focus Groups.* Lawrence, KS: KU ScholarWorks, 2011.

———. "Police Officer Focus Group Interview." In *Reconstructing Law on the Street: Transcripts of Interviews and Focus Groups.* Lawrence, KS: KU ScholarWorks, 2011.

———. "Traffic Officer Interview Archive." In *Reconstructing Law on the Street: Transcripts of Interviews and Focus Groups.* Lawrence, KS: KU ScholarWorks, 2011.

Farrell, John S. "Are More Traffic Stops and Fewer Citizen Complaints Mutually Exclusive?" *Police Chief,* July 1999, 35–38.

Feagin, Joe R. "The Continuing Significance of Race: Antiblack Discrimination in Public Places." *American Sociological Review* 56 (1991): 101–16.

Feldman-Barrett, Lisa, and Janet K Swim. "Appraisals of Prejudice and Discrimination." In *Prejudice: The Target's Perspective,* edited by Janet K. Swim and Charles Stangor, 12–37. San Diego, CA: Academic Press, 1998.

Ferrell, John S. "Are More Traffic Stops and Fewer Citizen Complaints Mutually Exclusive?" *Police Chief,* July 1999, 35–38.

Flournoy, James M. Jr., Steven Prentice-Dunn, and Mark R. Klinger. "The Role of Prototypical Situations in the Perceptions of Prejudice of African Americans." *Journal of Applied Social Psychology* 32, no. 2 (2002): 406–23.

Fogelson, Robert M. *Big City Police.* Cambridge, MA: Harvard University Press, 1977.

Foster, James A. "Narcotics Enforcement at the Street Level." *Law Enforcement Technology* 19, no. 5 (1992): 20–21.

Frank, James, Steven.G. Brandl, Frances T. Cullen, and Amy Stichman. "Reassessing the Impact of Race on Citizens' Attitudes toward the Police: A Research Note." *Justice Quarterly* 13 (1994): 321–34.

Fridell, Lori, and Mary Ann Wycoff, eds. *Community Policing: The Past, Present and Future.* Washington, DC: Annie E. Casey Foundation and the Police Executive Research Forum, 2004.

Gaines, Larry K. *An Analysis of Traffic Stop Data in the City of Riverside.* Riverside, CA: City of Riverside, 2003.

Gau, Jacinta M., and Rod K. Brunson. "Procedural Justice and Order Maintenance Policing: A Study of Inner-City Young Men's Perceptions of Police Legitimacy." *Justice Quarterly* 27, no. 2 (2010): 255–79.

Gelman, Andrew, Jeffrey A. Fagan, and Alex Kiss. "An Analysis of the New

York City Police Department's 'Stop-and-Frisk' Policy in the Context of Claims of Racial Bias." *Journal of the American Statistical Association* 102 (2007): 813–23.

Georges, William P. "Traffic Safety Strategies Yield Tangible Benefits." *Police Chief*, July 2000, 53–54.

Gibson, Chris L., Samuel Walker, Wesley G. Jennings, and J. Mitchell Miller. "The Impact of Traffic Stops on Calling the Police for Help." *Criminal Justice Policy Review* 21, no. 2 (2010): 139–59.

Gilliam, Franklin D., and Shanto Iyengar. "Prime Suspects: The Influence of Local Television News on the Viewing Public." *American Journal of Political Science* 44 (2000): 560–73.

Goffman, Alice. "On the Run: Wanted Men in a Philadelphia Ghetto." *American Sociological Review* 74 (June 2009): 339–59.

Goffman, Erving. *Frame Analysis: An Essay on the Organization of Experience.* New York: Harper & Row, 1974.

———. *Interaction Ritual: Essays in Face-to-Face Behavior.* Chicago: Aldine, 1967.

Goldstein, Herman. "Police Discretion: The Ideal versus the Real." *Public Administration Review* 23 (1963): 148–56.

Goldstein, Joseph. "Police Discretion Not to Invoke the Criminal Process: Low-Visibility Decisions in the Administration of Justice." *Yale Law Journal* 69, no. 4 (1960): 543–94.

Gomez, Laura E. "Looking for Race in All the Wrong Places." *Law & Society Review* 46, no. 2 (2012): 221–46.

———. "A Tale of Two Genres: On the Real and Ideal Links between Law and Society and Critical Race Theory." In *The Blackwell Companion to Law and Society*, edited by Austin Sarat, 453–70. Malden, MA: Blackwell, 2004.

———. "Understanding Law and Race as Mutually Constitutive: An Invitation to Explore an Emerging Field." *Annual Review of Law and Social Science* 6 (2010): 487–505.

Gotham, Kevin Fox. *Race, Real Estate, and Uneven Development: The Kansas City Experience.* Albany, NY: SUNY Press, 2002.

Gottschalk, Marie. *The Prison and the Gallows: The Politics of Mass Incarceration in America.* New York: Cambridge University Press, 2006.

Gould, Jon B., and Stephen D. Mastrofski. "Suspect Searches: Assessing Police Behavior under the Constitution." *Criminology & Public Policy* 3 (2004): 316–62.

Graham, Sandra, and Brian S. Lowery. "Priming Unconscious Racial Stereotypes about Adolescent Offenders." *Law and Human Behavior* 28, no. 5 (October 2004): 483–504.

Greene, Jack R. "Community Policing in America: Changing the Nature, Structure, and Function of the Police." In *Policies, Processes, and Decisions of the Criminal Justice System: Criminal Justice*, vol. 3, edited by Juley Horney. Washington, DC: Department of Justice, 2000.

Greenwald, Anthony G., T. Andrew Poehlman, Eric Luis Uhlmann, and Mahzarin R. Banaji. "Understanding and Using the Implicit Association Test: III. Meta-Analysis of Predictive Validity." *Journal of Personality and Social Psychology* 97, no. 1 (2009): 17–41.

Grogger, Jeffrey, and Greg Ridgeway. "Testing for Racial Profiling in Traffic Stops from Behind the Veil of Darkness." *Journal of the American Statistical Association* 101 (2006): 878–87.

Groves, Robert M., Floyd J. Fowler Jr., Mick P. Couper, James M. Lepkowski, Eleanor Singer, and Roger Tourangeau. *Survey Methodology*. 2nd ed. Hoboken, NJ: John Wiley & Sons, 2009.

The *Guardian* and the London School of Economics and Political Science. *Reading the Riots: Investigating England's Summer of Disorder*. http://s3 .documentcloud.org/documents/274239/reading-the-riots.pdf.

Gurin, Patricia, and Aloen Townsend. "Properties of Gender Identity and Their Implications for Gender Consciousness." *British Journal of Social Psychology* 25 (1986): 139–48.

Habermas, Jurgen. *The Structural Transformation of the Public Sphere: An Inquiry into a Category of Bourgeois Society*. Translated by Berger Thomas. Cambridge, MA: MIT Press, 1989.

Hagan, John, and Celeste Albonetti. "Race, Class, and the Perceptions of Criminal Injustice in America." *American Journal of Sociology* 88 (1982): 329–55.

Hahn, Harlan, and Judson L. Jeffries. *Urban America and Its Police: From the Post Colonial Era through the Turbulent 1960s*. Boulder: University Press of Colorado, 2003.

Hallett, Tim. "The Myth Incarnate: Recoupling Processes, Turmoil, and Inhabited Institutions in an Urban Elementary School." *American Sociological Review* 75, no. 1 (2010): 52–74.

Hallett, Tim, and Marc J. Ventresca. "Inhabited Institutions: Social Interactions and Organizational Forms in Gouldner's 'Patterns of Industrial Bureaucracy.'" *Theory and Society* 35, no. 2 (April 2006): 213–36.

Hamilton, David L., and Tina K. Trolier. "Stereotypes and Stereotyping: An Overview of the Cognitive Approach." In *Prejudice, Discrimination, and Racism*, edited by Samuel L. Gaertner, 127–63. Orlando, FL: Academic Press, 1986.

Hamilton, Lawrence C. *Regression with Graphics*. Pacific Grove, CA: Brooks/ Cole, 1992.

Harcourt, Bernard E. *Against Prediction: Profiling, Policing and Punishing in an Actuarial Age*. Chicago: University of Chicago Press, 2006.

Harris, David A. *Profiles in Injustice: Why Racial Profiling Cannot Work*. New York: The New Press, 2002.

——. "When Success Breeds Attack: The Coming Backlash against Racial Profiling Studies." *Michigan Journal of Race & Law* 6 (2001): 265.

Henry, Patrick Justin. "The Role of Group-Based Status in Job Satisfaction: Workplace Respect Matters More for the Stigmatized." *Social Justice Research* 24 (2011): 231–38.

Heumann, Milton, and Lance Cassak. *Good Cop, Bad Cop: Racial Profiling and Competing Views of Justice*. New York: Peter Lang, 2003.

Hicklin, Matthew J. "Traffic Stop Data Collection Policies for State Police, 2004." Washington, DC: Department of Justice, Bureau of Justice Statistics, 2005.

Hollander-Blumoff, Rebecca. "The Psychology of Procedural Justice in the Federal Courts." *Hastings Law Journal* 63 (2011): 127.

Hurwitz, Jon, and Mark Peffley. "Explaining the Great Racial Divide: Perceptions of Fairness in the U.S. Criminal Justice System." *Journal of Politics* 67, no. 3 (2005): 762–83.

"Immigrant Driver's License Restrictions Challenged in Some States." *Immigrants Rights Update* 16, no. 6 (Oct. 21, 2002): 13.

International Association of Chiefs of Police. "Condemning Racial and Ethnic Profiling in Traffic Stops (a Resolution Adopted at the 106th Annual Conference, 3 November 1999)." *Police Chief*, July 2000, 19.

——. "Ensuring Professional Traffic Stops: Recommendations from the First IACP Forum on Professional Traffic Stops." *Police Chief*, July 1999, 15–23.

International Association of Chiefs of Police Highway Traffic Safety Committee. "Looking Beyond the License Plate Program Underscores Diligent Police Work." *Police Chief*, July 2000, 70–72.

——. "Policies Help Gain Public Trust: Guidance from the IACP Highway Safety Committee." *Police Chief*, July 2000, 26.

Inman, Mary L., and Robert S. Baron. "Influence of Prototypes on Perceptions of Prejudice." *Journal of Personality and Social Psychology* 70 (1996): 727–39.

Jackson, Pamela Irving. *Minority Group Threat, Crime and Policing*. New York: Praeger, 1989.

Jacobs, David. "Inequality and Police Strength." *American Sociological Review* 44 (1979): 913–25.

Johnson, Cathryn, Timothy J. Dowd, and Cecilia L. Ridgeway. "Legitimacy as a Social Process," *Annual Review of Sociology* 32 (2006): 53–78.

Johnson, Kevin R. "How Racial Profiling in America Became 'the Law of the Land': *United States v. Brignoni-Ponce* and *Whren v. United States* and the Need for Rebellious Lawyering." *Georgetown Law Journal* 98 (2010): 1006–77.

Jones-Brown, Delores. "Forever the Symbolic Assailant: The More Things Change, the More They Stay the Same." *Criminology & Public Policy* 6, no. 1 (2007): 113–14.

Kaiser, Cheryl R., and Brenda Major. "A Social Psychological Perspective on Perceiving and Reporting Discrimination." *Law & Social Inquiry* 31, no. 4 (2006): 801–30.

Kane, Robert. "The Social Ecology of Police Misconduct." *Criminology* 40 (2002): 867–96.

Kelling, George L., Anthony Plate, D. Dieckman, and C. E. Brown. *The Kansas City Preventive Patrol Experiment: A Summary Report.* Washington, DC: Police Foundation, 1974.

Kelling, George L., and William H. Sousa. "Do Police Matter? An Analysis of the Impact of New York City's Police Reforms." New York: Manhattan Institute Center for Civic Innovation, 2001.

Kelling, George L., and James Q. Wilson. "Broken Windows: The Police and Neighborhood Safety." *The Atlantic*, March 1982. http://www.theatlantic .com/magazine/archive/1982/03/broken-windows/304465/.

Kennedy, David M. *Don't Shoot: One Man, a Street Fellowship, and the End of Violence in Inner-City America.* New York: Bloomsbury, 2012.

Kime, Roy Caldwell. "U.S. Supreme Court Rules on Asset Forfeiture and Traffic Stop Evidence." *Police Chief*, August 1996, 101–16.

Kinder, Donald R., and Lynn M. Sanders. *Divided by Color: Racial Politics and Democratic Ideals.* Chicago: University of Chicago Press, 1996.

King, Gary, Michael Tomz, and Jason Wittenberg. "Making the Most of Statistical Analysis: Improving Interpretation and Presentation." *American Journal of Political Science* 44, no. 2 (April 2000): 347–61.

Knowles, John, Nicola Persico, and Petra Todd. "Racial Bias in Motor Vehicle Searches: Theory and Evidence." *Journal of Political Economy* 109 (2001): 203–99.

Knowles, Louis, and Kenneth Prewitt, eds. *Institutional Racism in American.* Englewood Cliffs, NJ: Prentice-Hall, 1969.

Kohut, Andrew, Scott Keeter, Carol Doherty, Michael Dimock, and Leah Christian. "Assessing the Representativeness of Public Opinion Surveys." Washington, DC: Pew Research Center for the People and the Press, 2012.

Koper, Christopher S., and Evan Mayo-Wilson. "Police Crackdowns on Illegal Gun Carrying: A Systematic Review of the Impact on Gun Crime." *Journal of Experimental Criminology* 2 (2006): 227–61.

Krieger, N., and S. Sidney. "Racial Discrimination and Blood Pressure: The Cardia Study of Young Black and White Adults." *American Journal of Public Health* 86 (1996): 1370–78.

Lamberth, John L. "Revised Statistical Analysis of the Incident of Police Stops and Arrests of Black Drivers/Travelers on the New Jersey Turnpike between

Exits or Interchanges 1 and 3 from the Years 1998 through 1991." In *Report of the Defendant's Expert in* State v. Pedro Soto, 734 A 2d 350: NJ Supr Ct. Law Div, 1996.

——. "Report of John Lamberth." American Civil Liberties Union, 1996. http://homepage.stat.uiowa.edu/~gwoodwor/statsoc/lectures/w2/lamberth.html.

Landers, Amber J., David Rollock, Charity B. Rolfes, and Demietrice L. Moore. "Police Contacts and Stress among African American College Students." *American Journal of Orthopsychiatry* 81, no. 1 (2011): 72–81.

Lane, Kristin A., Jerry Kang, and Mahzarin R. Banaji. "Implicit Social Cognition and Law." *Annual Review of Law and Social Science* 3 (2007): 427–51.

Langan, P. A., L. A. Greenfeld, S. K. Smith, M. R. Durose, and D. J. Levin. *Contacts between Police and the Public: Findings from the 1999 National Survey.* Washington, DC: Department of Justice, 2001.

Lange, James E., Kenneth O. Blackman, and Mark B. Johnson. *Speed Violation Survey of the New Jersey Turnpike: Final Report.* Trenton, NJ: Office of the Attorney General, 2001.

Lee, Taeku. "Between Social Theory and Social Science Practice: Toward a New Approach to the Survey Measurement of 'Race.'" In *Measuring Identity: A Guide for Social Scientists*, edited by Abdelal Rawi, Yoshiko M. Herrera, Alastair Iain Johnston and Rose McDermott, 113–44. Cambridge: Cambridge University Press, 2009.

——. "Race, Immigration, and the Identity-to-Politics Link." *Annual Review of Political Science* 11 (2008): 457–78.

Leiber, Michael, Mahesh Nalla, and Margaret Farnsworth. "Explaining Juveniles' Attitudes toward the Police." *Justice Quarterly* 15 (1998): 151–73.

Lepore, Lorella, and Rupert Brown. "Category and Stereotype Activation: Is Prejudice Inevitable?" *Journal of Personality and Social Psychology* 72, no. 2 (1997): 275–87.

Levinson, Justin D., and Robert J Smith, eds. *Implicit Racial Bias across the Law.* New York: Cambridge University Press, 2012.

Levitas, Daniel. *The Terrorist Next Door: The Militia Movement and the Radical Right.* New York: St. Martin's Griffin, 2002.

Lichtenberg, Illya D. "Driving While Black (DWB): Examining Race as a Tool in the War on Drugs." *Police Practice and Research* 7, no. 1 (2006): 49–60.

Lind, E. Allan, and Tom R. Tyler. *The Social Psychology of Procedural Justice.* New York: Plenum Press, 1988.

Liska, Allen, and Paul Bellair. "Violent-Crime Rates and Racial Composition." *American Journal of Sociology* 101 (1995): 578–610.

Liska, Allen, Mitchell Chamlin, and Mark Reed. "Testing the Economic Production and Conflict Models of Crime Control." *Social Forces* 64 (1985): 119–38.

Logan, John, and Brian Stults. "Racial Differences in Exposure to Crime." *Criminology* 37 (1999): 251–76.

Lohman, Joseph D., and Gordon E. Misner. *The Police and the Community*. Washington, DC: Government Printing Office, 1966.

Long, J. Scott. *Regression Models for Categorical and Limited Dependent Variables*. Thousand Oaks, CA: Sage, 1997.

Lopez, Ian Haney. *White by Law: The Legal Construction of Race*. New York: NYU Press, 1996.

Loury, Glenn C. *Race, Incarceration, and American Values*. Cambridge, MA: MIT Press, 2008.

Luckenbill, David F. "Criminal Homicide as a Situated Transaction." *Social Problems* 25, no. 2 (1977): 176–86.

Lundman, Richard. "City Police and Drunk Driving: Baseline Data." *Justice Quarterly* 15 (1998): 527–46.

———. "Demeanor and Arrest: Additional Evidence from Previously Unpublished Data." *Journal of Research in Crime and Delinquency* 33 (1996): 306–23.

———. "Demeanor or Crime? The Midwest City Police-Citizen Encounters Study." *Criminology* 32 (1994): 631–56.

Lundman, Richard, and Robert Kaufman. "Driving While Black: Effects of Race, Ethnicity, and Gender on Citizen Self-Reports of Traffic Stops and Police Actions." *Criminology* 41, no. 1 (2003): 195–220.

Lundman, Robert J. "Organizational Norms and Police Discretion: An Observational Study of Police Work with Traffic Law Violators." *Criminology* 17 (1979): 159–71.

Lunier, R. A. "Stress Balance and Emotional Life Complexities in Students in a Historically African American College." *Journal of Psychology* 131 (1997): 175–86.

Lyman, Stanford M., and Marvin B. Scott. *A Sociology of the Absurd*. Pacific Palisades, CA: Goodyear, 1970.

MacDonald, Heather. "The Racial Profiling Myth Debunked." *City Journal*, Spring 2001. http://www.city-journal.org/html/11_2_the_myth.html.

Marshall, Kenneth B. "Managing Successful Criminal Patrol Interdiction Programs." *Police Chief*, July 1999, 30–33.

Mashaw, Jerry L. "Administrative Due Process: The Quest for a Dignitary Theory." *Boston University Law Review* 61 (1981): 885.

Mastrofski, Stephen D., Michael D. Reisig, and John D. McCluskey. "Police Disrespect toward the Public: An Encounter-Based Analysis." *Criminology* 40, no. 3 (2002): 519–51.

McGarrell, Edmund. "Reducing Firearms Violence through Directed Police Patrol." *Criminology & Public Policy* 1, no. 1 (2001): 119–48.

McGarrell, Edmund, Steven Chermak, and Alexander Weiss. "Reducing Firearms Violence through Directed Patrol: Final Report on the Evaluation of the Indianapolis Police Department's Directed Patrol Project." In *Report to the National Institute of Justice*. Indianapolis, IN: Crime Control Policy Center, Hudson Institute, 2000.

——. "Reducing Gun Violence: Evaluation of the Indianapolis Police Department's Directed Patrol Project, Ncj-188740." Washington, DC: National Institute of Justice, United States Department of Justice, 2002.

Meares, Tracey. "The Legitimacy of Police among Young African-American Men." *Marquette Law Review* 92, no. 4 (Summer 2009): 651–66.

Meehan, Albert J., and Michael C. Ponder. "Race and Place: The Ecology of Racial Profiling African American Motorists." *Justice Quarterly* 19, no. 3 (September 2002): 399–430.

Memorandum for the Secretary of the Treasury, the Attorney General, the Secretary of the Interior. "Memorandum on Fairness in Law Enforcement." Public Papers of the Presidents of the United States, William J. Clinton, June 9, 1999.

Mettler, Suzanne. "Bringing the State Back in to Civic Engagement: Policy Feedback Effects of the G.I. Bill for World War II Veterans." *American Political Science Review* 96, no. 2 (2002): 351–65.

Milazzo, Carl, and Ron Hansen. "Race Relations in Police Operations: A Legal and Ethical Perspective." Paper presented at the 106th Annual Conference, International Association of Chiefs of Police, Charlotte, North Carolina, October 30–November 3, 1999.

Miller, Jerome G. *Search and Destroy: African American Males in the Criminal Justice System*. 2nd ed. New York: Cambridge University Press, 2011.

Moody, Bobby D. "Professional Traffic Stops vs. Biased Traffic Stops." *Police Chief*, July 1998, 6.

Moona, Byongook, and Charles J. Corley. "Driving across Campus: Assessing the Impact of Driver's Race and Gender on Traffic Enforcement Actions." *Journal of Criminal Justice* 35, no. 1 (2007): 29–37.

Morford, Garrett, Michael Sheehan Jr., and Jack Stuster. "Traffic Enforcement's Role in the War on Crime." *Police Chief*, July 1996, 48–49.

Murakawa, Naomi, and Katherine Beckett. "The Penology of Racial Innocence: The Erasure of Racism in the Study and Practice of Punishment." *Law & Society Review* 44, no. 3/4 (2010): 695–730.

National Advisory Commission on Civil Disorders (Kerner Commission). *Report of the National Advisory Commission on Civil Disorders*. Washington, DC: Government Printing Office, 1968.

National Highway Traffic Safety Administration. *Traffic Enforcement: Saving Lives and Combating Crime*. Washington, DC: National Highway Traffic Safety Administration, 1995.

Neubauer, Ronald S. "Untitled Statement Introducing the IACP's Recommendations on Police Stops." *Police Chief*, July 1999, 15.

New York Attorney General's Office. *The New York City Police Department's 'Stop and Frisk' Practices*. New York: New York Attorney General's Office, 1999.

Obasogie, Osagie K. "Race in Law and Society: A Critique." In *Race, Law and Society*, edited by Ian Haney Lopez, 445–64. Burlington, VT: Ashgate, 2007.

Omi, Michael, and Howard Winant. *Racial Formation in the United States: From the 1960s to the 1990s*. 2nd ed. New York: Routledge, 1994.

Packer, Jeremy. *Mobility without Mayhem: Safety, Cars, and Citizenship*. Durham, NC: Duke University Press, 2008.

Penner, Andrew, and Aliya Saperstein. "How Social Status Shapes Race." *Proceedings of the National Academy of Sciences of the United States* 105 (2008): 19628–30.

Persico, Nicola, and Daniel A. Castleman. "Detecting Bias: Using Statistical Evidence to Establish Intentional Discrimination in Racial Profiling Cases." *University of Chicago Legal Forum* (2005): 217–35.

Persico, Nicola, and Petra Todd. "Generalizing the Hit Rates Test for Racial Bias in Law Enforcement, with an Application to Vehicle Searches in Wichita." *Economic Journal* 116 (2006): F351–F357.

Petrocelli, Matthew, Alex R. Piquero, and Michael R. Smith. "Conflict Theory and Racial Profiling: An Empirical Analysis of Police Traffic Stop Data." *Journal of Criminal Justice* 31 (2002): 1–11.

Pew Center on the States. *One in 100: Behind Bars in America 2008*. Washington, DC: Pew Research Center, 2008.

Phillips, Coretta. "Institutional Racism and Ethnic Inequalities: An Expanded Multilevel Framework." *Journal of Social Policy* 40, no. 1 (2011): 173–92.

Pilant, Lois. "Spotlight on Traffic Enforcement." *Police Chief*, June 1995, 23–24.

Provine, Doris Marie. *Unequal under Law: Race in the War on Drugs*. Chicago: University of Chicago Press, 2007.

Quillian, Lincoln, and Devah Pager. "Black Neighborhoods, Higher Crime? The Role of Racial Stereotypes in Evaluations of Neighborhood Crime." *American Journal of Sociology* 107 (2001): 717–67.

Rao, C. R., H. Toutenburg, A. Fieger, C. Heumann, T. Nitter, and S. Scheid. *Linear Models: Least Squares and Alternatives*. New York: Springer Series in Statistics, 1999.

Reinarman, Craig, and Harry G. Levine. "Crack in Context: Politics and Media in the Making of a Drug Scare." *Contemporary Drug Problems* 16, no. 4 (1989): 535–78.

Reiner, Robert. *The Politics of the Police*. 4th ed. Oxford: Oxford University Press, 2010.

Reisig, Michael D., and Mark E. Correia. "Public Evaluations of Police Performance: Analysis across Three Levels of Policing." *Policing* 20, no. 2 (1997): 311–25.

Reisig, Michael D., John D. McCluskey, Stephen D. Mastrofski, and William Terrill. "Suspect Disrespect toward the Police." *Justice Quarterly* 21, no. 2 (2004): 241–68.

Lou Reiter, "Affidavit/Preliminary Expert Report of Lou Reiter," in the case of *Chavez v. Illinois State Police*, 7. http://www.clearinghouse.net/chDocs/public/PN-IL-0003-0002.pdf.

Remsberg, Charles. *Tactics for Criminal Patrol: Vehicle Stops, Drug Discovery and Officer Survival.* Northbrook, IL: Calibre Press, 1995.

Riksheim, Eric, and Steven Chermak. "Causes of Police Behavior Revisited." *Journal of Criminal Justice* 21 (1993): 353–82.

Ritterhouse, Jennifer. *Growing up Jim Crow: How Black and White Southern Children Learned Race.* Chapel Hill, NC: University of North Carolina Press, 2006.

Rojek, Jeff, Richard Rosenfeld, and Scott Decker. "The Influence of Driver's Race on Traffic Stops in Missouri." *Police Quarterly* 7, no. 1 (2004): 126–47.

Rosenbaum, Dennis P. "The Limits of Hot Spots Policing." In *Police Innovation: Contrasting Perspectives*, edited by David Weisburd and Anthony A. Braga. 245–63. Cambridge: Cambridge University Press, 2006.

Rosenbaum, Dennis P., Amie M. Schuck, Sandra K. Costello, Darnell F. Hawkins, and Marianne K. Ring. "Attitudes toward the Police: The Effects of Direct and Vicarious Experience." *Police Quarterly* 8, no. 3 (September 2005): 343–65.

Ruby, C. L., and John C. Bringham. "A Criminal Schema: The Role of Chronicity, Race, and Socioeconomic Status in Law Enforcement Officials' Perceptions of Others." *Journal of Applied Social Psychology* 26, no. 2 (1996): 95–112.

Rudman, Laurie A. "Social Justice in Our Minds, Homes, and Society: The Nature, Causes, and Consequences of Implicit Bias." *Social Justice Research* 17, no. 2 (June 2004): 129–42.

Ruiz, Jim, and Matthew Woessner. "Profiling, Cajun Style: Racial and Demographic Profiling in Louisiana's War on Drugs." *International Journal of Police Science & Management* 8, no. 3 (2006): 176–96.

Runge, Jeffrey W. "The Role of Traffic Law Enforcement in Homeland Security." *Police Chief*, October 2002, 93.

Russell-Brown, Katheryn. *Underground Codes: Race, Crime, and Related Fires.* New York: New York University Press, 2004.

Sampson, Robert J. "Urban Black Violence: The Effect of Male Joblessness and Family Disruption." *American Journal of Sociology* 93, no. 2 (Sept. 1987): 348–82.

Sampson, Robert J., and Dawn Jeglum Bartusch. "Legal Cynicism and (Subcultural?) Tolerance of Deviance; the Neighborhood Context of Racial Differences." *Law & Society Review* 32, no. 4 (1998): 801.

Sampson, Robert J., and Jacqueline Cohen. "Deterrent Effects of the Police on

Crime: A Replication and Theoretical Extension." *Law & Society Review* 22 (1988): 163–89.

Sampson, Robert J., and Janet Lauritsen. "Racial and Ethnic Disparities in Crime and Criminal Justice in the United States." In *Crime and Justice*, vol. 22, edited by Michael H. Tonry, 311–74. Chicago: University of Chicago Press, 1997.

Sampson, Robert J., and Stephen W. Raudenbush. "Systematic Social Observation of Public Spaces: A New Look at Disorder in Urban Neighborhoods." *American Journal of Sociology* 105, no. 3 (Nov. 1999): 603–51.

———. "Seeing Disorder: Neighborhood Stigma and the Social Construction of 'Broken Windows.'" *Social Psychology Quarterly* 67, no. 4 (2004): 319–42.

Sampson, Robert J., Stephen W. Raudenbush, and Felton Earls. "Neighborhoods and Violent Crime." *Science* 277 (1997): 918–24.

Saperstein, Aliya. "(Re)Modeling Race: Moving from Intrinsic Characteristics to Multidimensional Marker of Status." In *Racism in Post-Race America: New Theories, New Directions*, edited by Charles Gallagher, 335–50. Chapel Hill, NC: Social Forces, 2008.

Scaglion, Richard, and Richard Condon. "Determinants of Attitudes toward City Police." *Criminology* 17 (1980): 485–94.

Schacter, Daniel L. *The Seven Sins of Memory*. Boston: Houghton Mifflin, 2001.

Schafer, Joseph A., David L. Carter, and Andra Katz-Bannister. "Studying Traffic Stop Encounters." *Journal of Criminal Justice* 32 (2004): 159–70.

Schafer, Joseph A., and Stephen D. Mastrofski. "Police Leniency in Traffic Enforcement Encounters: Exploratory Findings from Observations and Interviews." *Journal of Criminal Justice* 33 (2005): 225–38.

Schauer, Frederick F. *Playing by the Rules: A Philosophical Examination of Rule-Based Decision-Making in Law and Life*. New York: Oxford University Press, 1991.

———. *Profiles, Probabilities, and Stereotypes*. Cambridge, MA: Harvard University Press, 2003.

Schellenberg, Kathryn. "Policing the Police: Surveillance and the Predilection for Leniency." *Criminal Justice and Behavior* 27 (2000): 667–87.

Schuman, Howard, Charlotte Steeh, Lawrence Bobo, and Maria Krysan. *Racial Attitudes in America: Trends and Interpretations*. Cambridge, MA: Harvard University Press, 1997.

Selznick, Philip. *Leadership in Administration: A Sociological Interpretation*. Berkeley: University of California Press, 1957.

Sharkey, Patrick. *Stuck in Place: Urban Neighborhoods and the End of Progress Toward Racial Equality*. Chicago: University of Chicago Press, 2013.

Shaw, J. Wilford. "Community Policing to Take Guns Off the Street." *Behavioral Sciences and the Law* 11 (Fall 1993): 361–74.

Sheller, Mimi, and John Urry. "The City and the Car." *International Journal of Urban and Regional Research* 24, no. 4 (2000): 737–57.

Sherman, Lawrence W., Patrick R. Gartin, and Michael E. Buerger. "Hop Spots of Predatory Crime: Routine Activities and the Criminology of Place." *Criminology* 27 (1989): 27–55.

Sherman, Lawrence W., Denise Gottfredson, Doris MacKenzie, John Eck, Peter Reuter, and Shawn Bushway. *Preventing Crime: What Works, What Doesn't, What's Promising: A Report to the United States Congress.* Washington, DC: National Institute of Justice, 1997.

Sherman, Lawrence W., and Dennis P. Rogan. "Effects of Gun Seizures on Gun Violence." *Justice Quarterly* 12, no. 4 (1995): 673–93.

Sherman, Lawrence W., James W. Shaw, and Dennis P. Rogan. "The Kansas City Gun Experiment." *Research in Brief,* January 1995, 1–11.

Sigelman, Lee, and Steven A. Tuch. "Metastereotypes: Blacks' Perceptions of Whites' Stereotypes of Blacks." *Public Opinion Quarterly* 61, no. 1 (Spring 1997): 87–101.

Simon, Jonathan. *Governing through Crime: How the War on Crime Transformed American Democracy and Created a Culture of Fear.* New York: Oxford University Press, 2007.

Sklansky, David Alan. "Not Your Father's Police Department: Making Sense of Law Enforcement's New Demographics." *Journal of Criminal Law and Criminology,* 96, no. 3 (Spring 2006): 1209–243.

———. "Traffic Stops, Minority Motorists, and the Future of the Fourth Amendment." *Supreme Court Review,* 1997: 271–329.

Skogan, Wesley. "Citizen Satisfaction with Police Encounters." *Police Quarterly* 8 (2005): 298–321.

Skogan, Wesley, and Susan M. Hartnett. *Community Policing: Chicago Style.* New York: Oxford University Press, 1997.

Skolnick, Jerome H. "The Color Line of Punishment." *Michigan Law Review* 96, no. 6 (1998): 1474–85.

———. *Justice without Trial: Law Enforcement in Democratic Society.* 3rd ed. New York: MacMillan, 1994.

Smedley, Brian D., Adrienne Y. Stith, and Alan R. Nelson, eds. *Unequal Treatment: Confronting Racial and Ethnic Disparities in Health Care.* Washington, DC: National Academy Press, 2003.

Smith, Michael R., and Matthew Petrocelli. "Racial Profiling? A Multivariate Analysis of Police Traffic Stop Data." *Police Quarterly* 4 (2001): 4–27.

Smith, Paul, and Richard Hawkins. "Victimization, Types of Citizen-Police Contacts, and Attitudes toward the Police." *Law & Society Review* 8 (1973): 135–52.

Smith, Robert J, and Justin D. Levinson. "The Impact of Implicit Racial Bias on the Exercise of Prosecutorial Discretion." *Seattle Law Journal* 35 (2012): 795–826.

Smith, William, Donald Tomaskovic-Devey, Matthew Zingraff, Marcinda Mason, Patricia Warren, and Cynthia Pfaff Wright. "The North Carolina Highway Traffic Study." Final report to the National Institute of Justice under grant 1999-MU-CX-0022. July 2003.

Soss, Joe. "Lessons of Welfare: Policy Design, Political Learning, and Political Action." *American Political Science Review* 93, no. 2 (1999): 363–80.

Soss, Joe, Richard C. Fording, and Sanford F. Schram. *Disciplining the Poor: Neoliberal Paternalism and the Persistent Power of Race*. Chicago: University of Chicago Press, 2011.

Soss, Joe, Jacob S. Hacker, and Suzanne Mettler, eds. *Remaking America: Democracy and Public Policy in an Age of Inequality*. New York: Russell Sage Foundation, 2007.

Stewart, Jim. "Police Appear to Target Minorities in Efforts to Catch Criminals." *CBS Evening News*, May 22, 1996.

Stock, Margaret. "Online Symposium: The Court Throws Arizona a Tough Bone to Chew." *SCOTUSblog*, June 17, 2012. http://www.scotusblog.com/2012/06/online-symposium-the-court-throws-arizona-a-tough-bone-to-chew/.

Stroshine, Meghan, Geoffrey Alpert, and Roger Dunham. "The Influence of 'Working Rules' on Police Suspicion and Discretionary Decision Making." *Police Quarterly* 11, no. 3 (2008): 315–37.

Stuntz, William J. "Local Policing after the Terror." *Yale Law Journal* 111, no. 8 (June 2002): 2137–94.

Sugrue, Thomas J. "Driving While Black: The Car and Race Relations in Modern America." Automobile in American Life and Society website, http://www.autolife.umd.umich.edu/Race/R_Casestudy/R_Casestudy.htm.

Sullivan, Peggy, Roger G. Dunham, and Geoffrey P. Alpert. "Attitude Structure of Different Ethnic and Age Groups Concerning the Police." *Journal of Criminal Law & Criminology* 78 (1987): 177–96.

Sweeney, Earl M. "Combating Crashes and Crime through Professional Traffic Stops." *Police Chief*, July 1999, 39–42.

———. "Traffic Enforcement: New Uses for an Old Tool." *Police Chief*, July 1996, 45–46.

Sykes, Richard, and John Clark. "A Theory of Deference Exchange in Police-Civilian Encounters." *American Journal of Sociology* 81, no. 3 (1976): 584–600.

Terrill, William, and Michael D. Reisig. "Neighborhood Context and Police Use of Force." *Journal of Research in Crime and Delinquency* 40 (2003): 291–321.

Tillyer, Rob, and Robin Shepard Engel. "Racial Differences in Speeding Patterns: Exploring the Differential Offending Hypothesis." *Journal of Criminal Justice* 40 (2012): 285–95.

Tomaskovic-Devey, Donald, Cynthia Pfaff Wright, Ronald Czaja, and Kirk Miller. "Self-Reports of Speeding Stops by Race: Results from the North Carolina Reverse Record Check Survey." *Journal of Quantitative Criminology* 22 (2006): 279–97.

Tonry, Michael H. *Punishing Race: A Continuing American Dilemma*. New York: Oxford University Press, 2011.

Totman, Molly, and D. Steward. *Searching for Consent: An Analysis of Racial Profiling Data in Texas*. Austin: Texas Criminal Coalition, 2006.

"Top Ten Lies in Traffic Enforcement." *Police Chief*, July 1997.

Tribe, Laurence H. *American Constitutional Law*. 2nd ed. Mineola, NY: Foundation Press, 1988.

Tversky, Amos, and David Kahneman. "Judgment under Uncertainty; Heuristics and Biases." *Science* 185 (1974): 1124–31.

Tyler, Tom. "Procedural Justice, Legitimacy, and the Effective Rule of Law." *Crime and Justice* 30 (2003): 342.

——."Public Trust and Confidence in Legal Authorities: What Do Majority and Minority Groups Members Want from Law and Legal Institutions?" *Behavioral Sciences and the Law* 19 (2001): 215–35.

——. *Why People Obey the Law*. New Haven: CT: Yale University Press, 1990.

Tyler, Tom, P. Dogoey, and H. Smith. "Understanding Why the Justice of Group Procedures Matters: A Test of the Psychological Dynamics of the Group-Value Model." *Journal of Personality and Social Psychology* 70 (1996): 913–30.

Tyler, Tom, and Yuen J. Huo. *Trust in the Law: Encouraging Public Cooperation with the Police and Courts*. New York: Russell Sage Foundation, 2002.

Tyler, Tom, and E. Allan Lind. "Intrinsic Versus Community-Based Justice Models: When Does Group Membership Matter?" *Journal of Social Issues* 46 (1990): 83–94.

——. "A Relational Model of Authority in Groups." In *Advances in Experimental Social Psychology*, edited by M. P. Zanna. 115–91. San Diego, CA: Academic, 1992.

Tyler, Tom, and Cheryl J. Wakslak. "Profiling and Legitimacy of the Police: Procedural Justice, Attributions of Motive, and Acceptance of Social Authority." *Criminology* 42, no. 2 (2004): 253–81.

United States General Accounting Office. 'Racial Profiling: Limited Data Available on Motorist Stops." In *Report to the Honorable James E. Clyburn, Chairman Congressional Black Caucus*. Washington, DC: General Accounting Office, 2000.

United States Census Bureau, "Census 2000, Summary File 3, Table P53, Median Household Income in 1999." Washington, DC: Census Bureau, 2000.

Urry, John. *Mobilities*. Malden, MA: Policy Press, 2007.

Van Maanen, John. "The Asshole." In *Policing: A View from the Street*, edited by Peter K. Manning and John Van Maanen. 307–28. Santa Monica, CA: Goodyear, 1978.

Verniero, Peter, and Paul H. Zoubek. *Interim Report of the State Police Team Regarding Allegations of Racial Profiling.* Newark, NJ: New Jersey Office of the Attorney General, 1999.

Walker, Samuel. *A Critical History of Police Reform: The Emergency of Professionalism.* Lexington, MA: Lexington Books, 1977.

———. *The New World of Police Accountability.* Thousand Oaks, CA: Sage, 2005.

———. "Origins of the Contemporary Criminal Justice Paradigm: The American Bar Foundation Survey, 1953–1969." *Justice Quarterly* 9 (1992): 47.

———. "Searching for the Denominator: Problems with Police Traffic Stop Data and an Early Warning System Solution." *Justice Research and Policy* 3, no. 1 (2001): 63–95.

———. *Taming the System: The Control of Discretion in Criminal Justice, 1950–1990.* New York: Oxford University Press, 1993.

Warren, Patricia Y. "Perceptions of Police Disrespect During Vehicle Stops: A Raced-Based Analysis." *Crime & Delinquency* 57, no. 3 (2011): 356–76.

Warren, Patricia Y., and Donald Tomaskovic-Devey. "Racial Profiling and Searches: Did the Politics of Racial Profiling Change Police Behavior?" *Criminology & Public Policy* 8, no. 2 (May 2009): 343–69.

Weaver, Vesla M., and Amy E. Lerman. "Political Consequences of the Carceral State." *American Political Science Review* 104, no. 4 (November 2010): 817–33.

Webb, Gary. "DWB: Tracking Unspoken Law Enforcement Racism." *Esquire,* April 1, 1999, 118–28.

Weisburd, David, and Rosanne Greenspan. *Police Attitudes toward Abuse of Authority: Findings from a National Study.* Washington, DC: National Institute of Justice, 2000.

Weisburd, David, and Lorraine Green Mazerolle. "Crime and Disorder in Drug Hot Spots: Implications for Theory and Practice of Policing." *Police Quarterly* 3 (2000): 331–49.

Weiss, Alexander, and Edmund McGarrell. "Traffic Enforcement & Crime: Another Look." *Police Chief,* July 1999, 25–28.

Weitzer, Ronald. "Racialized Policing: Residents' Perceptions in Three Neighborhoods." *Law & Society Review* 34, no. 1 (2000): 129–56.

Weitzer, Ronald, and Rod K. Brunson. "Strategic Responses to the Police among Inner-City Youth." *Sociological Quarterly* 50 (2009): 235–56.

Weitzer, Ronald, and Steven A. Tuch. *Race and Policing in America: Conflict and Reform.* New York: Cambridge University Press, 2006.

Wells, Julia C. *We Now Demand! The History of Women's Resistance to Pass Laws in South Africa.* Johannesburg: Witwatersrand University Press, 2001.

Westley, William A. *Violence and the Police: A Sociological Study of Law, Custom, and Morality.* Cambridge, MA: MIT Press, 1970.

Whalen, Michael J. "Supreme Court Rulings Acknowledge Practical Considerations of Law Enforcement." *Police Chief,* April 2002, 11.

Wilkinson, Deanna L., and Jeffrey A. Fagan. "The Role of Firearms in Violence 'Scripts': The Dynamics of Gun Events among Adolescent Males." *Law and Contemporary Problems* 59, no. 1 (1996): 55–89.

Williams, Terry. *Crackhouse.* Reading, MA: Addison-Wesley, 1992.

Wilson, James Q. "Just Take Away Their Guns." *New York Times Magazine,* March 20, 1994, 1.

Wilson, James Q., and Barbara Boland. "The Effect of Police on Crime." *Law & Society Review* 12, no. 3 (1978): 367–90.

Wilson, William Julius. *More than Just Race: Being Black and Poor in the Inner City.* New York: W. W. Norton, 2009.

Winter, Nicholas J. G. *Dangerous Frames: How Ideas About Race & Gender Shape Public Opinion.* Chicago: University of Chicago Press, 2008.

Withrow, Brian L. "Driving While Different: A Potential Theoretical Explanation for Race-Based Policing." *Criminal Justice Review* 15, no. 3 (2004): 344–64.

———. "Race-Based Policing: A Descriptive Analysis of the Wichita Stop Study." *Police Practice and Research* 5, no. 3 (2004): 223–40.

Worden, Robert E., and Robin L. Shepard. "Demeanor, Crime, and Police Behavior: A Reexamination of the Police Services Study Data." *Criminology* 34 (1996): 83–105.

Zimring, Franklin E. *The City That Became Safe: New York's Lessons for Urban Crime and Its Control.* New York: Oxford University Press, 2011.

Index

Page numbers followed by an *f* or *t* refer to figures or tables, respectively.

Provine, Doris Marie, 9, 11, 33
punishment, of African American drivers
vs. white drivers, 110–12

race: concept of, 41; meaning of, 23–24
race relations, research on stereotyping
and implicit bias and understanding, 45
racial disparities: investigatory stops and,
13–16, 64–71, 100–110, 127–33, 135–36,
155–56; police stops and, 2–4
racial equality, police stops and, 3
racial framing, 42; African American drivers and, 47; institutionalized, 50–51;
white drivers and, 47–48
racial identity, police stops and shaping of,
148–50
racial justice, police stops and, 152–55
racial minorities, police stops and, 3.
See also African American drivers;
Hispanics
racial profiling: assumptions about, 4–6;
IACP's model policy on, 49–50; police response to, 48–50; police training
manual on, 39–40
racism: color blind, 41; debates over, 6; deliberate, 3, 12, 26, 92; institutional, 11;
as perceived attribute of police, 47;
as personal animus, 4; reforms of police on, 28, 29. *See also* implicit bias;
stereotypes
rapport, establishing, and investigatory
stops and, 40
Remsberg, Charles, 36–38, 162
riots, police stops as triggers for, 30–31
Ritterhouse, Jennifer, 92
Rosenbaum, Dennis, 156
Ruby, C. L., 45
Russell-Brown, Katheryn, 47

Sagar, Andrew, 43
Sanchez, Marco, 13
Sanders, Lynn, 41
Saperstein, Aliya, 148
Schofield, Janet, 43
Schram, Sanford, 11
Scott, Marvin, 76
scripts, for traffic-safety and investigatory
stops, 78–84
searches, consent to: fictitious quality of,
162; IACP resolution on racial profil-

ing and, 49; narratives on, 63, 98, 126;
targeting for, 40; training manual on,
37, 38
searches, person, 3, 9, 31, 32, 37, 81
searches, vehicle: court rulings on, 34–35;
crime-fighting utility of, 32; as element of stop, 2, 14; examples of, 2,
150; harms of, 134, 136, 137, 138; as influence on perceptual frame, 118–19,
121–22, 126; as invasion of privacy, 5–6;
narratives of, 63–64, 115–16; and New
Jersey profiling controversy, 34; proposed reform of, 162; racial disparities
in, 3, 8, 81, 83, 105–8; summary of data
on, 155–57, 158; training manual on,
36–38, 39; as trigger for riots, 31; type
of stop and, 105
segregation, neighborhood, investigatory
stops and, 145–48
Selznick, Philip, 12
Sherman, Lawrence, 32
shooter bias, 44, 162–63
Skolnick, Jerome, 30, 45
Smith, Robert, 45
Soss, Joe, 11, 15
stereotypes: of black criminality, 46; defined, 42; implicit, 3, 6, 12, 26, 41–47;
meta, 47; research on, and understanding race relations, 41–47; scientific
study of, 42–43; training and, 164–65.
See also implicit bias
Stolzberg, Lisa, 47
stops. *See* investigatory stops; police stops;
traffic-safety stops
Stuntz, William, 4–5, 114, 119, 120
Suchman, Mark, 27–28
Sugrue, Thomas, 18, 58

Tactics for Criminal Patrol (Remsberg),
36–38
targeted enforcement, 164
targeting harm, 5
Terry stops, 4–5
tit-for-tat hypothesis, 84–92
Tomaskovic-Devey, Donald, 163
Tonry, Michael, 30
traffic-safety stops, 53; African American complaints during, 110–12; African American vs. white experiences
of, 71–73; fairness and, 15; intrusions

The Chicago Series in Law and Society
Edited by John M. Conley and Lynn Mather